Stroup * HUNGARY IN EARLY 1848:
THE CONSTITUTIONAL STRUGGLE
AGAINST ABSOLUTISM IN
CONTEMPORARY EYES

STATE UNIVERSITY OF NEW YORK
COLLEGE AT BUFFALO'S

Program in East European and Slavic Studies
Publication Number 11.

General Editor:
Joseph M. Értavy-Baráth

Previous publications:

1. POEMS OF ENDRE ADY — Nyerges
2. Mécs: ARANYGYAPJÚ
3. ATTILA JÓZSEF — Nyerges
4. Komlós: LOUIS KOSSUTH IN AMERICA 1851-1852
5. PETŐFI — Nyerges
6. A.H. Várdy: A STUDY IN AUSTRIAN ROMANTICISM:
   HUNGARIAN INFLUENCES IN LENAU'S POETRY
7. Vucinich: GOD AND THE VILLAGERS:
   A STORY OF MONTENEGRO
8. Pujdak: ANTONI WISNIEWSKI:
   PREKURSOR FILOZOFII OSWIECENIA W POLSCE

# HUNGARY IN EARLY 1848:

## THE CONSTITUTIONAL STRUGGLE AGAINST ABSOLUTISM IN CONTEMPORARY EYES

EDSEL WALTER STROUP
University of Akron

Foreword by
STEVEN BÉLA VÁRDY
Duquesne University

HUNGARIAN CULTURAL FOUNDATION

Buffalo, New York — Atlanta, Georgia
1977

Library of Congress Catalog Card Number: 75-46400
I.S.B.N. 0-914648-07-1


Orders may be addressed to
HUNGARIAN CULTURAL FOUNDATION
P. O. Box 364, Stone Mountain, Ga. 30086


LECTORS
Steven Béla Várdy
Duquesne University

Zoltán Kramar
Central Washington State College

Andrew Ludányi
Ohio Northern University


Jacket design:
Magda Kerecseny Bárány

Printed by Classic Printing Corp., 9527 Madison Ave., Cleveland, Ohio 44102

# CONTENTS

TO
KÁROLY SERLY

# FOREWORD

Few events in Hungarian history have left an impact on the Magyar nation that could compare with that of the Revolution of 1848-1849. Despite its ultimate defeat by the Habsburg and Russian imperial forces, this event has been hailed ever since as one of the truly great moments in the history of the Magyars. Books written about it would fill a small library, and even today there seems to be no end to the unceasing effort to study and to reinterpret the events and meaning of this great popular uprising. As an example, in 1976 alone at least two new interpretations have appeared in Hungary.[1] But what is even more interesting and significant, the Revolution of 1848-1849 has always been viewed as a positive historical phenomenon by everyone concerned — be he an arch-conservative or a radical in his political convinctions. The interpretation of the meaning of the Revolution naturally varies with the interpreter. But one has yet to see a Hungarian historian, or any historian for that matter, who would classify it as a negative and reprehensible event in the history of Hungary.

While this positive view of the Revolution as a whole has remained unchanged for close to 130 years, the assessment of the roles of individuals, groups, political factions and social classes has varied considerably. Thus, during the first century after the Revolution — an epoch that encompassed the age of post-revolutionary absolutism (1849-1867), the age of dualism (1867-1918), and the interwar period (1918-1945) — the Revolution and most of its leaders were idealized. Moreover, there was a general tendency to emphasize the positive and unselfish role of the majority of the Hungarian nobility in voluntarily dismantling the remnants of feudalism (serfdom, entail, etc.), even against their very own economic interests. True, the chroniclers of the events of 1848-1849 were divided in their views on Kossuth, Széchenyi and a number of other noted personalities: the partisans of the anti-Habsburg independence movement (and most of the masses) idealizing Kossuth, and the more conservative and pragmatic scholars often opting for the similarly more pragmatic Széchenyi. It is also true that the "official position" on the relative significance of these two inspiring leaders of reform has changed with time, gradually shifting in the direction of Széchenyi, particularly during the interwar period. But the view about the basically constructive and unselfish role of the Hungarian nobility in the reforms of 1848 had remained unchanged until after 1945.

With the collapse of the old order in that year, and the rise of Marxist historiography soon thereafter, the situation changed completely. The Revolution of 1848-1849 still retained its position as one of the great events

---

1. *A negyvennyolcas forradalom kérdései*, ed. György Spira and Jenő Szűcs. Budapest: Akadémiai Kiadó, 1976; and Géza Várady, *Ezernyolcszáznegyvennyolc, te csillag*. Budapest: Gondolat, 1976.

in modern Hungarian history (although it had to take a backseat to the events of 1919 and 1945), but the relative significance of the participating personalities, groups, political factions and social classes was reinterpreted and altered completely. Thus, in addition to reversing the significance of Széchenyi and Kossuth in favor of the latter, historians discovered the role of the hitherto unappreciated or unknown radicals and the masses in general. Simultaneously, they also reinterpreted the role of the nobility. The nobility's vote in favor of the dismantlement of feudalism — which hitherto was thought to be the result of unselfish patriotism — was declared to be the result of their fear and inability to withstand the feverish pace of the revolution emanating from below. Thus, while differences still remained among Marxist scholars relative to small details, as well as about the significance of one radical group as opposed to the other, the new view about the alleged reactionary role of the Hungarian nobility in 1848-1849 became a basic tenet of post-1945 Hungarian historiography. But is this a view that we can accept with confidence?

This is precisely the question tackled by Mr. Edsel Walter Stroup, a young and promising American scholar, who immersed himself thoroughly into the study of the Hungarian Revolution of 1848-1849, going so far as to acquire a degree of fluency in the difficult language of the Magyars. He completed his self-assigned goal largely by re-examining many of the older, largely Anglo-Saxon sources, and by reading much of the secondary material published during the past century and a quarter.

As the reader will find, his conclusions do not quite rhyme with those of current Hungarian Marxist historiography. Instead of perceiving the Hungarian nobility of that period as reactionaries who were simply trying to hold on to their privileges, he sees them as basically honest and conscientious patriots, who were willing to forgo their traditional social and economic position of preeminence for the general good of their nation, and did so without compensation. In this they may have been unique in all of contemporary Europe.

The reader may or may not agree with the author's conclusions. But I am certain that he will detect the scholarly effort, the labor of love, and the honest search for truth that went into the making of this book. It is a work that deserves our attention and respect. And whatever one's personal views about the problems discussed, it will undoubtedly represent well the "other side," the currently less popular view about the role and significance of some of the makers of the Revolution of 1848-1849.

Pittsburgh, Pennsylvania  
Fall, 1976  

*Steven Béla Várdy*  
Duquesne University

# PREFACE

Hungary in early 1848 provided the exception to the dictum that "1848 was the turning point at which modern history failed to turn."[1] Standing on the base of an eight hundred year old Constitution, the Hungarian State and society did, in fact, execute the "turn" in a rather adroit manner considering the difficult circumstances in which it was accomplished. This, at least, was the judgment expressed by many contemporaries and subsequently by some historians. Friedrich Engels, an acute observer of the period, wrote in a January, 1849 issue of the *Neu Rheinische Zeitung* that between 1831 and 1848 the political life of Hungary had "brilliantly" caught up and come forward. He thought that "the feudal forms of the old Hungarian Constitution served democratic interests better than the modern forms of the south German constitutions."[2] Another contemporary source, in this case originating in Austro-German circles which have never been regarded as historically or innately of a pro-Hungarian disposition, observed:

> On whatever points our conditions are superior to those in Hungary, a higher standard of general education, greater prosperity, all that is counterbalanced and supplemented by the freer political institutions in Hungary, the greater freedom of speech and resolution, the perfect parliamentary training . . ., We have the basis of a free and strong constitution, they have the constitution itself.[3]

---

1 Attributed to G. M. Trevelyan, in Melvin Kranzberg (ed.), *1848 A Turning Point?* "Problems in European Civilization," (Boston: D. C. Heath, 1959), p. ix.

2 Quoted by E. Andics, "Der Widerstand der feudalen Krafte· in Ungarn am Vorabend der bürgerlichen Revolution des Jahres 1848," *Acta Historica*, IV, nos. 1-3 (1955), 206 and n. 225 cited from Franz Mehring (ed.), *Aus dem literarischen Nachlass von Karl Marx, Friedrich Engels und Ferdinand Lassalle* (Stuttgart: 1902), III, 239. This reference is also cited by Robert A. Kann in noting Engels' attitude and the pro-Hungarian sentiment for the Hungarian Liberal cause which then existed in Central and Western Europe. *The Multinational Empire: Nationalism and National Reform in the Habsburg Monarchy 1848-1918* (2 vols.; New York: Octagon Books, 1970), I, 125, 384 n. 44.

3 This quote provided by Kann, *Multinational Empire*, I, 382, n. 32 and obtained by him from Josef Redlich, *Das österreichische Staats-und Reichsproblem* (Leipzig: 1920), I, 36 who drew it from an Austro-German Liberal pamphlet, *Guter Rat für Österreich Mit Bezugnahme auf des Programm der liberalen Partie in Ungarn* (Leipzig: 1847).

A century later, the well-known Habsburg specialist Professor Robert A. Kann, whose sympathies are Austrian centralist rather than Hungarian, noted that the entire content of the Hungarian reform legislation of 1848 derived from the pre-1848 period.[4] Again, Priscilla Robertson, in her comprehensive effort to penetrate the social circumstances in which the revolutions of 1848 occurred, wrote:

> Of all the peoples and nations engaged in revolution in 1848, Hungary was the single one which kept its demands strictly on a legal basis. If the Habsburgs had had any respect for their oaths, Hungary could have used its ancient constitution as a neat springboard from which to leap over absolutism into the . . . more modern camp of democratic constitutional states like England and France.[5]

Such statements, repeated over the years, provide insight into the events in Hungary in early 1848 and are in accord with the viewpoint traditionally held by Hungarian historians which claimed that Hungary was at that time a *centre du rayonnement* in Central Europe, an advocate of reforms which fought for national and individual liberty.[6] This positive viewpoint, with some modification, has continued to be upheld by a number of Marxist historians in Hungary. István Barta, for example, has noted the evolutionary approach and non-violent progression of the reform movement which contrasted sharply with the bloody clashes that change appeared to necessitate in the States of Western Europe.[7] All these favorable interpretations of the Hungarian 1848 point toward the constitutional continuity of the Hungarian national demands of that year and the merger of these demands with the ideology of classical Liberalism.

Due to this favorable stream of interpretation, Western scholars interested in nineteenth century European conditions

---

4 Kann, *The Multinational Empire*, I, 122.

5 *Revolutions of 1848: A Social History* (Harper Torchbook ed.; New York: Harper and Brothers, 1960), p. 260.

6 Dominic G. Kosáry, *A History of Hungary* (Cleveland: The Benjamin Franklin Bibliophile Society, 1941), p. 185.

7 "A magyar polgári reformmozgalom kezdeti szakaszának problémái" (Problems of the Opening Phase of the Hungarian Bourgeoise Reform Movement), *Történelmi Szemle*, XI, nos. 3-4 (1963), 325, 331.

and the phenomenon of Liberalism should find the Hungary of this period a promising and worthwhile area for research. This is especially the case when the most cursory examination of Hungarian developments prior to 1848 reveals that the political, social, and economic transformation of Hungary undertaken in early 1848 was the product of nearly twenty years of mounting agitation and legislative debate known in Hungarian history as the Reform Era. Yet, the fact remains that there has been scarcely one, recent, full-length work in the English language entirely devoted to an investigation of the Hungarian Reform Era or the early Hungarian 1848.[8]

There are several reasons for the lack of recent Western studies of Hungary oriented toward the watershed year of 1848; especially ones which employ the constitutional and legal framework of the State as a basis. First, Western scholarship has traditionally approached the Habsburg Monarchy from the outside, as it were, and relied on the German language works of Austrian historians who have understandably tended to reflect the centralist viewpoint of Austrian Statesmen. This has produced a certain amount of genuine ignorance and inadvertently, if not consciously, a general disparagement of the Hungarian Constitution. It is, moreover, an interpretation whose influence is still evident in Western historiography today.[9] Secondly, present day Hungarian historians, who are doing impressive work and would be best qualified to present assessments of the influence of the historic Constitution, have their attention largely directed toward socio-economic studies. In Western historiography there has also been an increased interest in socio-economic history and, broadly speaking, a simultaneous decline in the

8 Recent and welcome exceptions are a translation from the Hungarian into English of a biography of Count Stephen Széchenyi during 1848 by György Spira and the current work of István Deák on a biography of Kossuth in 1848, one chapter of which has been published as an article. See the bibliography of this work for full references.

9 A very brief centralist-minded overview of the Monarchy's modern history by a scholar who lived through some of it and who was sincerely loyal to the concept is available in Hans Kohn, *The Habsburg Empire 1804-1918* (New York: D. Van Nostrand Company Inc., 1961). For an erudite, cautious, and closely reasoned defense of the centralist viewpoint, see the work of Professor Robert A. Kann generally and his *Multinational Empire*, II, 286-298 specifically. In this extensive work the reader will find references to numerous, centralist Austrian historians.

study of constitutional-legal influences. Thirdly, the truly tragic Hungarian nationality conflicts, which first made their appearance with significant force at the end of 1848 and which subsist to this day in altered context as one of the potentially most explosive conditions in East Central Europe, have taken their toll of the susceptibilities of all concerned, including historians. The result has been that scholars in the Successor States of Hungary almost invariably refer to the Hungarian State according to their perception of it in negative terms. The cumulative effect of this cannot help but contribute to a similar negative image in Western historiography.[10]

In response to these influences Western historiography has tended to revise its originally favorable opinion of the Hungarian 1848. Despite the virtual absence of full-length studies of the period in Western languages, strongly worded references condemning the Hungarian 1848 have appeared in English language studies which usually center in some manner around three major objections. The oldest objection, essentially Austrian in origin, states that before 1848 Hungary was an integral part of the Habsburg Monarchy or at best simply a somewhat privileged province. According to this interpretation, the Hungarian struggle in 1848 was illegal almost from its inception because inherent within it was the abrogation of legitimate Imperial powers and the inevitable separation of Hungary from the Monarchy. This was not only legally inadmissible, but also invalid on the grounds of maintaining the Monarchy as a major power. The second objection sees the Hungarian 1848 as originated and led by radical republican intellectuals who were supported by the peasantry's widespread hatred of the privileged nobility who manipulated the Constitution, produced some sham Liberal legislation and managed to retain control in the face of class violence. According to this interpretation, the whole Hungarian 1848 acquires a semi-conspiratorial character and its real nature consisted of a plot

---

10 See, for example, the excellent collection of articles by various scholars in "The Nationality Problem in the Habsburg Monarchy in the Nineteenth Century: a Critical Appraisal, Part II The National Minorities," *Austrian History Yearbook*, III, pt. 2 (1967). This is an informative and valuable collection by fine scholars who do, however, uniformly leave the Hungarian Constitution virtually unmentioned and whose references to the Hungarian State are largely negative.

to "preserve the gentry."[11] The third objection, which is presently perhaps the most widespread, insists that however beneficial the Hungarian Liberal legislation of 1848 might have been on paper, it contained provisions directed against the several minority language groups of historic Hungary.[12] The nationalities' problem in the Hungarian 1848 is thus promoted by this interpretation into a commanding position as its predominate and characteristic feature; the cultural imperialism of the Magyars, that is those Hungarians who spoke Hungarian as a primary language, was so oppressive and racially oriented, as to cancel out the Liberal achievements of the Hungarian 1848.[13]

The general object of the present study is to shed more light for the English reader than has been previously readily available on the nature of the early Hungarian 1848. The first two objections listed above are treated in its chapters. However, the complexities of the nationalities' problem are touched only briefly in this work since their major eruptions occurred later in 1848. Still, due to the negative influence which assessments of this problem have exercised on evaluations of the entire period, the reader is reminded that there are two sides to every conflict and a few words are addressed to it here. As 1848 unfolded from one crisis to the next, the Hungarian government and Kossuth, in particular, did, indeed, make serious mistakes in dealing with Hungary's several linguistic minorities. But it has often gone unmentioned that the leaderships of the various nationalities frequently matched or excelled the Hungarian in their obstinancy and unwilling-

---

11 A. J. P. Taylor, *The Habsburg Monarchy 1809-1918* (New York: Harper and Row, 1965), p. 59, see also pp. 51-52, 60.

12 Professor Kann sees the Hungarian Liberal legislation of 1848 as requiring knowledge of Hungarian for immigration, naturalization, and settlement in Hungary. Although such measures were discussed in the Diet, they were not sanctioned as part of the April Laws of 1848 whose only language provision was the requirement of a working knowledge of Hungarian to stand for election as a representative to future national Parliaments. Kann, *Multinational Empire*, I, 123, 239, and 419, n. 16; D. Kosáry, "Széchenyi in Recent Western Literature," *Acta Historica*, IX, no. 3 (1963), 269; C. A. Macartney, *The Habsburg Empire 1790-1918* (New York: Macmillan, 1969), p. 292.

13 Kann, *Multinational Empire*, I, 122-24.

HUNT LIBRARY
CARNEGIE-MELLON UNIVERSITY
PITTSBURGH, PENNSYLVANIA 15213

ness to compromise their extreme objectives.[14] Even the fact that Kossuth actually negotiated and extended plans for mutual compromises of the differences involved is often left obscure. Linguistic grievances on the part of the minorities quickly escalated into political demands and Kossuth had some justification for his adamant policy in the face of the territorial disintegration of a State faced with invasion. In reality, workable compromises might well have been concluded except for the encouragement received by the nationalities from the false promises extended by the Court centralists in Vienna. An honest attempt to assess this entire tragic and complex problem is available for the English reader in an extensive article by Zoltán I. Tóth.[15]

Specifically, the purpose of this study is to establish in some detail the true nature of the Hungarian struggle in early 1848. The substance of the Hungarian demands for national and social reform is described. The often neglected constitutional structure of the Hungarian State is employed as an unifying background and a proper appreciation of it is seen as essential for a full understanding of the narrated events. This approach stresses the legal progression as well as the constitutionally evolutionary elements in the Hungarian struggle and presents an alternative focus to more extreme and sensationalist interpretations of what is usually referred to collectively as the "Hungarian Revolution of 1848." The fundamental issue of the early Hungarian 1848 is seen as the nation's constitutional struggle with Habsburg absolutism. At stake was the establishment of an equitable relationship of a Hungary modernized by the April Laws with the Crown, and through it, with the rest of

---

14 For example, on April 14, 1848 a Serbian Church Council at Karlovic demanded an autonomous State which appropriated for itself five large counties of Inner Hungary, the population of which would have consisted mostly of non-Serbs. The Hungarian historian of the period, Mihály Horváth, using statistics compiled by the Austrian government, gives the totals 688,000 Serbs to 1,434,270 non-Serbs of various nationalities. See his comments and table in *Magyarország függetlenségi harczának története 1848 és 1849-ben* (History of Hungary's War for Independence in 1848 and 1849) (3 vols.; Geneva: Miklós Puky, 1865), I, 157.

15 This is virtually the only English summary of the Hungarian negotiations with the nationalities and the proposed compromises, "The Nationality Problem in Hungary in 1848-1849," *Acta Historica*, IV, no. 4 (1955), 235-77; especially 248; 256-57, 263-64, 269-70.

the Habsburg Monarchy. It is argued that in the reform-minded atmosphere of 1848, a mutually satisfactory settlement of these problems was the precondition for the swiftest, most complete, and most secure realization of social reforms. In other words, the achievement of social reform depended on the achievement of national goals. The efforts of the radicals and of Hungary's legally constituted leadership in pursuit of these goals are set forth. Attention directed toward establishing the exact sequence of events has resulted in conclusions which greatly modify the frequently encountered distortions and suppositions contained in English language references concerning the attitudes, participation, and interrelationships of Hungary's major historic classes during this struggle for reform. In sum, this work traces and evaluates the constitutional and related social developments during the early Hungarian 1848 struggle for meaningful progress.

It would be a loss to general knowledge as well as to the history of nineteenth century Europe if the Hungarian 1848 should become completely misunderstood in Western historiography, since the incidence of genuine, naturally-evolved constitutional societies with ideals of equitable governance is rather rare in human history. Many present day societies are struggling with the perennial problem of justly exercising political power in a constitutional fashion under conditions not entirely dissimilar from those confronting the Hungarian State and society in 1848. Moreover, without studies of the Hungarians during this and other crucial periods in their historical experience as well as of all the peoples of the former Danubian Monarchy, Western peoples and their policy-makers can only possess a less than adequate knowledge of the values, aspirations, and legal patterns which have helped to shape a significant portion of Europe. Collective values are in many respects more elusive and difficult to assess than purely material considerations, but attempts must be made toward building a truly complete picture of the historical development of East Central Europe, an area where special values have traditionally been important and which encompassess a complex of cultures distinguishing it from Eastern Europe as well as the West.

15

Since I have not been able to do research in Hungary, my account is limited in some aspects, but one cannot always wait for the ideal situation to materialize. The sources obtained to support my efforts represent a mixture of both old and new works. If any preference has been expressed, it is for those whose authors had some immediate experience of the events of which they wrote and whose accounts readily lend themselves to direct quotations. It is, of course, axiomatic that no two writers would select exactly the same sources or employ them in the same manner. With this in mind, criticism of this account is welcome and hopefully encouraged for it is only through honest disagreement and many studies that those interested in the developments of this era can begin to increase general awareness of its significance and to dispel some of the more flagrant inaccuracies encountered in English language surveys. Finally, a minor note, geographic place names are generally given in the text in the form used during the period discussed while personal names are rendered in their English form in the initial introductory section. However, the Hungarian and German (for Habsburg Kings of Hungary, members of the Imperial family and Austrian Statesmen) forms are used in the subsequent chapters.

It is with greatest pleasure that I take this opportunity to thank those whose help was instrumental in bringing this manuscript to completion. I thank the Graduate School and the Department of History of the University of Akron for extending a Graduate Teaching Assistantship which was a great support in the pursuit of this study. I am grateful to the faculty, students, and graduate students of the Department of History of the University of Akron for providing the friendly and scholarly atmosphere which encourages such efforts and I am especially grateful to Professor Robert H. Jones, Professor Boris Blick, Professor Warren F. Kuehl, and Professor Sheldon B. Liss, whose kind interest and efforts have helped to straighten the paths of graduate study. I wish to particularly express my thanks and appreciation to my advisors, Professor David C. Riede and Professor June K. Burton, who read this manuscript in its original form when it was submitted as a thesis and provided valuable criticism and comment. I also

16

thank Professor Vincent H. Cassidy who subsequently read it and extended helpful criticism as well as Professor Howard S. Reinmuth Jr. for his consistent interest and encouragement. Again, I am very grateful to Professor Boris Blick for his critical reading of the enlarged introduction.

Improvement of the manuscript was also facilitated by the librarians, staff, and especially the interlibrary loan librarian, Mrs. Dorothy M. Kantosky, of the University of Akron's Bierce Library. In a similar vein, I am in addition indebted to Mr. Dénes Dietrich and Mrs. Ferenc Bárány of the Hungarian Bookstore in Cleveland for the expert knowledge, ability, and persistence with which they obtained those Hungarian language works which I preferred to personally own.

I am immeasurably indebted and deeply grateful to Professor Steven Béla Várdy of Duquesne University for his kind interest and generous expenditure of time without which this manuscript would never have proceeded toward publication. I am sincerely grateful to Professor Zoltán Kramar of Central Washington State College, and to Professor Andrew Ludányi of Ohio Northern University, each of whose comments and suggestions were extremely valuable and greatly improved the manuscript. I am also indebted and grateful to Professor Joseph M. Értavy-Baráth, General Editor of the Hungarian Cultural Foundation, for his interest, reading of the manuscript, and knowledgeable facilitation of the publication process.

To Messrs. Ernst, Eberhard, Uwe and Volker Molesch I extend my thanks for their continued interest and comments and I also would be remiss if I did not recognize with appreciation the patient cooperation and exceptional ability of Mrs. Robert Baucher and Mrs. Joyce Harris in typing the manuscript. Lastly, and above all, my sincere thanks go to Mrs. Elemér Gyarmathy without whose unfailing encouragement and understanding this work would not have been completed.

Cleveland, January, 1976

EDSEL WALTER STROUP

# HUNGARIAN CONSTITUTIONAL DEVELOPMENT
## TO 1848

The Hungarian struggle of early 1848 can be most clearly understood as yet another, though profound, phase in a long history of constitutional conflict between the Habsburg dynasty and their Hungarian subjects. Before the Habsburgs had ever acceded to the throne, the Hungarians knew a full five centuries of independence during which time national institutions and attitudes toward government were so firmly established that the most determined efforts of the House of Austria to eliminate or weaken them were at most only partially successful. The following account of Hungary's constitutional development and its ambivalent relations with the Habsburgs provides an often ignored dimension that elucidates the imperfectly understood Hungarian grievances and objectives during the critical year 1848.

\* \* \*

The Hungarians, under an elected leader, Árpád, first came in force into the Carpathian Basin, then essentially a political vacuum, in 896 A.D., a time when the general European tribal migrations had almost ended. For a brief period, known as the "Era of Adventures," they launched, with the connivance of Western Princes, a series of daring and swift raids throughout Europe in which their forces penetrated as far as Basel, Bremen, Otranto, Cambrai, Orléans and Nimes; their unbounded audacity even led them to cross the Pyrenees and ride toward Córdoba. The Holy Roman Emperor finally ended these astonishing forays by defeating the federated Hungarian tribes at the Battle of Lechfeld in the summer of 955. But the really arresting feature of the period and its essential significance, was the swiftness of the Hungarians, in contrast to other nomads who passed through the Basin before them, in occupying and organizing the areas west and east of the Danube inside the Carpathian rim. They have good claim to be the first people to have unified both halves, and as early as 900 the conquest was an accomplished fact.

During the extraordinary process of the gradual transformation of these nomadic warriors into an agricultural people assimulating European concepts of property rights, the Hungarians, traditionally tolerant in religious matters, embraced Christianity. Their first Christian King, St. Stephen (997-1038), secured recognition from Pope Sylvester II who conferred apostolic authority on him and sent the Holy Crown used at his coronation on Christmas Day in the year 1000 A.D. This most important event in Hungarian history recognized Hungary as a European State with all the then acknowledged prerogatives; thus it was geographically adjacent to the Holy Roman Empire, but completely independent of the Emperor's authority.

The Hungarian State was also singularly fortunate in its development under the patrimonial Kings of the Árpád line. Before the dynasty's extinction in 1301 it had successfully developed most of the country's institutions. In 1222 the middling class of free men (the spiritual, if not actual, descendants of Árpád's warriors) won the famous Golden Bull from King Andrew II. The Golden Bull exerted a deep constitutional and psychological influence on successive generations due to its crucial clauses which, like those of the Magna Carta, limited the King's power over life and property. In addition, the Golden Bull expressed the Hungarians' strong national consciousness in forbidding the bestowal of office or land on foreigners. Above all, it protected the free "common nobility" (*köznemesség*) against encroachment of the Magnates by reaffirming the nobles' legal equality, irrespective of office or wealth. Although this provision suffered erosion, it markedly differentiated Hungarian society from the hierarchical system of hereditary office and sub-vassalage which developed in the States of Western Europe.

Other thirteenth century development rivaled the Bull's importance in the emergence of basic political institutions. While the term "noble" had actually been imported from the West, a certain amount of two-way social mobility continued to exist between the lower orders of society and the ranks of free men. The autonomous noble county emerged as a replacement for the purely administrative royal counties initiated by St. Stephen. The new county assemblies (*congregationes*) composed of the small and medium nobles chose their own officers and very quickly defended their own interests and those of the King against the oligarchical tendencies of the great Magnates and high churchmen. A royal decree of 1267 initiated the practice of each county electing two or three representatives to an annual gathering of free men at Székesfehérvár called for the purpose of deliberating the condition of the country. But this hardly stopped many nobles who often preferred to appear in person.[1] By the end of the century, these national gatherings, whose origins can be traced to St. Stephen's "days of law," acquired legislative power. Under the last Árpád, Andrew III, "the first truly constitutional Hungarian King . . . who submitted voluntarily to restrictions of his power,"[2] the national gatherings were moved in 1298 to the Field of Rákos outside Pest. There it became customary for the legislative proposals of these embryonic national assemblies to acquire the force of law when they received the seals of King and Magnates.[3] The constitutional concept of shared political power thus definitely existed at the end of the Árpád line.

In the two succeeding centuries the nation elected a veritable parade of foreign lines to rule the Kingdom and remained forever after divided over the benefits and drawbacks of foreign dynasties. Under the first two Anjou Kings, Hungary experienced such sustained material prosperity and potent international prestige, that these seemingly compensated for the fact that constitutional ground was lost. Along with an efficient fiscal policy, both rulers introduced Western European concepts of feudal hierarchy and legislated nearly at will. Charles Robert (1308-1342), especially, after he first beneficially broke the power of the "kinglets," heavily favored the

---

1 Charles d'Eszlary, *Histoire des Institutions publiques hongroises* (3 vols.; Paris: Librairie Marcel Riviere et Cie, 1959-65), I, 229.

2 *Ibid.*, p. 231.

3 *Ibid.*, p. 228.

Magnates at the expense of lesser mortals. But he did give major impetus toward improvement and sophistication of the legal system and even delegated authority to the county assemblies whose administrative and judicial powers under their own elected officials actually increased. This development continued during the "Golden Age" of his son and successor, Louis the Great (1343-1382), who confirmed the Golden Bull in 1351 and expressly stated that all nobles had one and the same liberty; it was also he who standardized the peasant's obligation to his lord at one-ninth of his crop yield, upheld the peasant's right of free movement, and entailed land holdings with the *aviticitas* (*ősiség*) law.

With Louis' death, the usual election crisis eventually brought as King Sigismund (1387-1437), whose rule produced a blend of bad and good effects, among the latter in a constitutional sense being his prolonged absences from Hungary due to his positions as Holy Roman Emperor and Bohemian King. These absences permitted the nation to regain constitutional ground and the Palatine (*Nádor*) to transform his office from chief administrator and judge into constitutional arbiter between the interests of King and nation. Sigismund was followed, briefly, by an able Habsburg, Albert (1437-1439), who died prematurely of dysentery, a Jagiello, Wladislaw I, (1440-1444), the Regent, Hunyadi (1446-1452), and the boy-King, Ladislas V (1452-1458). In an elective monarchy Hunyadi's regency was unprecedented. Originally a Transylvanian landowner of modest means, Hunyadi rendered extremely valuable service to the nation in a difficult period by eventually beating the divisive Magnates at their own game of building personal power. His persistence was rewarded with a certain amount of national unity and by a stunning defeat inflicted on the Turks before Belgrade in 1456. The Turkish threat was consequently neutralized for at least a generation and this prepared the ground for the reign (1458-1490) of his son, Matthias Corvinus, who was Hungary's last great national King.

Elected on the January ice of the Danube by a host of common nobles, King Matthias swore to respect the nation's constitutional forms which he did in a perfunctory manner, and was in every other respect a true Renaissance prince. Learning and the arts flourished under his rule as did taxes, a large army, and the condition and numbers of the general population. He set a high standard of justice, favored the common nobles in the counties, and promoted the interests of the growing agricultural towns (mezővárosok) whose obligations he simplified and protected against the ever rapacious Magnates. Internationally, he divided his efforts between containing the growing ambitions of the Habsburg, Frederick III, and throwing back the Turk. He has been understandably criticized for not paying sufficient attention to the Turkish threat in the south where the Hungarian speaking population was thick. But it appears that he wished to secure the Imperial Crown and Habsburg resources before turning again southward and mounting an effort sufficient to sweep the Turk from Europe.

The nation's remarkable progress under Matthias was reversed after his death by a resurgence of the Magnates who supported two weak Kings and whose selfish political and economic aggrandizement so weakened the country that many antagonized common nobility and the newly oppressed inhabitants of the numerous mezővárosok sensed approaching disaster. The extractions of the Magnates so profoundly antagonized the lower social orders that a crusade called by the Cardinal Primate Thomas Bakócz against the infidel degenerated into a social jacquerie in 1514 under the leadership of a Transylvanian noble, George Dózsa. But this jacquerie was liquidated with such unspeakable cruelty, even for that age, that it further demoralized the Hungarians who were approaching their darkest hour.

In the midst of such disorder and social conflict, it is ironic that in the fifteenth century and the opening decades of the sixteenth, the Hungarian Constitution and parliamentary forms reached a high level of sophistication. The autonomous counties' administrative, judicial, and ordinance-making powers as well as their relation to the central government were established in considerable detail. The county assemblies and their representatives to the national assembly or Diet were composed of nobles having one and the same liberty.[4] Besides

4 *Ibid.*, II, 86-87, 311.

electing the King, the Diet also elected the nation's major office holders (Palatine, Lord Justices, and members of the Royal Council) who were accountable for their official actions. The Diet, acting in its judicial capacity, could try them for treasonous "infidelity."[5] The immensely important "power of the purse" came under the control of the Diet as new taxes required its affirmative vote. Organization and direction of the military forces were also subject to the Diet's consent.[6] Because of these powers, especially that of impeachment, the Diet's opinion had to be taken into account concerning decisions of war and peace and it even asserted the right to ratify peace treaties.[7] Above all, tradition strongly held that the King derived his powers from the "political nation," i.e. from the free men or nobles.

The King, the nation, and the nation's territory together formed a corporate entity symbolized by the Holy Crown.[8] National legislation could be sponsored by either the co-equal King or nation and their mutual consent was necessary for a Dietal bill to become a Law, considered highest expression of sovereignty superior to and unalterable by royal decree.[9] These principles with practical and detailed procedural regulations were codified by a common jurist, István Werbőczy, in his *Tripartitum* approved by a Dietal commission and Wladislaw II in 1514. Although Werbőczy's work never received the royal seal (due in all probability to Magnate opposition), it was edited and published in 1517.[10] Together with the official compilation of Laws contained in the *Corpus Juris Hungarici*, the *Tripartitum* was universally employed as the nation's fundamental codex until 1848.[11] Werbőczy's work registered the nobles' extensive privileges and condemned those serfs who followed Dózsa to "perpetual servitude." Historians with

---

5 *Ibid.*, pp. 80-81.
6 *Ibid.*, pp. 81-84.
7 *Ibid.*, pp. 84-85.
8 *Ibid.*, pp. 12-13.
9 *Ibid.*, p. 79, 98. This principle was formulated in 1514 in Werbőczy's *Tripartitum* (II, title 4), see *ibid.*, III, 88 and n. 51.
10 *Ibid.*, II, 20-21.
11 *Ibid.*, pp. 23-24.

reason have condemned the psychologically deleterious and long lasting effects of dividing the nation between the privileged and non-privileged. Still, the critics of Werbőczy's work unfairly ignore the advanced nature of its provisions for a truly national and parliamentary governance and take out of context its class provisions formulated in an extraordinary social crisis of the early sixteenth century. This undeserved error of appreciation is magnified when it also goes unmentioned that Werbőczy's "perpetual servitude" was reversed in 1556 by sanctioned Dietal Laws. Later, under somewhat different circumstances when the peasant's right of free migration was again restricted by the effect of Law XIII of 1608 (thus bringing his status in accordance with general East Central European developments), this was not the direct result of Dózsa's revolt or even Werbőczy's code of nearly a century before.[12]

However, the promising evolution of Hungary's uniquely national parliamentary institutions soon sustained a seemingly fatal blow from the Turks who were experiencing their last great renaissance under Suleiman the Magnificent. Many Hungarians clearly foresaw the threat, but their lucidity encountered a familiar excess of Magnate "liberty" and self interest. A period of mismanagement common enough to all States was especially fatal in Central Europe. The young and not untalented Louis II (1516-1526) could not reverse this situation with sufficient speed. As Suleiman took Belgrade and reduced two southern fortresses, messengers scoured Europe for support against what was truly a European threat. Only the Papacy stood ready to help; Bohemia was indifferent, Poland occupied with the Tartars, and the Valois, Francis I, was basically hostile. The Habsburg Archduke Ferdinand, although inclined to extend active support, had little to offer because his family was concerned with the French, and the Princes of the Empire were occupied with their eternal parochial introspection. In the end, the eighteen year old King Louis left Buda in July of 1526 and proceeded southward at

---

12 Laws XXVII—XXXIII of 1556 broke the serf's ties to the soil, reestablished his migration and property rights and specified severe penalties for nobles who disregarded them. *Ibid.*, II, 351-52; III, 314.

the head of only 3,000 men who included Hungary's highest Magnates and prelates. They faced the Sultan's 120,000 troops, a high proportion of which were regulars. On August 29th the Hungarian forces, increased to 20,000 by volunteers, met the entire Turkish force near the village of Mohács on the right bank of the Danube in Baranya county. With a magnificent courage born of sheer desperation and force of will, the Hungarians threw themselves at the Turkish center in a staggering assault which was impossible to maintain. Methodically, the Turks cut down isolated groups at will and by evening the King, the nation's highest Magnates, and nearly all their followers were slain, having paid for their errors and misrule with their lives. The defeat was not at first irreversible. But it eventually became so due to the Hungarians' failure to unify in the fifteen years following Mohács. John Zápolyai, Hungary's last "national" King (1526-1540), was elected by the Diet on November 10th by a majority of the nobility. But on December 17th a rump Diet elected Ferdinand of Austria as King (1526-1564) in the mistaken hope that this brother of Charles V could command the resources of the Empire to clear Hungary of the Turk. The confused rivalry of these two parties resulted by 1541 in an Ottoman occupation of the central portion of the country for 150 years.

*　*　*

Thus, the year 1526 simultaneously initiated the nation's 300 year association with the Habsburg dynasty and marked the first signal emergence of the "Austrian Empire" since Ferdinand also acquired the Bohemian Crown that year. In the very confused and turbulent decades which followed one on another in nightmare fashion, the Diet sat in Pozsony (Pressburg, Bratislava) under Habsburg tutelage while the Turks dug up the Christian graves, destroyed buildings, and exacted slaves and taxes at will throughout the richest portion of the nation. It diminishes nothing from the Ottoman military and administrative achievements to note they brought little to Hungary except an unbelievable devastation and a hierarchy of values which refused as oil and water to mix with Hungarian concepts. While Hungarians, such as Jurisics at Kőszeg and in Zrínyi's epic defense of Szigetvár, bled time and again to throw off the Turkish yoke, the Habsburgs and their generals were preoccupied with Imperial affairs to the degree they missed successive opportunities to free Hungary from the weakening Ottoman grip. The dynasty's inaction in this regard as well as its fierce persecution of Protestants eventually led many Hungarians to view the Habsburgs as a threat to be equated with the Turks and drove them into tactical alliances with the latter. Yet, the complete restoration of the State remained the ultimate goal of all Hungarian parties and was held with amazing tenacity in the face of the most adverse developments. A seventeenth century English traveller noted the Turks' unceasing desire to secure the Holy Crown and the Hungarians' extraordinary attachment to it which increased rather than diminished as the century wore on.

The Habsburg Emperor Leopold I's (1657-1705) capitulation to the Turks in the 1664 Vasvár Treaty prompted the Wesselényi Conspiracy. Leopold reacted with an especially vicious persecution of Hungarian Protestants and suspended the Constitution in 1673 provoking the Thököly rebellion (1678-1682) which forced him to restore the Constitution in 1681 and reconvoke the Diet. This was little better than a truce and when the "Liberation" of Hungary from the Turk was finally achieved (1683-1699) with Hungarian auxiliaries by a bumbling international army under Habsburg auspices, the devastation of the country equaled or excelled that inflicted by the Turks. Leopold's advisors urged him to treat Hungary as territory taken *jure belli*, to try traitors, and redistribute land among his supporters in a large scale fashion. At Imperial invitation waves of Slavic peoples inundated most of depopulated southern Hungary and for years thereafter every footloose nationality in Europe was encouraged to settle there with only Hungarians excluded (especially for example in the Banate of Temesvár after 1718) in the hope of weakening Hungary's political structure. The Habsburgs normally accommodated their rule to existing political structures with some grace and their drastic policy in Hungary constituted inadvertent testimony to their respect for the potency of the Hungarians' devotion to their State. The dynasty's establishment of the Military Border, so effective a problem for

Hungary in 1848, was finalized at this time and was anti-Hungarian as well as anti-Turk; the Habsburg rulers of the day must in fact bear a part of the responsibility for the subsequent nationality problems. In the celebrated view of Leopold's advisor, Kollonich, Hungarians should first be made beggars, then Catholics, and, finally, Germans. It was a truly inauspicious beginning for nation and dynasty.

Leopold I, beset on several fronts with major problems, was less extreme than his advisors. In 1687 he convoked a Hungarian Diet and agreed to uphold the Constitution as affirmed in 1681. The nation in return by Law IV of 1688 renounced article thirty-one of the Golden Bull (the *jus resistendi* or right of resistance) and agreed to accept the Habsburg dynasty as hereditary in the male line by Laws II and III of 1688. As assurance of constitutional government in the face of this significant concession, the Diet also provided in Laws II and III of 1688 that at the moment of a monarch's death his successor as *rex hereditarius* possessed only normal administrative powers. He was prevented from sponsoring or sanctioning legislation, conferring pardons or titles, or in any way altering Hungary's fundamental structure or practices until his coronation as *rex legitimus*. This in turn depended on his acceptance of the articles of the *diploma inaugurale* and the Coronation Oath.[13]

---

13 These were intended to secure the Constitution against arbitrary rule and had venerable origins. At the very founding of the State, a public oath was sworn by the Árpád leaders creating a tradition which was reflected in several aspects of the coronation ceremony under the Habsburgs. The first *diploma,* issued by King Andrew III at his coronation in July of 1290, was simply a royal decree which promised that the monarch would fulfill certain generally acknowledged duties. So long as dynastic lines remained elective, these documents were rather flexible and irregular since the nation would never submit to an anticonstitutional monarch nor did any national King object to undertaking such commitments which actually rendered his power more secure. The new monarch's obligation to take a Coronation Oath was well established by the accession of Wladislaw II in 1490. His obligation to issue a *diploma* (to be entered in the *Corpus Juris*) was made definite in 1608 and an absolute condition of coronation by 1637. The election of the Habsburgs as a hereditary dynasty only served to increase the importance of these documents. Without adhering to them the new King could not be crowned and exercise full constitutional powers. Upon the death of the previous monarch, a specially elected joint-House Dietal commission "edited" both documents and presented them to the new hereditary King for his inspection before his coronation. The Diet's obligation in this matter was first to verify that the new King acceded according to the correct hereditary lines of succession and secondly to preserve the Constitution intact as it existed at the death of the previous monarch until the

This settlement was eroded and eventually torn asunder by Vienna's religious persecution and the flagrantly illegal land grabbing activities of a commission established in 1690. These imperialist policies provoked the Rákóczi rebellion (1703-1711) which united the country as seldom before or since under the leadership of a most reluctant rebel, a Roman Catholic, who commanded many Protestants and who was among the most admirable and selfless leaders in all Hungarian history. With rebellion well under way, the first Habsburg to accede under the 1687 agreement, Joseph I (1705-1711), did so with a "false clause" inserted in his *diploma* permitting the King to declare void any previous Hungarian Law which he refused to accept.[14] This was one of the stated reasons for the dethronement of the dynasty by the Rákóczi party at the Diet of Ónod in 1707. Even though Rákóczi's forces were unable to win Hungary's complete independence, the rebellion did achieve the compromise Peace of Szatmár in 1711. This promised religious freedom, restoration of the 1687 settlement guaranteeing the Constitution, and the convocation of a Diet.

\* \* \*

The new King, Charles III and VI as Emperor (1711-1740) shared nothing of his father's dislike of Hungary and the rebellion had convinced even his advisors of the desirability of

coronation of the new King. Thus, the texts of these documents in which the King swore to safeguard the Constitution and rule according to the law remained essentially unchanged from the accession of Joseph I in 1688 through that of Charles IV in 1917. Any Dietal insertion of a novel clause or reform in these documents as a precondition for coronation would have been just as illegal as an act by the hereditary King to unilaterally abolish a previously sanctioned Law before his coronation. In either case, the very purpose of these documents — to preserve the Constitution unaltered until the two co-equal elements of sovereignty, the legally crowned King and the nation, might mutually agree on changes — would have been defeated. The only alternations which the Dietal commission could make were "inevitable" ones; that is, if a Law sanctioned in the previous reign contradicted something in the texts, a good example being alterations necessary to accommodate female succession. The commission might also propose to insert a previously sanctioned Law to underline a new problem or changed conditions, but the new monarch was free to reject the proposal without prejudice to his right of coronation provided he adhered to the original texts. *Ibid.,* II, 44-58; III, 38-49.

14 This was done in a clandestine manner by a group of Magnates tied to Habsburg pretensions as Joseph I acceded in May at nine years of age. The Diet protested the clause when it was detected and refused to enter Joseph's *diploma* in the *Corpus Juris. Ibid.,* III, 43-44.

establishing a workable relationship. Charles III sanctioned Law III of 1715 which repaired the false clause loophole by stating that the validity of the Laws did not depend upon renewed or subsequent agreement.[15] The future thus promised a more stable Hungarian-Habsburg relationship, and all the more so because Charles was anxious to secure universal recognition of the Pragmatic Sanction providing for his Dominions' territorial integrity under a probable female succession. This he achieved in nearly all the Western Lands of the Monarchy as of 1720 by simply informing them they had no right to propose conditions for acceptance and reading the Sanction to them somewhat as a riot act.[16]

The Kingdom of Hungary was a different matter and only in 1723 by Laws I-III of that year did the Diet establish the essence of the Sanction without using its title. The nation thereby accepted female succession in default of male in three strictly defined Habsburg lines with the additional condition that the successors be legitimate Roman Catholic Archdukes or Archduchesses.[17] The nation recovered its right of election in the event of the extinction of all these lines. So long as these legitimate Habsburg lines succeeded, Hungary was bound in article seven of Law II to be ruled by them and "administered indivisibly and inseparably, mutually and simultaneously"[18] with the other Hereditary Dominions and Kingdoms of the Monarchy. Whatever the subsequent interpretation by Austrian centralist historians, a complete reading of this Hungarian implementing legislation reveals that the link or union established by it was essentially dynastic.[19] It was an agreement

---

15 The "false clause" was retained in *diploma inauguralia* but never again employed in its original sense except in a futile dynastic effort in 1741, and, remarkably, just prior to the first World War by the "Great Austrian School of Public Law" which exhumed it to question the binding force of Hungarian Laws. *Ibid.,* pp. 44-45 and n. 54.

16 It was first read to a chosen gathering of privy councillors on the morning of April 19, 1713. Although some of the extra-Hungarian Lands of the Monarchy attempted to propose conditions for their acceptance, they were informed they had no right to do so and virtually all adhered to the document by the end of 1720. C. A. Macartney (ed.), *The Habsburg and Hohenzollern Dynasties in the Seventeeth and Eighteenth Centuries* (New York: Walker, 1970), p. 83.

17 d'Eszlary, *Institutions,* III, 32-34.

18 Macartney (ed.), *Habsburg and Hohenzollern Dynasties,* p. 93.

19 *Ibid.,* p. 85.

strictly between the nation and its legitimate Kings, in no way dependent upon assent or alteration by other political entities within the Monarchy. Charles bound his successors to maintain a constitutional rule by the requirement of accepting the traditional and mutually confirmed *diploma inaugurale* and Coronation Oath at their coronation. His sanction of Laws I-III further bound the dynasty to respect and safeguard all of Hungary's "rights, liberties, privileges, immunities, prerogatives, recognized customs, and Laws already enacted"[20] and to enforce them in respect also to the dynasty's "other subjects without regard to Estate, rank, or position."[21] The dynasty was also committed to defend and keep intact the territorial integrity of Hungary which was understood to be "indivisible."[22] This 1723 Hungarian legislation implementing the Pragmatic Sanction clearly established that the nation's sole deducible obligation to the other political entities in the Monarchy was mutual cooperation with them under the auspices of its legitimate King in matters of common concern, especially those relating to defense.[23] As the Hungarian Law commented on the nature of the union, it was to be valid "for all events and also against external enemies."[24] Charles for himself and his successors swore to rule Hungary as an independent polity, having its own Constitution, and not "after the pattern of other provinces."[25]

With this fundamental constitutional settlement completed, the best part of the eighteenth century passed in relative peace for Hungary giving the nation a sorely needed opportunity to reverse the recent and extensive material devastation. Charles left the Hungarian office of Palatine vacant,

---

20 Article one of Law III in *ibid.*, p. 93.

21 Article three of Law III in *ibid.*, p. 94.

22 Article four of Law I in *ibid.*, p. 92.

23 In Law VIII of 1715 the Diet had authorized Hungarian participation in a regular standing army to be composed of "indigenous and foreign" persons. By Laws VI and C of 1723 the nation by implication acknowledged further cooperation in the Monarchy's common defense force, yet retained some civil control over the internal regulation of Imperial units and left as a legal possibility the raising of purely national military units. See, d'Eszlary, *Institutions*, III, 165-66 and n. 66, 174 and n. 92.

24 Macartney (ed.), *Habsburg and Hohenzollern Dynasties, p. 7.*

25 *Ibid.*

convoked the Diet only once more (1734) and died unexpectedly in 1740. He left his daughter and youthful successor, Maria Theresa (1740-1780), to face Frederick II's aggression with the Monarchy's Western Lands in a disorganized and bankrupt condition. As is well known, she turned to Hungary for help and the 1741 Diet's loyal and speedy granting of it saved the Habsburg Monarchy from disintegration at a time when Upper Austria and Bohemia swore allegiance to the enemy. In return, Maria Theresa promised to fill the office of Palatine and sanctioned Laws confirming the nation's constitutional privileges and requiring that Hungarian affairs be conducted by Hungarians through Hungarian governmental bodies. In the Laws of 1741 the Royal Hungarian Court Chancellory, the Hungarian Treasury (*Camera*), and the Hungarian Vice-Regal Council (the *Consilium* or national administrative and executive body established by Laws XCVII—CII of 1723) were guaranteed independence on a footing of complete equality with the Court administrative institutions for the Western Lands. These Hungarian governmental institutions were not to be "interfered with" or "impeded by other authorities."[26]

Maria Theresa's sanction of these Laws at her accession, her gratitude for Hungarian support, and the very size of Hungary all promted her to leave the nation's institutions relatively intact. However, under the guidance of Baron Haugwitz, she did undertake a governmental consolidation of the smaller Western Lands of the Monarchy which made her reign the single most constructive in its history. These reforms in the interest of centralized efficiency (leading in the end to bureaucratic absolutism) which were necessary and timely in the Western Lands, could not have been introduced in Hungary "except," in Maria Theresa's words, "at a legally convoked Diet."[27] But she convoked the Hungarian Diet on only two more occasions during her long reign indicating her basic satisfaction with the nation. She regarded Hungarians as

---

26 Phrases drawn from Law XIII of 1741, *ibid.*, p. 135, see pp. 132-37 for other excerpts from the 1741 Laws. On the *Consilium*, see also d'Eszlary, *Institutions*, III, 119.

27 Macartney (ed.), *Habsburg and Hohenzollern Dynasties*, p. 126.

31

"fundamentally a good people, with whom one can do anything if one takes them the right way."[28] She also wrote with acerbity about the past selfishness and hatred in her officialdom. She was especially critical of the overbearing Austrian bureaucracy which endeavored to exclude Hungarians from all the Monarchy's central services.[29] This open-minded attempt to be even-handed was the key to her Hungarian policy and responsible for its success. She had the knack of rendering the Hungarians satisfied with less than they demanded and the limited recognition she extended made the "woman-King" more popular in Hungary than any previous Habsburg ruler.

Still, Maria Theresa's fundamentally sound rule was not of unqualified benefit to Hungary. However much the nation replaced material devastation with a simple and abundant prosperity, constitutional ground was lost. Her father had initiated the practice of ruling Hungary by decree in every conceivable area where legislation did not require consultation with the nation. She continued this policy issuing no less than 2,340 royal decrees during her forty year reign,[30] a policy opposed to the Hungarian constitutional concept that the monarch had few powers not specifically granted by the nation or exercised in concord with it. The sanctioned Laws of 1741 were only nominally honored and, most importantly, Maria Theresa acquiesced to Austrian and Bohemian interests in establishing a "temporary" discriminatory tariff (1754) and adopting a generally oppressive economic policy toward Hungary. The rationale for this was that Austrian nobles had submitted to taxation while the Hungarian had not. The argument,

---

28 C. A. Macartney, *Hungary: A Short History* (Chicago: Aldine, 1962), p. 97.

29 This is from Maria Theresa's "Political Testament," discovered in the late nineteenth century and originally written under her close supervision about 1750. Macartney (ed.), *Habsburg and Hohenzollern Dynasties*, p. 112.

30 Béla K. Király, *Hungary in the Late Eighteenth Century: The Decline of Enlightened Despotism* (New York: Columbia University Press, 1969), p. 97, n. 36. Maria Theresa did try to get a Diet convoked in 1764 to approve her *urbarium*. This set minimum sizes for peasant holdings, extended to him legal protection, and attempted to register all land in the interests of State taxation and the general prosperity. When the Diet refused, she promulgated it by rescript in 1767. Macartney, *Hungary: A Short History*, pp. 114-15.

however, had flaws since the nobles of the Western Lands paid at a reduced rate with much land left "hidden" while the Hungarian political nation had some justification in resisting direct taxation which was irresponsibly expended. In any event, the "temporary" became permanent and was carried to a degree that some historians have viewed Hungary in this period as an economic colony. It is possible to over emphasize the bad effects of this policy on Hungary in view of the relative lack of economic activity in eighteenth century Central Europe. Yet even before Maria Theresa's time, Hungarians felt economic discrimination emanated from Vienna. Virtually every Hungarian Diet from 1723 to 1848 demanded changes in the Crown's discriminatory licensing and tariff policies with several submitting detailed proposals.[31]

In the social sphere, Maria Theresa created special schools and an elite Hungarian Bodyguard to attract the common nobles' sons to Vienna. She also built strong ties with the Magnates. The great Viennese residences of the Hungarian Magnates, so admired by the outer world and viewed with a mixture of envy and apprehension by lesser Hungarians, date from her reign. While many Hungarian Magnates became rather denationalized and cosmopolitan in their outlook, the political backbone of Hungary rested with the common nobles in their county assemblies. There the Constitution was very much alive during the long periods when the national Diet remained unconvoked.

The Crown appointed a lord-lieutenant (*főispán*) in each county, but his legal powers were purely formal and his actual status that of an observer and liaison officer.[32] Real power rested in the county assemblies, which could be called at any time and operated under their own elected officials who served virtually unpaid for roughly three year terms. The chief administrative officer, the *alispán*, took an oath acknow-

31 G. Heckenast, "Magyarország ipara 1726-ban" (Hungarian Industry in 1726), *Történelmi Szemle*, XIV, nos. 3-4 (1971), 320-39; Ferenc Eckhart, *A bécsi udvar gazdaságpolitikája Magyarországon Mária Terézia korában* (The Economic Policy of the Viennese Court in the Age of Maria Theresa) (Budapest: Budavári Tudományos Társaság, 1922); *A bécsi udvar gazdaságpolitikája Magyarországon, 1780-1815* (The Economic Policy of the Viennese Court, 1780-1815) (Budapest: Akadémiai Kiadó, 1956).

32 d'Eszlary, *Institutions*, III, 205.

ledging his responsibility to the assembly and his obligation to defend its interests; his election was invalid and no one obliged to obey him if he refused to do so.[33] The assembly exercised a wide degree of executive and judicial authority over all inhabitants, villages, and towns (except Royal Boroughs) within the county borders. Its activities included the regulation of such diverse matters as roads, health, lord-subject relations, land disputes, trade, prices, interest rates, recruitment, supply, and the quartering of Imperial Army units. The promulgation and enforcement of Vienna's directives handed down from the *Concilium* and the preparation of statistics and reports necessary for reform projects were also among its duties. By the mid-eighteenth century standards the county administrations were "stable, efficient, professional, well-organized, self-confident and effective."[34] The counties' statute-making powers were only limited by national Laws and constitutional custom; they were not subject to review by the central government and required no confirmation from it.[35] The counties' cooperation was necessary in the collection of taxes and their influence decisive when it fell time to negotiate via the national Diet, a new assessment for the war-tax (*contributio*) or other extraordinary levies requested by the Crown.[36] Such extraordinary direct taxation was levied exclusively on the productivity of the subject peasants since several Laws, notably Law VIII of 1741, stated all Hungarian land and all nobles were tax exempt.[37] As recognized in Law XXXIII of 1444, the counties had the constitutional right to question the legality of any rescript, decree, order, or policy of the King and the central government which they felt to be unconstitutional. They could protest these in writing or with a delegation to the originating authority and had the legal right to receive a considered reply. They could also raise such points in grievances (*gravamina*) at the national Diet. Whether they did

---

33 *Ibid.*, p. 206.

34 Király, *Hungary*, p. 110.

35 d'Eszlary, *Institutions*, III, 208.

36 Henry Marczali, *Hungary in the Eighteenth Century* (New York: Arno Press, 1971), pp. 353-54.

37 Macartney (ed.), *Habsburg and Hohenzollern Dynasties*, p. 134.

any of these things or not, they were legally entitled to exercise the "right of passivity" and to lay aside (*cum respectu ad acta*) an illegal royal decree and refuse to execute it.[38] Each county elected two Delegates to the national Diet who were bound by their assemblies' instructions on national questions, a system which required considerable alacrity and forethought by all concerned. Moreover, the counties legally could, and from the time of Maria Theresa with increasing frequency did, exchange views with one another concerning questions of national importance.[39] However much at the service of class interest, the Hungarian county system in the eighteenth century was also the conservator of the national and constitutional concept that political power was shared between King and nation under the rule of law.

Such Hungarian constitutional independence was in fundamental opposition to the absolutism and bureaucratic centralization which were the predominate political concepts in the Western half of the Monarchy by the end of the eighteenth century. Maria Theresa's son and successor, Joseph II (1780-1790), eagerly acceded to his long anticipated position of power determined to push these concepts to their "logical" culmination throughout the Monarchy. Influenced since youth by Enlightenment abstractions, he refused coronation as King of Hungary, nor would he employ his other titles. He saw himself instead as the animating force and absolute ruler of a rationalized empire for which he never did devise a name. He fostered the modern and beneficial objectives of opening careers to talent and improving the material welfare of society — especially that of the subject peasant whose obligations he set out to standardize but whom he did not necessarily intend to liberate. Some Hungarians initially supported these goals but their merits were canceled by his impatient and extreme political absolutism.[40] While Hungarians resisted

38 d'Eszlary, *Institutions*, III, 209; M. Bernath, "Ständewesen und Absolutismus im Ungarn des 18. Jahrhunderts," *Südostforschungen*, XXII (1963), 353.

39 d'Eszlary, *Institutions*, III, 207.

40 P. Sugar, "The Influence of the Enlightenment and the French Revolution in Eighteenth Century Hungary,"*Journal of Central European Affairs*, XVII, no. 4 (January, 1958), 331, 336, 340, 351, 354-55; George Barany, *Stephen Széchenyi and the Awakening of Hungarian Nationalism, 1791-1841* (Princeton, New Jersey: Princeton University Press, 1968), pp. 15-16, 145-46.

arbitrary and irresponsible taxation, Joseph refused to convoke the national Diet. He tried to Germanize the country and flooded it with bureaucrats dependent on his will as he tightened the colonial system of economic discrimination to the point of strangulation in order to secure political capitulation. This intensified Hungary's chronic lack of economic diversification and consigned the Emperor's own measures on behalf of the peasantry to the realm of ineffectual theory.[41] In 1785 he attacked the Hungarian counties in a series of decrees which would have destroyed the Constitution[42] and provoked determined resistance from the previously complacent nobility. Finally, the astute Catherine II enticed him into a common policy of Balkan adventurism and his inveterate militarism was the immediate cause of his failure. Even Viennese opinion[43] turned against his insistence on a tremendous anti-Turk war effort while the alienation of all classes in Hungary was virtually complete. This included even the peasants in southern Hungary who were expected to support with their all what was widely perceived as a Russian road to glory. At the time of his death, Joseph's policies had brought Hungary to the edge of a violent "feudal"[44] revolt, surpassed in the Habsburg Dominions only by that other political entity with definite concepts of constitutional government, the Austrian Netherlands. Hungary seethed with Enlightenment terminology and the "Balogh Program" of 1790 flatly demanded a written constitution with vice-regal powers to the Palatine and the establishment of a national administration responsible to the Diet.[45] A party of Hungarian nobles claimed that Joseph had broken his "contract" with the nation and the nobility in general formed paramilitary units, a movement which received considerable support from several Hungarian units in the Imperial Army.[46] Negotiations were conducted

41 E. Balázs, "Die Lage der Bauernschaft und die Bauernbewegungen 1780-1787," *Acta Historica*, III, no. 3 (1956), 300.

42 d'Eszlary, *Institutions*, III, 212-13.

43 See the assessment of Joseph by the eminent Austrian historian Friedrich Walter in "Autklärung und Politik am Beispiele österreichs," *Österreich in Geschichte und Literatur*, XI, no. 7 (September, 1965), 354-55.

44 Király, *Hungary*, p. 1.

45 *Ibid.*, p. 181.

46 *Ibid.*, p. 189.

rather openly for the election of a Prussian King, the legality of which being curiously enough supported with sincerity by the knowledgeable Imperial Chancellor, Prince Kaunitz, who had long and unsuccessfully tried to influence Joseph toward a policy of moderation.[47] This was the critical situation inherited by Joseph's brother and successor, Leopold II (1790-1792).

Leopold had constitutional inclinations and mastered the crisis with great skill being considerably aided by the withdrawal of Prussian support for Hungary. To the horror of his Imperial Austrian advisors, he conducted private negotiations with the Hungarians.[48] The resulting compromise was the abandonment of the Balogh program, the coronation of Leopold II as *rex legitimus,* and a legal revision to the *status quo ante* Joseph with the exception of his Peasant, Toleration, and Livings Patents which the Diet had the satisfaction of enacting on the basis of fourteenth and seventeenth century Hungarian Laws. Most importantly, Leopold agreed to consider at the Diet convoked on June 10, 1790 a corpus of Laws reconfirming Hungary's national and constitutional status.

The most famous of the "fundamental" Hungarian Laws of 1791 was the often cited Law X which stated in part that:

> Hungary with its annexed Parts shall be a free Kingdom and independent in respect of its entire lawful administration . . . that is, not subject to any other Kingdom or people, but having its own political entity and Constitution and consequently to be ruled and governed by its own lawfully crowned hereditary King . . . according to its own laws and customs, and not after the fashion of other Provinces . . . [49]

Many of the other 1791 Laws were hardly less important and taken as a whole their national as opposed to class interest was abundantly clear. Laws I and II recorded Leopold II's *diploma inaugurale* in the *Corpus Juris* in essentially the same form as had become traditional since 1711.[50] Law I repeated

---

47 *Ibid.,* pp. 193-94.
48 *Ibid.,* p. 237.
49 Macartney (ed.), *Habsburg and Hohenzollern Dynasties,* p. 142.
50 *Ibid.,* p. 141.

earlier legislation[51] which obliged the King to spend a part of each year in Hungary and article 2 of Law II also repeated older legislation requiring the guardians of the Holy Crown to be laymen without regard to their religion.[52] Law VI stated that the Holy Crown should be kept and guarded at Buda (Joseph II had removed it) and, in conformity with the sense of Law XXXVIII of 1715, stated that only in case of danger was it to be transported elsewhere.[53] Law IV recorded the election of the King's brother as Palatine, stated that he was supreme commander of the nation's armed forces, and required him to reside in Buda, the location of the nation's central administrative institution (the *Consilium*).[54] To seal Joseph II's loophole, Law III required the King to issue the proper *diploma* and be crowned within six months of "the day of death" of his predecessor.[55] Law XII stated that "the right of enacting, rescinding, and interpreting legislation" was vested "jointly in the lawfully crowned Prince and the Estates of the Realm, lawfully assembled in the Diet and cannot be exercised outside it."[56] The King was to "preserve this right of the Estates uninfringed," to transmit it intact, and Hungary was "never to be governed through Edicts or so-called Patents" which were to be employed only in "cases where the law is unaffected."[57] The King was not to interfere in the functions of the lawfully established judiciary; he was to appoint judges without discrimination concerning religion and to exercise his executive powers "in the sense of the laws only."[58] Law XIII required the King to convoke the Diet every three years or "earlier should the public welfare" make it desirable.[59] The Dietal members were not to be impeded in any manner from assembling or discussing the

51 Laws LVII of 1536, XVIII of 1546, XXII of 1547, article four of Law III of 1563, XLVI of 1567, XVIII of 1608, VIII of 1723, VII of 1741, I of 1751, d'Eszlary, *Institutions*, III, 66 and n. 112.

52 *Ibid.*, p. 65 and n. 108.

53 *Ibid.*, p. 64.

54 Macartney (ed.), *Habsburg and Hohenzollern Dynasties*, p. 141.

55 *Ibid.*

56 *Ibid.*

57 *Ibid.*, p. 142.

58 *Ibid.*, p. 143.

59 *Ibid.*

"business of the Realm with lawful liberty" and all affairs "shall at every Diet be dealt with effectively and in full."[60] Law XIX stated that the size of the *contributio* for the maintenance of the military was to be negotiated at the Diet and fixed until the next convocation. Most importantly, all taxes "whether in cash, kind, or recruits" were not to be levied on "nobles or non-nobles" without the consent of the Diet.[61] Law XVIII required all Hungarian officeholders to take an oath to observe the Constitution. Laws XIV and XVII,[62] referring to previous legislation, notably that of 1741, obligated the King to conduct Hungarian affairs through the Hungarian *Consilium.* "Equipped with all necessary authority to execute the law, . . . it was directly subordinate"[63] to the monarch, and independent of all other institutions. The King was to be "duly advised" by Hungarians on Hungarian affairs and, if, "by any mishap unlawful commands reach the country," the King was bound to "pay due heed" to representations concerning them while he bound himself and successors to maintain the law, the counties, and other jurisdictions "intact."[64] Finally, it was established that "His Majesty has also declared himself ready to satisfy the wishes of the Estates in that Hungarian internal affairs shall be conducted by Hungarians, and foreign affairs with the participation of Hungarians."[65]

These Hungarian Laws of 1791 were patently of fundamental constitutional and national importance. Before the Diet of 1790/91, Austrian efforts to weaken the Hungarian Constitution had stood on the shaky legal basis[66] that the Hungarian Constitution, due to its organic growth, was not a closed legal code but a partially unwritten collection of custom, privilege, and sometimes paradoxical Laws; a compilation which was the product of centuries of growth, struggle

---

60 *Ibid.*

61 *Ibid.*, p. 144.

62 *Ibid.*, pp. 143-44.

63 *Ibid.*, p. 143.

64 *Ibid.*, pp. 143-44.

65 *Ibid.*, p. 144.

66 Bernath, "Ständewesen und Absolutismus im Ungarn des 18. Jahrhunderts," p. 353.

and change. Therefore, the advantage of the 1791 Laws was that they explicitly codified, updated, and adapted to Habsburg rule the essentials for Hungarian constitutional government in the span of a single Diet. They reiterated the independence and integrity of the Hungarian State in such a unified manner that future policies of procrastination or subversion toward Hungary on the part of Viennese policy makers were much more difficult. Critics of these Laws subsequently attempted to obscure their obvious national and constitutional meaning by popularizing the simplification that they were nothing more than a codification of the privileges of the Hungarian nobility.[67] However, Győző Ember was one of many who arrived at a more realistic assessment of the role of the nobility in the eighteenth century when he stated that "the ruling class fought not only in its own interest, but in the interest of the entire nation. The rights and privileges which they defended were not only those of their class, but also national rights and privileges."[68] Even as trenchant a critic of the Hungarian State as Louis Eisenmann noted the constitutional and national nature of the 1791 Hungarian legislation, and its direct legal continuity in these respects with the Hungarian 1848 legislation. He also claimed that Hungary's Laws were a "legal fiction" since they remained largely unobserved,[69] but this observation cannot really detract from the legal and moral validity of Hungary's constitutional compact with the dynasty as expressed in the Laws of 1791.

Yet, on the debit side, the Hungarian Laws of 1791 constituted a restoration rather than an innovation. The Balogh radical proposals to place the preponderance of power in the legislature with an executive responsible to it had been withdrawn. Leopold's concessions to Hungary in the vital areas of finances, military, and foreign affairs were formal rather

---

67 C. M. Knatchbull-Hugessen gives an old example of the Austrian view with critical comment. *The Political Evolution of the Hungarian Nation* (2 vols.; London: National Review Office, 1908), I, 232, n. 1. More recently, this view of the Leopoldian settlement has been repeated by Taylor, *The Habsburg Monarchy 1809-1918*, p. 20.

68 "Der österreichische Staatsrat und die ungarische Verfassung 1761-1768," *Acta Historica*, VI, nos. 1-2 (1960), 114.

69 *Le Compromis austro-hongrois* (Paris: Société nouvelle de Librairie et d'Édition G. Bellais, 1904), p. 639.

than substansive in nature. The monarch retained his right of absolute veto over legislation and a great deal continued to depend on his will. This was not an inherently detrimental situation in view of the fact that Hungary, evaluated by its Laws, was a throughly constitutional monarchy. However, the real obstacle to the realization of constitutional governance, left ùnmastered by the Hungarian Laws of 1791, derived from the simple fact that the Habsburgs were not truly national Kings. The dynasty commanded non-Hungarian resources in an absolute manner which normally allowed it to act with complete independence of any financial clout mounted by the Hungarian Diet. This hindered Hungarian development toward a parliamentary system with ministerial responsibility such as evolved over many generations in England. Moreover, the pervasive influence of the Austrian Secret Police, so much a part of life before 1848, really got under way in Leopold's reign.

However, in late 1790 some hope of further progress continued to exist. When the Diet rose on March 13, 1791, it had established in Law LXVII nine commissions whose members were influenced by Enlightenment thought.[70] This, plus the recent ferment at home and that of the French Revolution abroad prompted them to set about devising proposals for a thoroughgoing overhaul of Hungarian conditions in a conservative, but entirely serious manner.[71] Even the Hungarian peasant, whose legal status had been debated in a patriarchical fashion at the Diet[72] and fixed according to Law XXXV, might well have received eventual benefit from their work since the commercial and economic proposals were reportedly well thought out. As fate had it, this potentially beneficial work of the Dietal commissions, in which the his-

---

70 d'Eszlary, *Institutions*, III, 90-91, 98.

71 *Ibid.*; Barany, *Stephen Széchenyi*, pp. 32-33.

72 One member recommended that non-noble officials of peasant communities present the views of their inhabitants on a regular basis at the county assemblies. But he also believed that the non-privileged members were in need of guidance and that "the French pattern of events has clearly demonstrated that the people, imprisoned for a long period in a dark jail, cannot stand sharp rays if they reach their eyes too abruptly." Bálint Hóman and Gyula Szekfű, *Magyar történet* (Hungarian History) (5 vols.; 7th ed.; Budapest: Királyi Magyar Egyetemi Nyomda, 1941-1943), V, 63.

torian István Barta sees the true genesis of the subsequent Hungarian Reform Era,[73] was halted for the span of a full generation.

\* \* \*

Leopold II died unexpectedly on March 1, 1792, as the French Revolution which he originally welcomed degenerated toward terrorism and the Monarchy entered a quarter century of nearly constant war effort. The tragedy of Leopold's death was compounded by the conversative temperament of his successor, Francis I (1792-1835), as well as the discovery of the so-called "Martinovics Conspiracy" in Hungary, an affair which even with its Austrian counterpart would have been innocuous and almost comical save for its far reaching results. In Hungary it resulted in the execution or imprisonment of several of the nation's best patriots many of whom were likely completely innocent of treasonous activity or intention.[74] These events conspired to turn Hungary's ruling classes firmly against considerations of reform while the Emperor Francis employed his capacity as Hungarian King to call one Diet after another demanding extensive votes of men and supplies. His demands were met loyally enough since many Hungarians, including numerous writers and poets, who had originally believed Napoleon to be the true standard bearer of French revolutionary principles rather quickly came to distrust his intentions and methods. By 1800 they turned against him nearly to a man.[75] As one Hungarian wrote, Napoleon was great in the sense of Frederick II or Catherine II, but he would not choose to live under any one of the three.[76] Still, Hungarians were under no illusions concerning Habsburg solicitude toward the nation and resentment grew over Francis' habit of illegally dissolving the Diet immediately upon achieving his objects without ever hearing Dietal proposals. Faced with war-

---

73 "A magyar polgári reformmozgalom kezdeti szakaszának problémái." pp. 336-42.

74 C. Benda, "Les Jacobins hongrois," *Annales historiques de la Révolution française,* XXXI (January-March, 1959), 55, 57-59.

75 Édouard Sayous, *Histoire des Hongrois et de leur Littérature politique de 1790 a 1815* (Paris: Librairie Germer-Bailliere, 1872), pp. 109-10, 118-21, 127-28.

76 Béla Grünwald, *A régi Magyarország 1711-1825* (The Old Hungary 1711-1825) (3rd ed.; Budapest: Franklin-Társulat, 1910), p. 71.

time conditions, the Hungarians perforce swallowed this practice and neither the incursion of French troops in November, 1805, nor Napoleon's consumate public appeal to the nation in May, 1809[77] (which touched every sore spot in its relationship with the dynasty) was sufficient to sever Hungarian adherence to its hereditary and legitimate King. Many Hungarians even keenly resented the dynasty's forced obeisance to Napoleon in that year. The Hungarian consensus concerning Napoleonic imperialism was confirmed by the incorporation of Croat territory associated with the Holy Crown into the "Illyrian Provinces." Yet, Vienna interpreted the independent-mindedness of Hungarian loyalty as near if not actual treason.

Predictably, it was the Monarchy's desperate financial condition which brought Hungary and the Habsburgs to a constitutional nadir in 1811. Early in the year, the Vienna government replaced the expedient of the printing press with a stroke of the pen, recalling all notes and small coins in circulation and replacing them with a new issue on the ratio of one new for five old notes, which naturally increased State taxation five fold. This brutal attack on inflation pressed especially hard on debtors (the State recommended scale of conversion did not hold) and on the poorer peasants who were heavily dependent on small coins.[78] Moreover, the measure never did demonstrate its dubious merits because it was soon wrecked by the 1813 war effort. But, even before this, the Crown also chose 1811 to violate Law XX of 1791 as well as Francis' rescripts of September 23, 1802 and December 14, 1807 by arbitrarily increasing the important salt tax.[79] Vienna next demanded a one hundred per cent increase in the Hungarian *contributio* and that Hungary assume the amortization of 100 million forints of the Monarchy's 212 million State debt—to be met at 1,885,000 forints per annum payable in

---

77 See L. Lanyi, "Napoléon et les Hongrois," *Annales historiques de la Révolution francaise,* XXVII, nouvelle serie (October-December, 1955), 368-69.

78 This *Finanzpatent* of 1811 was completed on February 20th and officially extended to Hungary in May. Grünwald, *A régi Magyarország,* p. 436; Hugessen, *Political Evolution,* I, 250-51.

79 Hugessen, *ibid.,* p. 250 and n. 2.

silver[80] The Hungarian Diet which sat from August 25, 1811 to May 30, 1812[81] protested on the practical grounds that the salt and small coin measures alone were ruinous to the poor peasants and furthermore protested, as usual, the preferential tariff long maintained against Hungarian interests. In addition, the Diet's theoretical and constitutional protests were also accurate. The Crown's traditional prerogatives concerning coinage were reaffirmed, but the Delegates ardently argued that these recent Vienna-decreed paper manipulations constituted and unprecedented form of hidden, irresponsible, and uncontrolled taxation. This was injurious to all classes in Hungarian society. Nothing in the Pragmatic Sanction, they stated, justified these sweeping fiscal measures which were taken completely outside Dietal control.[82] The hard pressed Crown thereupon dismissed the Diet and ruled Hungary unconstitutionally for the following thirteen years which was small consideration in return for the nation's material sacrifices and the steadfastness of its troops during the preceding decades of crises. Although few historians have noted it, the Crown's cavalier treatment of the Hungarian Constitution at this time created, in effect, a debt which was presented with accumulated interest by Hungary in 1848.

\* \* \*

The *de facto* loss of financial sovereignty to "Vienna" in the opening years of the nineteenth century paradoxically called attention to a gradual qualitative transformation in the importance of economic activity for the nation. During the Napoleonic Wars, the increased demands for Hungarian cereal products had resulted in several periods of boom prosperity which implanted the idea of large scale production for a cash market. The centuries-old cyclical production for a self-sufficient local market slowly began to retreat before the uneven advance of a monied economy. The necessities and opportunities of incipient "capitalism" encouraged land speculation and sponsored an unprecedented desire for credit which

---

80 Hóman and Szekfű, *Magyar történet*, V, 190.

81 *Ibid.*, pp. 189-90; d'Eszlary, *Institutions*, III, 129.

82 Hóman and Szekfű, *ibid.*; d'Eszlary, *ibid.*

touched small nobles and peasants as well as the big men. In 1825, an aristocrat, later known to the English speaking world as Count Stephen Széchenyi, first appeared in the public eye by offering a year's income to found the Hungarian Academy. He soon wrote a book in 1830 entitled, *Hitel* (Credit), which was followed by other works demanding a revision of Hungarian Laws and conditions. Széchenyi argued that land must be freed of entail (the *ősiség* of 1351) and that the labor of a subject peasant was only one-third as productive and therefore less profitable than paid labor. Entirely selfless and deeply patriotic, his essentially moral purpose of regenerating Hungary was frequently misunderstood by his fellow countrymen. But he tirelessly promoted his persuasive efforts on behalf of beneficial change via a nearly inexhaustible series of practical and non-political projects. Among these were the construction of a Buda-Pest suspension bridge, the improvement of roads, and making the Tisza river navigable. Due to his efforts, increasing numbers of patriotic Hungarians became aware that their nation must make necessary changes or fall hopelessly behind the advances of Western Europe. [83]

The Hungarian Reform Era was unquestionably under way by the 1830s. But whichever way Hungarians turned to express the concerns of reform, they encountered the ever-present obstacle of Vienna's censorship and Secret Police.[84] When they

---

83 Széchenyi's call for reform commanded attention because of his social position as a Magnate, but he was not alone in his recognition of the necessity. Recent Hungarian research has thrown light on the many works of John Balásházy, a poor member of the middling nobility who won national recognition and awards from the Academy. His first work, a guide to sheep raising, stated that its purpose was "to help the middle class and those even lower" and his 1829 "Advice to Hungarian Agriculturalists" stressed the need for credit to the extent the names Balásházy and Széchenyi were often linked in the public mind. Balásházy especially complained about the usurious practice of the private money lenders (with whom he had personal experience) who easily evaded the legal six per cent interest limitation. He urged the education and liberation of the subject peasants. The Palatine, Archduke Joseph, had a high opinion of him and Széchenyi as well as other great landowners purchased hundreds of copies of his 1830 "Reader" which they distributed free of charge among their subjects. See L. Tilkovszky, "Balásházy János élete és munkássága" (The Life and Works of János Balásházy), *Századok*, XCVI, nos. 3-4 (1962), 409, 412, 414-15, 416, 418, 422, 425.

84 Balásházy's criticism of the tariff and his general advocacy of sweeping legal reforms brought him under the watchful eye of the Austrian Secret Police. The pressure proved too great for him and in the 1840s he refrained from public comment on any problems involving Hungary's relationship to Austria. *Ibid.*, pp. 417, 425-27.

turned to the Crown, they found it dedicated to a system of immobility. Széchenyi's efforts to secure Metternich's support for his essentially moderate and non-political projects of material improvement met with far more procrastination than affirmation.[85] In Vienna, Hungarians saw their constitutional system of government held so tightly in the illegal handcuffs of a monarchic and bureaucratic absolutism that legal redress of their nation's retarded conditions often appeared permanently precluded. Looking abroad, Hungarians managed to be extremely well informed of European problems and conditions,[86] but found Europe hardly cognizant of their aspirations or constitutional order, so overshadowed had the Hungarian State become by its inclusion in the Habsburg Monarchy.

An illustration of Hungary's isolation from Europe at this time was the wonder with which Englishmen "discovered" the country. When the English traveller, John Paget, visiting Vienna in the summer of 1835, announced his intention of venturing into Hungary, he was strongly urged against the project. Neither his possessions nor his very life would be safe in that strange land. "Nothing," he later wrote, "can exceed the horror with which a true Austrian regards both Hungary and its inhabitants." But he was then sufficiently impressed to have his sturdy coach plentifully provided with arms, which were carefully loaded and "ready for immediate use."[87] Several hours of dusty posting out of Vienna brought him to a simple barrier in the road signifying the Hungarian border. Here he encountered the first of many surprises. Upon offering his passport to the guard it was declined with a bow and the as-

85 The long relationship between these two complex individuals was a fascinating one in which Metternich's esteem of the Hungarian Constitution as a guarantee of stability was abundantly clear. Barany, *Stephen Széchenyi*, pp. 124-31, 141, 214, 303, 319f, 375, 391, 401f, 454f, 460f.

86 See, for example, the intense interest with which Hungarians followed the agitation in England for repeal of the Corn Laws in the newspapers "Jelenkor" (Present Times), "Pesti Hírlap" (Pest News), "Hetilap" (Weekly), "Budapesti Hír- adó" (The Budapest News), "Hírnök" (News), and "Világ" (The World) in which many Hungarians argued for eventual industrialization in accordance with Hungary's capacities while at the same time taking care to avoid its attendant evils so apparent in England. E. H. Haraszti, "Contemporary Hungarian Reactions to the Anti-Corn Law Movement," *Acta Historica*, VIII, nos. 3-4 (1961), 381-403.

87 *Hungary and Transylvania with Remarks on their Condition, Social, Political and Economical* (2 vols.; New London ed.; Philadelphia: Lea and Blanchard, 1850), I, 13.

surance that in Hungary he no longer had need of it; an event which, as he noted, was most unusual in the Central Europe of that day. Altogether, Paget spent a year and a half in Hungary on his first trip during which time he travelled through the country extensively and thoroughly. He never once had need of his arms, but he did make effective use of a notebook and ended by producing an irreplaceable pen portrait of the nation and its people. This so far transcended the newly popular genre of travelogues in its detail and judgement as to become a classic of its type and extremely useful to historians in the absence of similar Hungarian accounts.[88] It is true that he wrote sympathetically of Hungary and subsequently settled there permanently, but his many well considered criticisms of society and legal conditions were often sharp and always honest. He observed and conversed with all manner of men, from innkeepers, peasants, and merchants through the common nobility to great aristocrats. What he discovered was a land of great contrasts. Many aspects of its day to day life had changed little since the time of Maria Theresa, yet everywhere there was talk of change and reform. Centuries of tradition fostered an innate conservatism, but this blended with a remarkable vitality. A rich diversity of peoples and cultures existed simultaneously with an underlying and unyielding sense of State unity. The highly deferential social system somehow successfully accommodated a national passion for extremely individualistic and self-assured expressions of opinion and argumentation. Despite the censorship, booksellers managed to stock a good collection of European literature which usually appeared in Hungarian, German and Latin translation. Paget found English journals in the national casino in Pest and encountered to his amazement an innkeeper in remote Upper Hungary with a great admiration for England who produced a well-worn copy of one of Sir Walter Scott's novels.[89] Yet, side by side with a growing dissatisfaction with Hungarian conditions and the notably wide-spread admiration for England, there also existed a strong sense of a unique State identity and deep attachment to Hungarian institutions.

88 J. Balogh, "John Paget," *The Hungarian Quarterly*, VI, no. 1 (Spring, 1940), 66-68, 71, 79.
89 *Hungary and Transylvania*, I, 25-26, 79-80, 143.

In 1840 slightly after Paget's first travels, the Kingdom of Hungary with Transylvania encompassed 125,000 English square miles and supported with ease an estimated total population of 12,880,900 souls.[90] Since 1782 the population of the Royal Free Boroughs had increased from 352,000 to 575,518 inhabitants.[91] But this was only a superficially progressive increase since the majority of these urban dwellers could not be considered bourgeoisie in the Western sense, nor did they play any significant role in the national political structure.[92] Rather, the growth in the urban population simply reflected a rapid overall increase in all classes which constituted an average population expansion of seventy per cent in the half century between 1787 and 1840.[93] Out of the total 1840 population, 680,000 persons or something in excess of five per cent regardless of age or sex, were in possession of noble status.[94] By 1848 when the estimated total population of Hungary stood at 15,000,000 those with noble status could be conservatively estimated at 700,000.[95] The Hungarian nobility of the Reform Era thus increased apace with the overall population growth and in some areas even surpassed that of other classes. This was explained in part by the phenomenon that "many families were able to prove to the satisfaction of the counties that they were noble, a fact previosly lost to memory." [96]

---

90 Gyula Szekfű, *Három nemzedék és ami utána következik* (Three Generations and What Followed) (Budapest: Királyi Magyar Egyetemi Nyomda, 1935), p. 70 and ns, 1, 2. Some contemporary statistics placed the total slightly higher. Bárány, *Stephen Széchenyi,* p. 149, n. 52.

91 Királyi, *Hungary,* p. 42; Szekfű, *Három nemzedék,* p. 70.

92 Szekfű, *ibid.* See also Hóman and Szekfű, *Magyar történet,* V, 242.

93 Hóman and Szekfű, *Magyar történet,* V, 209.

94 *Ibid.*

95 Kann, *Multinational Empire,* I, 119.

96 Hóman and Szekfű, *Magyar történet,* V, 208. Hungarian law made no distinction whatsoever on the basis of language in regard to the acquisition or retention of noble status, but in practice the great majority of Hungarian nobles were Hungarian-speaking from birth. Still, the very existence of Hungarian nobles whose mother tongue was other than Hungarian tends to discredit the belief that this class was racially restricted and indicates that stratification traditionally occurred along class lines and the support or nonsupport of the Hungarian State. In 1840 of the 544,372 nobles of Inner Hungary; 464,705 were Hungarian speaking by birth, about 58,000 spoke a Slavonic language by birth, and some 21,666 were primarily German or Roumanian speaking. Elek Fényes, *Magyarország statisztikája* (Hungary's statistics) (3 vols.; Pest: Trattner-Károlyi, 1842), I, 64.

The Hungarian nobles' exclusive possession of political rights in pre-reform Hungary made their activity, excepting that of the Crown, paramount in national politics. When virtually all minors and women are necessarily omitted from political considerations, those in possession of the franchise before 1848 may have constituted nine or ten per cent of the total adult male population.[97] Thus, in Hungary a higher proportion of the total population could exercise suffrage rights than in England with Wales prior to the Reform Act of 1832[98] or in France at any time prior to 1848. Concerning France, especially, this comparison is particularly striking. Before the July 1830 Revolution, the French Charter admitted about 94,000 individuals to the exercise of the franchise out of a total population of 30,000,000 souls.[99] This was .3% of the total population or one in every 322 individuals. After 1830, amendments to the electoral law increased the number of eligible voters to 188,000.[100] However, agitation for further suffrage extension as well as other reforms met with little satisfaction from the Guizot Ministry. In the general elections of 1846 when the largest number of voters were registered during the entire period of the July Monarchy, only 241,000 persons were admitted to the franchise. Hence, in the France of 1846, even in this extraordinary election, only a relatively small group of titled nobility, landed gentry, and upper bourgeoisie which constituted less than one per cent of the total population could exercise the suffrage.[101] Therefore, the Hungarian historian, Gyula Szekfű, was entirely correct when he stated that in democratic France fewer people had access to political

97 K. k. Direction der administrativen Statistik, *Tafeln zur Statistik der österreichischen Monarchie*, 1846, part I, table 2, p. 2 as cited by Jerome Blum, *Noble Landowners and Agriculture in Austria 1815-1848: A Study in the Origins of the Peasant Emancipation of 1848* (Baltimore: The Johns Hopkins Press, 1948), p. 36, n. 83.

98 Sir Llewellyn Woodward, *The Age of Reform 1815-1870*, Vol. XIII of *The Oxford History of England*, ed. Sir George Clark (14 vols.; 2nd ed.; Oxford: Clarendon Press, 1962), pp. 88, 599 and n. 1.

99 Szekfű, *Három nemzedék*, p. 74.

100 *Ibid.*

101 Sherman Kent, *Electoral Procedure under Louis Philippe* (New Haven: Yale University Press, 1937), p. 25.

power than in Hungary under the old, unreformed, feudal Constitution prior to 1848.[102]

Recently some historians have criticized comparisons between the old Hungarian political structure and Western States as deceptive and misleading since the relatively high percentage of enfranchised population in Hungary rested upon membership in a privileged class which "had no mandate to represent the rest of the population."[103] As Professor Barany has concisely described the problems of the Hungarian Reform Era:

> The Hungarian Diet was *not* a modern parliament in the Western sense . . . . A feudal system of representation, functioning in an essentially absolutist system of government, had come to grips with the demands put forward by Western liberal ideologies and by the economic necessities of incipient capitalist practices . . . [104]

Certainly there is no doubt that pre-1848 Hungary's constitutional structure as well as its experience, values, traditions, and the lamentable lack of economic diversification militated in many ways against the emergence of a modernized and democratically inclined State.

However, those who might be tempted to elevate these very correct observations to the exclusion of all other elements in the pre-1848 situation would be placing carts before horses in a real sense. Exclusive emphasis on how far Hungary was from functioning as an ideal democratic polity while ignoring the positive elements in the historic Constitution and the nobility's undeniable concept of public service, leaves one at a considerable loss to explain the nation's indigenous resistance to absolutism and the provision of greater political equity in early 1848. Paget, writing in the 1830s concerning the Hungarian nobles' legal exemption from taxation, had no difficulty in perceiving not only the negative elements in the situation, but also the crux of the constitutional problem. Standing armies had long since outmoded the original justification for the

---

102 *Három nemzedék*, p.74.

103 Barany, *Stephen Széchenyi*, pp. 149-50 and n. 56.

104 "The Hungarian Diet of 1839-40 and the Fate of Széchenyi's Middle Course," *Slavic Review*, XXII, no. 2 (June, 1965), 503.

exemption and he condemned the right of one class to enjoy this privilege at the expense of the rest of society. Yet, he also stated that the more progressive nobles had "some show of reason on their side when they declared that they will only yield up the privilege on obtaining a direct influence on the expenditure of revenue; in other words a budget and a responsible ministry."[105]

Paget's remark illustrates that virtually all reform proposals in early nineteenth century Hungary tended to become politicized when encountering "Vienna's" preference for unchanged conditions and the continuation of *de facto* absolutism.[106] The political obstacles to reform were seen as constituting the paramount issues by a poor noble from Upper Hungary who was subsequently widely known in the English-speaking world as Louis Kossuth. He came to the Lower House of the Diet in 1832 as the appointed representative of a Magnate's widow, a peculiar constitutional provision which restricted his activities. Even so, he effectively agitated for the proposition that reform should be achieved through the proper exercise of the political power guaranteed to Hungary by its sanctioned Laws. He built a considerable following among the reform-minded in the Lower House, but this group accomplished little in the face of Magnate resistance. In direct contravention of the Hungarian Constitution as codified by Werbőczy, a group in the Upper House at this juncture seriously maintained that the King's legal inviolability extended beyond his person to protect members of the government and their policies from criticism in the Lower House.[107] This sentiment was evidently an indication of "Vienna's" decision to adopt a repressive policy for when the Diet rose in 1836, Kossuth and several other members of the Liberal opposition were arrested for their pains.[108] This official violation of due process and *salvus conductus* (the immunity of Dietal

---

105 *Hungary and Transylvania,* I, 242-43.

106 See, for example, Jerome Blum's account of Vienna's adversion to change. "Transportation and Industry in Austria 1815-1848," *Journal of Modern History,* XV, no. 1 (March, 1943), 24-38.

107 d'Eszlary, *Institutions,* III, 141-42.

108 Macartney, *Hungary: A Short History,* p. 147; Barany, "The Hungarian Diet of 1839-40 and the Fate of Széchenyi's Middle Course," p. 291, n. 30.

members) provoked a storm of protest. When Vienna reversed itself by 1840, the net result was that the released Kossuth was more prominent than ever. His belief in the efficacy of liberty and his emphasis on direct political action carried infinitely more appeal for the Hungarian temperament than Széchenyi's Vienna-dependent program of cautions and gradual material improvement. Paget had automatically sensed the situation when visiting the Diet in 1835. He noted the general support in the Lower House for speeches against a measure of the Vienna government and the "dead silence" which weighed on the deliberations of the Upper House in which the minority of Liberal Magnates were "totally powerless."[109]

Agitation for reform in Hungary clearly mounted during the time of Paget's visit. Still, with all the lengthy debates in the Lower House,[110] the "Long Diet" of 1832-36 failed to secure sanction of a single major reform measure. Minor items were passed. Laws VI and X of 1836 recognized that subject peasants had collective property rights in the division of common lands.[111] Laws XXV and XXVI enacted the principle of expropriation and declared tolls should be paid by nobles on Széchenyi's proposed Buda-Pest suspension bridge.[112] But the crucial reform ideas remained stillborn in the legal sense.

The Diet of 1839-40 was somewhat more successful with its reform proposals since the Crown, in need of money and recruits, undertook consideration of a host of measures and extended sanction to several. Law XVII of 1840 was a bit ahead of its time in prohibiting unheated factories and restricting child labor, ages twelve through sixteen, to a nine hour day with a one hour break therein. Laws VI and VII of 1840 provided that the subject peasant could forever and irreversibly terminate his obligations and status by means of a voluntary agreement with his lord. The measure had considerable symbolic meaning in the altered economic milieu of the early nineteenth century, but its effects were negligible due to

---

109 *Hungary and Transylvania*, I, 28-31.
110 Hóman and Szekfű, *Magyar történet*, V, 288.
111 d'Eszlary, *Institutions*, III, 338.
112 Bárány, *Stephen Széchenyi*, pp. 275ff, 338.

the acute lack of credit facilities.[113] Consequently, from 1840, measures to facilitate adequate credit were of major concern to the reformers. A few attempts were made to initiate banks, but these were so inadequate they only served to illustrate the great need.[114]

Next, the Diet of 1843-44 drafted a bill for a large scale credit institution. But this measure, which originally had Crown support, fell through quickly enough due to arguments with Vienna concerning control of the institution, the Hungarians fearing that exclusive Vienna control would encourage political reprisals.[115] A similar fate awaited other constructive Dietal proposals for tariff revision, revision of the criminal code, and the extension of urban suffrage to elect magistrates and increase representation in the national Diet. Széchenyi's constructive proposal for a noble land tax was carried by the Lower House, but eventually it also failed. In the end, the only clear-cut advance was Law IV of 1844 which unequivocally stated that all non-nobles belonging to an "accepted" religion as well as nobles had the right to become freehold land-owners.[116]

When the Crown convoked the Hungarian Diet in 1847, the reformers' persistence and the increasing support which they received brought a belated recognition in Vienna that some consideration of reform was necessary. But the Hungarians' ever mounting desire for significant change plus the small amount of progress realized since 1832, gained supporters for the argument that only a complete implementation of the nation's Constitution could secure the necessary reforms. All proposals for change increasingly returned to the ultimate question of the constitutional exercise of political power versus continued absolutism. Therefore, this account of Hungary's simultaneous struggle to achieve national and social modernization in early 1848, properly begins with a consideration of the Hungarian Diet on the eve of "1848."

---

113 d'Eszlary, *Institutions*, III, 339.
114 *Ibid.*
115 Mihály Horváth, *Huszonöt év Magyarország történelméből 1823-1848* (Twenty-five Years from the History of Hungary 1823-1848) (3 vols.; 3rd ed.; Budapest: Mór Ráth, 1886), II. 266.
116 Hóman and Szekfű, *Magyar történet*, V, 327-32; d'Eszlary, *Institutions*, III, 339, and n. 222.

*Chapter I*

## A GLANCE INTO THE HUNGARIAN
## DIET PRIOR TO "1848"

Before the beginning of the year 1848 as well as "1848," a member of the Upper House of the Hungarian Diet observed that there was scarcely a county in Hungary in which the nobles had not for some years past been voluntarily contributing large sums in the form of subsidies for county purposes.[1] The new county hall in Pozsony, for example, had been paid for exclusively by a rate which the county nobles had voted upon themselves.[2] In fact, a system of general taxation of all classes, noble and non-noble without distinction, had been under discussion since 1845 and had been adopted on the part

---

1 Speech delivered by Count Emil Dessewffy before the conservative Magnates of the Upper House in a private debate shortly before the Diet's 1847 Christmas recess. Great Britain, Parliament, House of Commons, *Sessional Papers,* 1851, Vol. LVIII, *Correspondence Relative to the Affairs of Hungary, 1847-1849 Presented to Both Houses of Parliament by Command of Her Majesty August 15, 1850,* (hereinafter referred to as *CRAH*), p. 20, Mr. Blackwell, Presburg, ("Presburg" is a variant spelling of the more commonly used "Pressburg" and is retained in the *CRAH* references as originally written.), 3 February, 1848 to Viscount Ponsonby, Vienna. Blackwell refers to these debates among the Magnates having taken place after they received a *nuncium* from the Lower House on December 7, 1847. Summary of the Proceedings of the Hungarian Diet of 1847-48, *CRAH,* p. 11.

2 Mr. Blackwell to Viscount Ponsonby. Presburg February 3, 1848, *CRAH,* p. 20. Csongrád county in central Hungary had been one of the first counties (in the early 1840's) in which the nobles had voted taxes on themselves for domestic purposes. The seventh of the "Szatmár Points" of 1841 had called for noble taxation and nineteen of fifty-two counties in 1842 had recommended complete taxation in their instructions to the Dietal Delegates. The principle of general taxation was accepted by both Houses at the Diet of 1843-44. Hóman and Szekfű, *Magyar történet,* V, 322, 328 and 330. It should be noted that Mr. Blackwell writes from Pressburg and that the Hungarian Diet was situated there. Pressburg (in the Hungarian language "Pozsony") had been the seat of the Hungarian Diet since 1541 due to the Turkish occupation of central Hungary and had remained the seat of the Diet after the Turkish withdrawal because of the city's relative convenience to Vienna. The Hungarian national central administrative institutions had, however, been moved back to Buda by Joseph II in 1784. Andrew F. Burghardt, *Borderland: A Historical and Geographical Study of Burgenland Austria* (Madison: University of Wisconsin Press, 1962), pp. 124-26. Pozsony is presently Bratislava, the capital of Slovakia in the State of Czechoslovakia.

of the Liberal opposition in the Lower House in an "Oppositional Declaration" issued the previous summer in June, 1847.[3]

On November 29, 1847, a Delegate named Szemere delivered a speech on the question of general taxation before the Lower House. He represented Borsod, a very Protestant and one of the most Liberal counties of the period. He concluded his speech with three proposals. The first, asking if the nobles would be willing to pay conjointly with the non-nobles (largely the subject peasants) the *cassa domestica* (the local county taxation), was answered in the affirmative by a majority of seventeen votes. The second proposal, asking if the nobles would be willing to be assessed on a permanent basis for the *contributio* (the "war tax" which the Diet periodically voted to the Habsburgs), was defeated by fifteen votes. However, the third proposal calling upon the nobles to pay a direct tax into a national treasury was carried in the affirmative almost unanimously.[4] In the latter instance, the funds so raised would be applied to projects of national benefit, for example road construction on a national scale.

On December 7, 1847, a full-dress Dietal sitting of the Lower House formally passed these resolutions and sent them in the form of a communication (*nuncium*) to the Upper House of Magnates, urging the Magnates to adopt them as well. The *nuncium* also asked them to agree to the formulation of a joint two-House Dietal committee to draft appropriate legislation and to find a means by which the Diet could retain its control over any national revenues raised by this new taxation. Probably to make the recommendations more palatable to conservatives among the Magnates, the *nuncium* of the Lower House observed that it might be more advisable to raise funds for national purposes largely by indirect rather than direct taxation. But the overriding concern was that the proposed committee should devise the most stringent bills to ensure Dietal control over the administration of such funds to be raised from general taxation.[5]

3 Programme of the Opposition, Supplementary Documents, *CRAH*, p. 15; Macartney, *Habsburg Empire,* pp. 315-16 and n. 1.

4 C. General Taxation in Summary of the Proceedings of the Hungarian Diet of 1847-48, *CRAH*, p. 11.

5 *Ibid.*

No action was taken immediately by the Magnates upon receipt of the Lower House's *nuncium*. The Diet broke for its Christmas recess in mid-December with the Lower House not convening again until January 7, 1848, and the Upper House a few days later on the 12th. Each House then sent a deputation to wish the other a happy New Year at the outset of the new sessions. The head of the Magnates' deputation, the Bishop of Győr, told the Lower House with more truth than he could have known that 1848 would be an important and decisive year in which measures of a comprehensive nature would be adopted for the development of the nation. He quickly proceeded to the heart of the matter by recommending that the Delegates devote their attention exclusively to the eleven royal propositions which had been read before the Lower House on November 16th just after the November 11th opening of the Diet in 1847. Several of these royal propositions designated areas in which reform legislation was badly needed and they had in reality been rather recently taken over by the Crown from the program of the opposition which was centered in the Lower House. The propositions were: (1) election of a Palatine, (2) provisioning of troops in Hungary, (3) extension of the representation of the Royal Free Boroughs, (4) reform of ecclesiastical corporations, (5) review of Laws on mortgages, (6) review of the urbarial Laws in light of Law VIII of 1836 and Law VII of 1840, (7) review of the commercial relations between Hungary and Austria, (8) measures for extending trade and railways in Hungary, (9) consideration of the Crown documents on the reincorporation of the Transylvanian counties, (10) review of the criminal code, and (11) payment of 53,828£ to the Royal Treasury which was supposedly a national debt. Propositions five through eight were dear to the reformers' hearts, but the fact that the propositions carefully avoided the crucial question of political and financial responsibility had, naturally, not been lost on the opposition at their initial presentation. The fact that the Upper House deputation took the occasion of its 1848 New Year's greeting to reiterate the Crown's proposals while at the same time omitting any reference to the recently raised fundamental question of general taxation, meant, in effect, that the Magnates were telling the Lower House to be submissive to Vienna's policy.[6]

Following these exchanges, it was not until the 19th through the 23rd of January that the resolutions concerning a system of general taxation contained in the Lower House's *nuncium* were debated by the Magnates. Even though a conservative bloc of pro-Habsburg Magnates could normally command majorities in the Upper House, its adherents did not dare to raise direct objections to the Lower House's proposals on this matter. They were mindful of the strong feeling in the Lower House and throughout Hungary that reform in this area was indispensable. They did, however, attempt to defer the question of general taxation by associating it with the overall question of changes in county administration. This was a project inspired by the Habsburg Court with high hopes of increasing "Vienna's" influence in local Hungarian affairs.[7] The reform-minded and liberal among the Magnates, however, opposed any such obstructionist and Habsburg-inspired "tacking" and the debate ended in a compromise proposed by the new Palatine.[8] The Upper House agreed to the formation of a joint-House Dietal committee to make recommendations for legislation on the implementation of general taxation, but it reserved to itself full liberty to come to a final decision on the subject when the report of the committee was submitted. The

---

6 For the eleven royal propositions, see Summary of the Proceedings of the Hungarian Diet of 1847-48, *CRAH*, pp. 6-7; for the New Year's exchanges, see Summary of the Proceedings of the Hungarian Diet Since the Christmas Recess, *ibid.*, pp. 20-21. See also Macartney, *Habsburg Empire*, pp. 317-18.

7 Very simply, after the turbulent Diet of 1844 the Crown had undertaken to exercise its traditional right to appoint *főispánok* or Lord Lieutenants in the counties in a new manner by pushing aside the old, sometimes hereditary and previously unsalaried *főispánok* in favor of a new class of salaried administrators. By 1848, twenty-nine of fifty-two counties had these new administrators whose total annual salary was 17,400£. Through an unknown amount of secret service funds supplied by "Vienna" their institutions were to manage the county assemblies into sending "right-minded" Delegates to the national Diet. This new tactic was strongly objected to as *de jure* illegal and contrary to the spirit of the Hungarian Constitution. It was part of a program devised by the Chancellor, Count György Apponyi, to undermine the program of the Liberal opposition. Macartney, *Habsburg Empire,* pp. 293-94, 318; Mr. Blackwell to Viscount Ponsonby. Presburg, January 28, 1848, *CRAH*, pp. 17-19.

8 The Palatine by Law XXXII of 1492 was elected by the Diet and was the constitutional arbitrator between Crown and Diet. The office remained vacant through much of the eighteenth century under the Habsburg and then came to be filled by custom (not Law) with Habsburg Archdukes. d'Eszlary, *Institutions,* II, 121.

obstructionist attitude of the Upper House on this important issue is further revealed by the fact that this Dietal committee was still not definitely appointed by mid-February.[9]

The dating here is important since it shows that this program of tax reform was the will of the majority of the Hungarian "political nation" (i.e. the nobility) long before the French revolution of February, 1848, exercised any influence upon the situation.[10] It also reveals that the Habsburgs feared the loss of political control in Hungary, even at the very beginning of 1848 during a period of relative stability and that they employed the conservative-minded Magnates in the Upper House to obstruct tax reform in Hungary. It is very clear that the Hungarian nobles as a class had become increasingly convinced of the necessity of modifying their tax-exempt status in the interests of the national welfare and that they were fighting in a constitutional manner to make this concept a reality from the very beginning of 1848.[11]

Thus, long before the European upheavals of 1848, the desires for change were evident in the Diet. Already in the

---

9 The Magnates sent their compromise *renuncium* on this subject back to the Lower House on January 24, 1848. Mr. Blackwell to Viscount Ponsonby. Presburg, February 3, 1848. General Taxation, *CRAH*, p. 20; Mr. Blackwell to Viscount Ponsonby. Presburg, February 29, 1848, *CRAH*, p. 22.

10 The revolution in Paris occurred between February 22nd and 24th, 1848. Word of Louis Philippe's fall reached Vienna on the night of February 29th — March 1st, but apparently Austrian financial circles had gotten wind of the event slightly earlier since Baron Rothschild personally informed Metternich in the State Chancellery offices on February 29th before the *Augsburger Zeitung* made the news public very late on that date.

The news arrived in Pozsony on the next day, Wednesday, March 1st and caused, according to Mr. Blackwell, "the greatest sensation here" among the Delegates of the Hungarian Diet. On March 2nd the younger and more impatient reformers discussed the situation at Kossuth's quarters prior to his famous speech to the Diet of March 3, 1848. Mr. Blackwell to Viscount Ponsonby. Presburg, March 3, 1848, *CRAH*, p. 34; Macartney, *Habsburg Empire*, pp. 322-24; *Hungary: A Short History*, p. 155; Hugessen, *Political Evolution*, I, 155; Otto Zarek, *Kossuth* (Port Washington, New York: Kennikat Press, 1970), pp. 133-35.

11 The economic motivation for noble agrarian reform is summarized in Macartney, *Habsburg Empire*, pp. 242-45. See also B. Iványi, "From Feudalism to Capitalism: The Economic Background to Széchenyi's Reform in Hungary," *Journal of Central European Affairs*, II, no. 3 (October, 1960), 270-87; Blum, *Noble Landowners*, pp. 242-45; Barany *Stephen Széchenyi*, pp. 154, 278, 285, 369-70. Professor Barany gives many examples of the reforming attitude of Deák, Széchenyi, Hajnóczy, and others. Szekfű describes how eloquently Deák and others argued for urbarial reform at the 1832-1836 Diet from a moral convinction. Hóman and Szekfű, *Magyar történet*, V, 295, 245-46 and 280.

1830s and certainly by 1847 the reforming Dietal opposition was pushing for not only tax reform, but for the modernization of the entire Constitution, particularly for the adoption of a system of ministerial responsibility. Time and again the opposition had mustered commanding majorities in the Lower House in favor of modernizing reforms. The motivation behind these majorities was an essentially moral conviction brought about by no other pressure than the awareness of economic changes and the belief that the welfare of the Hungarian nation demanded them. The abolition of the noble's tax exemption, the introduction of the classless suffrage and of general taxation, the abolition of the subject status (i.e. "serfdom") and above all the inauguration of a system of ministerial accountability, were all Hungarians demands which pre-dated "1848."

News of the Paris February revolution altered the political situation in Hungary at the beginning of March, 1848, only by bringing an unexpected pressure upon the Habsburg dynasty to meet the existing demands of the Hungarian reformers. It also heightened the impatience of the reformers. However, their demands, expressed with increasing urgency, remained essentially unchanged as stated in the Hungarian Liberal "Oppositional Declaration" of June, 1847.[12]

---

12 Macartney, *Hungary: A Short History,* p. 155; *Habsburg Empire,* pp. 323-24; Denis Sinor, *History of Hungary* (New York: Frederick A. Praeger, 1959), p. 257.

*Chapter II*

## THE HUNGARIAN DIET: MARCH 3rd-13th

News of the Paris revolution and the abdication of Louis Philippe became public knowledge in Vienna on February 29, 1848, and the initial reaction of the Viennese had the merit of being practical if not spectacular. There was a run on the Austrian national and other banks to cash in notes for silver and in prompt confirmation of the public's instinctive financial judgment the banks quickly folded. As was correctly suspected, under Metternich's guidance, Habsburg policy was beginning to conceive a European crusade against the revolution,[1] one which would perforce be arbitrarily financed by a

---

1 Macartney, *Hungary: A Short History*, pp. 155; *Habsburg Empire*, pp. 322-23. Insight into this period is provided by knowledge of the fact that the Austrian Imperial Ministries when faced with these early March events became gripped by a sort of stubborn paranoia and sought to shift the responsibility for these upheavals anywhere but on their own reactionary and obscurantist policies of thirty-odd years standing. The fact that they struck out first at the Hungarian Liberal opposition is in itself an admission of the advanced and preeminent place of Hungarian political life in the Monarchy. A startled Metternich announced that Hungarian Liberal radicals had caused the run on the Vienna banks and then the Austrian Ministers managed to convince themselves that the Hungarian Diet and Kossuth, being in contact with Viennese radicals, were engaged in some sort of conspiracy which was responsible for the first Vienna revolution of March 13th, 1848; an idea reflected in a few old Austrian histories—for example, the Austrian Minister of the period, Count Franz Hartig, *Genesis der Revolution in Österreich im Jahre 1848* (3rd ed.; Leipzig, 1851), pp. 113, 121—but one so without merit that it went no further. Hugessen, *Political Evolution*, II, 1 and n. 1, 7 and n. 1. The simple truth seems to be that the Paris revolution was unexpected by everyone while Kossuth, as his whole life testifies, was an able politician but by no means possessed a conspiratorial temperament. Blackwell's observation is relevant:

> I am told that some of the Austrian Ministers fancy that the students were instigated . . . by Hungarian Liberals, that they were in secret correspondence with Kossuth and other leaders of the Liberal party. There cannot be a more erroneous notion . . . . The Liberals in their famous programme . . . stated their views without the least disguise, that they would use all the efforts in their power to obtain a responsible Ministry, liberty of the press, etc. at the same time recommending His Majesty to grant constitutions to the hereditary states of the empire . . . this is the only kind of conspiracy the Hungarian Liberals have been guilty of. They were determined to realize their views by constitutional means, and by constitutional means only. Mr. Blackwell to Viscount Ponsonby. Presburg, March 25, 1848, *CRAH*, p. 53.

new issue of uncovered paper money. In Hungary also the popular reaction was the same. Even before this crisis, it had been estimated that the total ratio of Austrian paper to silver in circulation in Hungary stood at 200 millions to twenty millions,[2] and the memory of "Vienna's" disasterous financial manipulations during the Napoleonic period had been deeply imprinted in the public mind. Blackwell wrote to Ponsonby from Pozsony on March 3, 1848, that there was a lack of public confidence in the Austrian paper notes and none were being changed in the city's shops without a purchase.[3]

On the same day, at a Circular Sitting of the Lower House of the Hungarian Diet, Kornel Balogh,[4] a Delegate of Győr county, delivered a speech urging the Diet to ask the Vienna government to abandon its habitual reticence concerning financial matters. He called on Vienna to issue an official statement on its current monetary policy, especially concerning the proportion of specie in reserve to the notes in circulation. This, he stated, would arrest public anxiety and avoid a more gloomy public view of the financial outlook than was perhaps justified by the facts.[5] It was a moderate rather than a revolutionary request. Moreover, it was a reasonable one to be placed before any government.

Following Balogh's speech, Lajos Kossuth, attending this Circular Sitting as a Delegate recently elected by a large margin from Pest county,[6] rose to speak. Alluding to the Győr Delegate's views, he delivered his famous address which was

---

2 Horváth, *Huszonöt év*, III, 336.

3 Mr. Blackwell to Viscount Ponsonby. Presburg, March 3, 1848, *CRAH*, p. 35.

4 As noted in the Preface, the Hungarian form of given or Christian names is followed in these chapters, although the Western usage of first name followed by surname as opposed to Hungarian practice is employed. Also, the German form of given or Christian names is rendered in the case of Habsburg Kings of Hungary, members of the Imperial family and Austrian Statesmen.

5 Horváth, *Huszonöt év*, III 337; Hugessen, *Political Evolution*, II, 1.

6 He was elected to the Diet October 19, 1847, by a margin of 2,948 votes to 1,314 votes following an active campaign mounted against him by the government in Vienna. Zarek, *Kossuth*, pp. 124-27. He came to the election without means, and Count Lajos Batthyány spent a princely sum to ensure his return which was ordinary practice but by no means always effective. Hóman and Szekfű, *Magyar történet*, V, 385.

subsequently hailed throughout the Habsburg Monarchy as the inauguration of the 1848 revolution.[7] Several of those present later recorded that as he spoke his whole frame shook under the weight of his convinced belief in the necessity for change and his vision of a new Hungary.[8] Although emotional, his speech was also factual and constitutional in every sense. It was, in effect, an exhortation to the Delegates of the Lower House to adopt a representation, that is a formal Address to the Crown, demanding nothing more nor less than the Crown's consent to the program of the Hungarian reformers which had been published as the "Oppositional Declaration" of June, 1847.[9] It was Kossuth's skill in utilizing the financial uncertainty to present with forceful clarity the necessity of a political change from absolutism to a *de facto* constitutional government as well as the publicity his speech received out of context outside Hungary which made it seem "revolutionary." Standing firmly upon the Hungarian Constitution and the traditional Hungarian sense of constitutional government, he warned that Hungary could not be guarded against financial chaos and hardship until she had control of her own finances.

The Crown's irresponsible manipulation of the value of the Austrian paper notes during the Napoleonic Wars had caused a form of hidden taxation injurious to all classes in Hungary. It forcefully called the Diet's attention to the fact that previous constitutional checks upon the Crown were no longer adequate. The experience was of major significance in

---

7 Hugessen, *Political Evolution*, II, 2, 7; Horváth, *Huszonöt év*, III, 337, 345ff.; Macartney, *Habsburg Empire*, p. 323. On the previous day, Thursday, March 2, 1848, Széchenyi, knowing of Kossuth's proposed address to the Diet, wrote in his Diary that it was "a splendid declaration," but that he as well as others, for example, Apponyi, felt that it went too far, too fast and was bound to lead to trouble. "I use all my eloquence . . . my words have no effect . . . I yield rather than pour oil onto the fire," Széchenyi concluded. Quoted by Zarek, *Kossuth*, p. 136. See also Hugessen, *Political Evolution*, II, 6; Zarek, *Kossuth*, p. 141; Macartney, *Habsburg Empire*, p. 327.

8 László Teleki and Lajos Batthyány were especially impressed with Kossuth's passionate appeal; his "pleasant" and imperiously "metallic voice as it filled his listeners' ears with the liberation of the subject peasants," etc. Árpád Károlyi, *Az 1848-diki Pozsonyi törvénycikkek az udvar előtt* (The Pozsony Laws of 1848 Before the Court) (Budapest: Magyar Történelmi Társulat, 1936), p. 3.

9 Sinor, *Hungary*, p. 257; Macartney, *Habsburg Empire*, pp. 323-24.

Hungary's constitutional development, and a reason for the mood of the nation to follow Kossuth's viewpoint.[10]

Kossuth continued by stating that, moreover, the time had come when their demands must not be limited to the nomination of a responsible Finance Minister. The Diet must tell His Majesty in plain language that the whole existing system of absolute government was bankrupt. It was imperative that the Diet demand the "transformation of our present system of government by committees into a responsible and independent Hungarian Ministry."[11]

In another passage of his speech (one which was to have great effect outside Hungary, especially in Vienna) Kossuth urged the Diet to advise the Royal and Imperial Throne to place all the peoples under its sceptre in enjoyment of constitutional freedom since constitutional government in Hungary would never be safe as long as absolutism prevailed in the rest of the Monarchy. The best guarantee against the Monarchy's dissolution would be the establishment of "Constitutional institutions with respect for the different nationalities."[12]

Kossuth is often said to have been the most eloquent and persuasive of men, but the written word—even if as eloquent as the following passage—can hardly convey his effect upon the Diet on March 3, 1848:

Let us draw strength from our civic duty for a resolution corresponding to such extraordinary circumstances . . . . Even unnatural political systems may last long; for there is a long way between the patience of peoples and despair. But political systems which have lasted a long time may have lost strength; their long life makes them ripe for death (Here Kossuth refers to the Habsburg governance of Hungary by collegial committees, for example the *Con-*

10 On Dietal protests in 1811 see Hóman and Szekfű, *Magyar történet*, V, 189-90. See also d'Eszlary, *Institutions*, III, 129. Hugessen, *Political Evolution*, I, 250; Macartney, *Habsburg Empire*, p. 196. The warnings of financial disaster delivered by Pál Nagy against the Vienna paper money issues at the Hungarian Diet of 1807 are treated in Sayous, *Histoire des Hongrois de 1790 à 1815*, p. 180.

11 Macartney, *Habsburg Empire*, p. 324.

12 *Ibid.*, see also Hugessen, *Political Evolution*, II, 5; Mr. Blackwell to Viscount Ponsonby. Presburg, March 15, 1848, *CRAH*, p. 46; Zarek, *Kossuth*, p. 138.

*silium,* responsible in theory to both the Crown and to the Diet but which in practice were subordinated illegally to the pan-Monarchic institutions and responsible only to the monarch.) But death is not a thing that one may share or stay. I know that for an old system, as for an old man, it is hard to separate from life. I know that it is hard to see the things which a long life has built up, crumble piece by piece. But where foundations are not truly laid collapse is the inevitable fatality.[13]

But the people is everlasting and we wish the fatherland of this people to be everlasting . . . a pestilential wind reaches us from the charnel house of the Vienna cabinet, an air which dulls our nerves and paralyzes our spirit . . . a glorious future awaits both the nation and the throne which derives its strength from the freedom of its subjects. Loyalty and enthusiasm for the dynasty can exist only in the hearts of free men whose interests are indissolubly bound up with those of the ruling family; for a bureaucracy no such sentiments can be entertained . . . [14]

Kossuth, who had spent three years of his life in a Habsburg prison for political activity, concluded:

The gallows and the bayonet are ill-contrived means to cement goodwill. Who can reflect without a shudder that sacrifices should be imposed upon the people without spiritual and material compensation? . . . We wish that the glory of the dynasty that rules over us be everlasting . . . . But only a dynasty relying on the liberty of its peoples . . . [15]

Kossuth's accurate and eloquent articulation of long-felt grievances was received with indescribable enthusiasm. The Crown-appointed Speaker of the Lower House quickly delivered an address in which he criticized Kossuth for expressing opinions concerning non-Hungarian Lands and in general tried to moderate the universal uproar, but to no avail.[16] The

---

13 Zarek, *Kossuth,* p. 137.

14 Hugessen, *Political Evolution,* II, 2. See also Macartney, *Habsburg Empire,* p. 323.

15 Zarek, *Kossuth,* p. 138.

16 Anton Springer, *Geschichte Oesterreichs seit dem Wiener Frieden 1809* (2 vols.; Leipzig: S. Herzel, 1865), II, 169.

Delegates of the Lower House immediately passed a resolution by acclamation to draft a formal Address to the Crown in the sense he had recommended.[17] It is virtually certain that some Delegates had doubts concerning the forcefulness of the measure, but it was genuinely popular. On this very same day, March 3, 1848, the Lower House drafted and passed its famous formal Address to the Crown, pertinent excerpts of which may be provided from Blackwell's full English translation with his comments included:[18]

May it please Your Majesty [Ferdinand V] . . .

The events which have recently taken place make it our irremissible duty to direct our attention to what our fidelity to your Majesty's dynasty, our lawful relations with the united monarchy, and our duty to our country demands.

On taking a retrospective view of our history, we acquire the sad conviction that for the last three centuries we have not only been unable to render our constitution

---

17 That is, rather than by a roll-call vote, it was carried by a thunderous voice vote with no one dissenting. On the local level this robust and previously adequate practice of the Hungarian nobility was often followed in the county assemblies for the election of officeholders. Both here and in the national Diet the presiding officer sometimes "weighed" the votes. Openly before the voting body he tended to give preference to the lead given by the more important and influential among the body, which, if no one dissented, often decided an issue. The head-count of votes after all speeches and opinions had been delivered was only necessary for closely contested issues which aroused great interest and division. The fact that this convenient practice sufficed for so long shows a considerable degree of solidarity among the nobility about fundamental concepts.

In the modern era, however, this practice was susceptible to influence-wielding, pre-arranged demonstrations, and occasionally rowdy confrontations so that it was held up to ridicule by József Eötvös in his novel, the *Village Notary,* and generally disapproved of by the Hungarian reformers. Hence, in the interests of "democratization," once it had been established that voting was no longer exclusively a class privilege, Article 32 of Law V of 1848 provided provisionally for local committees to maintain written lists of voters as was being done in England with the object of introducing the secret ballot. However, the noble tradition of voting had stamped a strong imprint on Hungary as shenanigans and the alternation of the secret with the public ballot into the twentieth century testify. See comments by Blackwell, Inclosure in No. 23 Acts passed by the Hungarian Diet, *CRAH*, pp. 67-68.

18 Representation respecting the Questions before the Diet, adopted at a Circular Sitting of the Delegates, March 3, 1848, *CRAH*, pp. 42-44. Mr. Blackwell's, Explanatory Remarks on the preceding representation, *CRAH*, pp. 44-45 are inserted in parentheses at the appropriate points in the quoted representation. The Address in English translation exists also in part in Hugessen, *Political Evolution*, II, 3-4. Comments on the solidarity of the Lower House in support of the Address, *ibid.,* p. 5 and n. 1.

conformable to the spirit of modern times, but have been obliged to use all our efforts for its maintenance.

The reason for this has been, that your Majesty's Imperial Government (In the original, *"Birodalmi Kormánya"* which may be rendered "the Governmental of the realm," but they evidently mean the Central or Imperial Government of the Austrian Empire, to which the Hungarian Government — in their opinion — has been unlawfully subjected.) has not had a Constitutional tendency, and therefore could not be brought in unison either with the independence of our Government or with the chartered rights of the nation.

This tendency has hitherto only prevented the development of our constitution; but we are now convinced that if such a system of policy be any longer maintained, your Majesty's throne and the monarchy, to which we are bound by the pleasing ties of the Pragmatic Sanction, will be involved in consequences of which it is impossible to foresee the final issue and our country, moreover, suffer an inappreciable [i.e. incalculable] detriment.

Your Majesty summoned us to the present Diet in order that we might lay the foundation for the reform of our social institutions. We hailed this summons as the fulfillment of wishes long entertained, and have proceeded to the task of legislation with redoubled ardour and activity.

With the adoption of the principle of General Taxation, we have resolved to share with the people those public burdens hitherto exclusively imposed for defraying the expenses of Comitatal administration, and to raise in the same manner the funds now required for regnicolar [i.e. national] purposes. ("People," *nép,* in these paragraphs is used for "peasants." "We nobles have resolved to share with you peasants," etc. In other paragraphs "People" seems to be used for peasants and burgesses.)

We have resolved, on the principle of an equitable compensation being afforded, to take the necessary steps for the liberation of the peasants from urbarial services, and by thus adjusting the conflicting interests of the people and the nobles, to augment the national welfare and strengthen the throne of your Majesty . . . the time has already come when our political rights must be shared with the people . . . . Our constitutional life also requires to be developed in a real representative direction.

The responsible administration of Hungarian State revenue and finances, with due publicity of the accounts, is a question that we cannot any longer postpone, as it is only in this manner that we can fulfill those constitutional duties relating to the expenses for defraying the splendour of your Majesty's Royal Throne and the exigencies of the country, as likewise all other lawful duties that can but tend to a wholesome result. (This, in plain English, is asking His Majesty to appoint a responsible Hungarian Chancellor of the Exchequer.)

In respect to several of these questions, it will be necessary that the conflicting interests of Hungary and the hereditary provinces of the empire be equitably adjusted, in order to effect which we shall always be ready, with the due maintenance of our independent national rights and interest, to lend a helping hand. (This paragraph more particularly alludes to the intermediate customs line, the removal of which was recommended in the Royal Propositions. And "the due maintenance of our independent national rights and interests" means that the fixation and regulation of the Hungarian customs duties belongs, *de jure,* exclusively to the Diet.)

We are moreover convinced that the laws which will have to be enacted for the development of our social institutitons, as well as for the promotion of the intellectual and material welfare of the nation, can only acquire vigour and reality when, for their execution, a national Government, totally independent and free from any foreign influence whatsoever, shall be called into existence, and which, in conformity with constitutional principles, must be a responsible Government, and the result of a majority of the people. We therefore regard the conversion of the actual Collegial system of government into a responsible Hungarian Ministry, as the principal condition and the essential guarantee for every measure of reform . . . . (By a "Collegial system of Government" they mean the administration of public affairs by irresponsible Government offices, colleges, as the Vice-Regal Council, the Hungarian Chancery, etc.)

To bring these questions with the agreement of your Majesty to a satisfactory conclusion during the present Diet, is our fixed and earnest design.

Our country expects this from us; millions expect it. It

is commanded by that impulse of loyalty and attachment that binds us, with indissoluble ties, to your Majesty's dynasty. We are moreover convinced that it is only in this manner that tranquility, peace, and concord can be so firmly established in our fatherland, that no unforeseen events or storms will be able to shake the solid foundation . . . .

We will not grieve your Majesty's paternal heart by entering into any details respecting these lamentable symptoms, neither will we examine the palpable effect which, in a financial point of view, they have already produced; (*Viz.*, a fall of 20 per cent, in the Austrian funds, and a run on the Austrian National Bank.) but the sentiments of loyalty by which we are animated, and the responsibility we are under compel us to declare that we can only look for a source of the evil now becoming so manifest, as well as for the principal cause of our social retardment, in the principles upon your Majesty's Imperial Government is founded. We are also throughly convinced that your Majesty will find the most secure guard against any possible untoward contingencies, as well as the most cordial agreement with your loyal people, and the most complete fusion of the different provinces of the Monarchy, and consequently the firmest support of the Throne and the reigning dynasty, when your Royal Throne is environed by those Constitutional institutions imperatively called for by the exigencies of the age, and which can no longer be postponed (This is also a way of telling His Majesty that he heterogeneus States of his empire can only be kept together when the present bureaucratic Administration is superseded by a Constitutional Government.) . . . . We regard the bringing of the above-mentioned questions of reform to a satisfactory conclusion, on constitutional principles, during the present Diet, as the irremissible means of allaying our anxiety; and we fear the usual course of Dietal business, and the tedious negotations with the Government, consequent on the actual collegial system, will dangerously retard our arriving at a result . . . . We therefore venture . . . to beseech your Majesty to be graciously pleased . . . to send to the Diet . . . members of the highest Government office . . . as the constitutional representatives of the executive power . . . to take an immediate part in the Dietal proceedings . . . in respect to your Majesty's gracious intentions . . . to afford such assistance in bringing the questions under discussion to a satisfactory conclusion, that the contemplated salutary laws may the sooner be submitted for your Majesty's sanction . . . .

It is difficult to imagine any more apropos, comprehensive, and succinct statement than this partially-quoted formal Address to the Crown which was unanimously voted by the Lower House on Friday, March 3, 1848. The rapidity with which it was formulated and passed following Kossuth's speech makes it all the more remarkable. The Lower House had the entire Address printed for public consumption and immediately turned to the practical drafting of bills (the beginning of the "April Laws" of 1848) which were intended to implement the points made in the Address once they were completed and received royal sanction.[19]

Thus, it is abundantly clear that as early as March 3, 1848, there existed a majority in the Hungarian Lower House committed to a comprehensive program of political and social reform.[20] Hungarian constitutional practice, however, required that an Address to the Crown must be approved by both Houses of the Diet, and here the unequivocally stated reforming desire of the Lower House encountered ten days of obstruction from the conservative pro-Habsburg Magnates. Even some of the more reform-minded Magnates had been completely taken aback by Kossuth's speech; Count Mihály Esterházy, for example, characterized the demands contained within it as the "fruits of his (Kossuth's) untimely vanity."[21]

The Magnates received the proposed Address to the Crown

---

19 Macartney, *Habsburg Empire*, p. 324.

20 Although March 3, 1848, was the most comprehensive and dramatic example, it was by no means the first instance of this development. During the preceding Diets of the Reform Era, the Lower House had regularly passed piece-meal reform bills only to have them "vetoed" by the Habsburg Crown acting through its Magnate allies in the Upper House. Thus, for example, at the Diet of 1832-1836 the best political talent in Hungary—Deák, Kölcsey, Széchenyi and Wesselényi—had objected to this inconsiderate usage of the Upper House of a "second veto" (the first being the King's) as being unconstitutional. Barany, *Stephen Széchenyi*, pp. 294, 300. Similarly, it was this conservative bloc among the Magnates which Kossuth meant when he wrote in no. 14 of the *Pesti Hírlap* on February 17, 1841: "It will come true with them and by them if they like it, without and even against them, if necessary." *Ibid.*, p. 300 and n. 174.

21 Károlyi, *Az 1848-diki Pozsonyi törvénycikkek az udvar előtt*, pp. 3-4.

from the Lower House on Saturday, March 4th, the day after it had been formulated. However, the presiding officer of the Upper House, the Palatine, had been called to Vienna on March 1st [22] and the interim head of the Upper House, the *Judex Curiae* (i.e. the *Országbíró* or, in English, the Lord Chief Justice of the Realm), ruled to defer the Magnates' consideration of the Address until his return. This ruling immediately caused considerable annoyance among the Delegates of the Lower House.

On Monday, March 6th, the Magnates did not meet, and when they did not do so again on Tuesday, March 7th, the Delegates began to complain loudly that the absence of the Palatine in Vienna was a mere pretext to delay the Address. They observed that constitutionally the deliberative and legislative powers of the Diet could not be rendered inoperative simply because of the absence of a single officer. The *Országbíró* as *ex officio* president of the Upper House had the power to conduct its affairs and in his absence the duty fell to the *Tavernicus* (Lord High Treasurer).

On Wednesday, March 8th, the continuing situation provoked several violent speeches, and it was decided to send the chairmen of the day[23] to the *Országbíró* and the *Tavernicus* for the purpose of urging them to call a sitting of the Upper House. On their return, the chairmen announced that these two dignitaries, as well as most of the other office-holders in the Upper House, had quietly followed the Palatine to Vienna on the previous day. This revelation snapped the patience of Kossuth and the most ardent reformers who immediately argued that the Magnates' inaction was an abdication of authority. They urged the Lower House to forward the Address to the Crown without further delay.

---

22 See Macartney, *Habsburg Empire,* p. 324. Information in this and the following paragraphs is drawn mostly from Mr. Blackwell to Viscount Ponsonby. Presburg, March 15, 1848. Inclosure 1 in No. 7 and Inclosure 2 in No. 7. Continuation of the Proceedings of the Hungarian Diet, *CRAH,* pp. 46-48. See also, Dániel Irányi and Charles-Louis Chassin, *Histoire politique de la Révolution de Hongrie 1847-1849* (2 vols.; Paris: Pagnerre, 1859-1860), I, 135-37.

23 Two Delegates were elected each day or at times by the week to preside over a Circular Sitting of the Lower House as opposed to the presidency of the *Személynök* (i.e. *Personalis* or Speaker who was the personal representative or alter ego of the King) over its formal sittings. György Spira, *A Hungarian Count in the Revolution of 1848* (Budapest: Akadémiai Kiadó, 1974), p. 53.

However, the majority in the Lower House, led by Dénes Pázmándy, hesitated to take such a constitutionally questionable action. The more conservative Delegates were inclined to be persuaded by certain Magnates who argued that in normal circumstances the Delegates would have just reason to complain, but due to the critical European situation it was only natural that His Majesty should have summoned the nation's highest officeholders, his Hungarian councillors, to advise him in Vienna. This, Kossuth bluntly replied, was sheer nonsense. As everyone was aware, these noble and learned office-holders were in Vienna to hold conferences on Hungarian affairs with the Austrian Ministers. That is to say, with gentlemen who had not the shadow of a right to interfere in any manner whatsoever, directly or indirectly, in the internal affairs of the Kingdom of Hungary. He observed that such conferences had always been unconstitutional and illegal.[24] Moreover, at this critical juncture they were highly dangerous to the liberties of the country.[25]

---

24 Law CI of 1723, Laws XI and XIII of 1741, Law XVII of 1791. Macartney (ed.), *Habsburg and Hohenzollern Dynasties*, pp. 134-35, 144.

25 Thus, Kossuth's views as stated in the Lower House on March 8, 1848, and recorded by Mr. Blackwell in his letter to Viscount Ponsonby, British Ambassador in Vienna, as of March 15, 1848, were publicly known and reflected a general political feeling in Hungary.

The attitude expressed on this point by the "heroic age" of Marxist historiography in Hungary (*ca.* late 1940s to 1956) indicates it was under ideological duress to emphasize the negative aspects of Hungary's association with the Monarchy. Thus, Hungarian Marxist historiography of that era appropriated to itself the "discovery" that there were conservatives in Hungary in 1848. The following quotes, from an article by Erzsébet Andics (in 1949, President of the Historical Society) are illustrative:

Kossuth did not and could not know of the plans of the neo-conservatives for counter revolution because on the one hand they were made in secret and on the other hand, they misfired, p. 210. The pro-Habsburg outlook of the Magnate reaction grew out of their economic and political position in Hungary and in Europe. Their position was tied to Vienna socially and politically, p. 207. The bourgeois writers of history have left several *terra incognita* in this period due to subjective interpretation, not because of lack of material. The high treason of the reactionary classes has not been revealed. In spite of great research done on 1848/49 there is evidence that Kossuth had to fight not only against foreign oppression but also against the reactionary classes in Hungary who wanted to retain Austrian oppression and were against social reform. The Magnates were on the side of the enemy and against the people. The new Marxist writing of history must bring out this theme, p. 151. "Der Widerstand der feudalen Kräfte in Ungarn am Vorabend der bürgerlichen Revolution des Jahres 1848," *Acta Historica*, IV, No. 7 (1955), 151-210.

However, since 1956 such uncompromising and extreme views are no longer characteristic of Hungarian Marxist historiography.

Kossuth's analysis was entirely correct. The typical, ever-present desire to delay decisions was now tempered with the current confusion dominating the Imperial Viennese Councils which Professor Sinor has described as "the rubber wall of Habsburg mediocrity."[26] As early as February 29th the Hungarian Chancellor, Count György Apponyi, had advised the dissolution of the Diet in the belief that new elections could produce a more amenable group of Delegates in the Lower House. The Austrian *Staatskonferenz* (State Council) had felt this would be a salutary measure and a royal rescript was drafted to that effect. Then news of Kossuth's March 3rd speech arrived from Pozsony via the good offices of Count Sedlnitzky's Secret Police and it was learned to the general amazement of the Court that the Hungarian Lower House had voted unanimously for its contents under the "terror" exercised by the Dietal Youth.[27] The amazement was swollen to shocked anger when it also became clear that the voted Address contained a request for His Majesty to grant the Austrian Lands a modernized Liberal constitution in place of absolute government.[28] It was then that Metternich had insisted on the desirability of questioning the Palatine about the political temper in Hungary and the Palatine in turn had wanted to call in the *Országbíró* and the *Travernicus* for their opinions. During the discussions held throughout March 7th, 8th and 9th, the *Staatskonferenz* could not arrive at any decision concerning a policy to be adopted toward Hungary. The option of dissolving the Diet, which was ardently urged by Apponyi and Count Antal Széchenyi on the 9th, was discarted as too risky. Széchenyi, who was present at several of these Vienna meetings, noted the stubborn attitude of the Court and grew more and more apprehensive of a collision between these centralists and the Hungarian nation.[29] As time passed, Apponyi fell ill and the rescript got lost somewhere in the *Staatsrat*. In the end, all the masterful Austrian men of the State could agree upon was Archduke Ludwig's idea that the Palatine *et alii* should delay

---

26 *Hungary*, p. 257.
27 Károlyi, *Az 1848-diki Pozsonyi törvénycikkek az udvar előtt*, p. 4 and n 3.
28 *Ibid.*, and n. 4.
29 *Ibid.*, pp. 4-5 and n. 6.

their return to the Hungarian Diet as long as possible in hope of preventing the Address to the Crown from reaching Vienna.[30]

In the meantime, naturally, the dissatisfaction in the Lower House of the Hungarian Diet in Pozsony was continuing to mount. On Thursday, March 9th, the Delegates voted a *nuncium* to the Magnates by acclamation expressing strong disapproval of the Upper House deferment of the Address to the Crown as unconstitutional and urging its immediate consideration. This was the atmosphere over the weekend of the 11th and 12th when most of the Hungarian dignitaries returned to Pozsony after the Vienna conferences,[31] although the Palatine himself did not return until Monday evening, the 13th.[32] A sitting of the Upper House was scheduled for that day, but it was agreed at informal conferences, with at least the tacit concurrence of the Delegates of the Lower House, to postpone the sitting until the following morning. During the night or sometime the following day, news could be expected from Vienna concerning the reaction of the Austrian Emperor and the Imperial government to a rather well publicized petition drafted by the Austrian Diet. However, it was agreed that in all events both Houses of the Hungarian Diet should meet at three o'clock in the afternoon of Tuesday, March 14th.[33]

---

30 Macartney, *Habsburg Empire*, p. 324 and n. 3; Hugessen, *Political Evolution*, II, 6. Széchenyi offered his services as royal commissioner to negotiate with the Diet, but his offer was rejected in Vienna. The conservative Count Emil Dessewffy who was in Vienna at this time recalled that the Hungarian high officeholders who were called to the Court on March 7th "accomplished nothing" in their deliberations and that Apponyi was "continuously ill and by March 10th was in bed." Manó Kónyi (ed.), *Deák Ferencz beszédei* (The Speeches of Francis Deák) (6 vols.; Budapest: Franklin-Társulat, 1882-1898), II, 26.

31 Mr. Blackwell to Viscount Ponsonby. Presburg, March 15, 1848. Inclosure 2 in No. 7 Continuation of the Proceedings of the Hungarian Diet, *CRAH*, p. 47.

32 Macartney, *Habsburg Empire*, p. 333.

33 Mr. Blackwell to Viscount Ponsonby. Presburg, March 15, 1848. Inclosure 2 in No. 7. Continuation of the Proceedings of the Hungarian Diet, *CRAH*, p. 47.

## Chapter III

## REVOLUTION IN VIENNA: MARCH 13TH

The situation in Vienna by the second week of March had become extremely agitated. What many in Europe had long believed to be impossible in that city was beginning to materialize, although in many respects subsequent events would simply confirm the deep and indelible loyalty which even the most critical Austrians of the *Vormärz* reserved for the Emperor and the Imperal family.[1] Further news from Paris, reports of Kossuth's March 3rd speech in Hungary,[2] and word of demonstrations in the Germanies prompted petitions to the Austrian Emperor. The elderly, sensible and popular Archduke Johann, who had been called up from Gratz, urged his brother to make concessions but his advice was overruled. By March 11th an *ad hoc* preparatory committee of the previously long-defunct Diet of Lower Austria had collected many signatures on a petition (Hugessen terms it a "monster petition") asking for the publication of the annual budget and the State debt, the convocation of corporate representative assemblies with the power to impose taxation and to audit expenditures, and, for good measure, a free press and public judicial proceedings.[3] The petition was to be formally

1 Márta S. Lengyel, *Reformersors Metternich Ausztriájában* (Fate of a Reformer in Metternich's Austria) (Budapest: Akadémiai Kiadó, 1969), pp. 39, 47-49, 87.

2 Kossuth's March 3rd speech before the Lower House was quickly sent down to Pest where Malvieux, a merchant of the capital and a fervent Liberal, immediately translated it into German and sent many copies to his numerous Viennese acquaintances. But even more directly, Ferenc Pulszky, who was in Vienna at the time, received a copy on the evening of March 4th. He translated it into German the same evening and forwarded it to the very influential Viennese *Juridisch-Politischer Leseverein*, a Liberal association, from which it spread with great speed. Károlyi, *Az 1848-diki Pozsonyi törvénycikkek az udvar előtt*, p. 6.

3 Macartney, *Habsburg Empire*, pp. 325-26; Hugessen, *Political Evolution*, II, 6-7. The Diet of Lower Austria had been essentially powerless and decorative since Maria Theresa's reign. Under Franz I it had been particularly under the thumb of the central Imperial bureaucracy. By 1848, however, a qualitative change distinguished the Lower Austrian Estates from those in the other Lands in the Western half of the Monarchy. Many people of bourgeois origins came to possess land in Lower Austria, giving the Estates by March 1848, an identification with "bourgeois" interests. Macartney, *Habsburg Empire*, p. 303 and n. 2.

presented to the Estates of Lower Austria when they assembled in their Diet on Monday, March 13th. By Sunday, the 12th, word of mouth, promoted especially by the university students who were busy concocting their own petition, had spread throughout Vienna the popular expectation that "the morrow was going to be the day."[4]

Quite early on Monday morning the streets of the Inner City around the *Landhaus* (Seat of the Provincial Diet) of the Lower Austrian Estates began to fill with a dense crowd, some of whom were obviously bent on mischief.[5] Many workers were present from their miserable suburban quarters due to the unofficial Viennese habit of "blue Monday" which left many workers idle on this day of the week.[6] Just after the Estates arrived to begin their deliberations, a body of students, marching in formation, appeared and forced their way into the *Landhaus* courtyard where several of their number began delivering speeches to the crowd on the subjects of a free press and public jury trials.[7] A young man named Goldmark called

---

4 Macartney, *Habsburg Empire*, p. 327.

5 Information on this first revolution in Vienna of early March, 1848, is drawn principally from Macartney, *Habsburg Empire*, pp. 327 and ns. 1 and 2, 328 and ns. 2, 3, and 4, 529 and n. 1, 330, 331 and ns. 1 and 3, 332, 333; *cf.* Zarek, *Kossuth*, pp. 140-42, and R. John Rath, *The Viennese Revolution of 1848* (Austin: University of Texas Press, 1957), pp. 57-89 and *passim.*, an excellent English language account.

6 The material causes of workers' discontent in Vienna in 1848 are not difficult to discover. The increase in population, the migration of people to this greatest urban center in the Monarchy, and the lack of industrialization as well as the influence of industrialized conditions all played their role. In Vienna by 1842 the average wage of an "industrial" worker had increased to forty-two kreutzers a day from an average of 40.9 in 1836 which lagged well behind the increase in the price of food staples. The uneven onset of industrialization in the Monarchy was brutal enough, with foremen more inhuman than the country lord's bailiff in their ability to inflict corporal punishment. See Victor-L. Tapié, *The Rise and Fall of the Habsburg Monarchy* (New York: Praeger, 1971), pp. 265-68.

7 In 1846, Vienna University carried some 3,719 students on its rolls. Most nobles and well-to-do bourgeoisie saw to their sons' education at home by tutors with the result that most of Vienna's University students were the sons of struggling peasants, artisans, and Jewish professional people. Their age and social origins combined with their often desperate poverty (the Jewish students, especially, found it generally more difficult than Christian students to earn a pittance for giving private lessons) would incline them, it seems likely, toward radicalism. Macartney, *Habsburg Empire*, pp. 303-304. According to Anton Johann Gross-Hoffinger, a petty Viennese bourgeois who attended the Universities of Vienna and Graz in the 1820s and wrote reform critiques under the pseudonym Hans Normann in the 1830s, the Austrian University system had good instructors in medical science and those fields preparing one for State service. But a premium was placed on conformity and

upon the crowd to enter the *Landhaus* and force the Diet to carry its demands to the Court. However, the crowd was not quite ready for this task. As a group was being chosen to attend the deliberations of the Estates (permission for this had been granted by Count Montecuccoli, the Estates' chief magistrate), a student named Goldner arrived with a bundle of recently and hurriedly prepared leaflets of Kossuth's March 3rd speech in German translation. This was then read aloud amid frenzied excitement and soon a deputation from the over-awed Diet of the Estates of Lower Austria was virtually rushed by the crowd to the Hofburg (Royal Palace) where they presented a double demand for Metternich's dismissal and the granting of a ready-made constitution.

The Archduke Ludwig told them that he had no authority to grant concessions diminishing the Emperor's absolute sovereignty without Ferdinand's consent. However, when the committee's report was read, the Sovereign would take action on it. This was hardly what the "constitutionalists" wanted to hear, and, as the crowd in the streets began to get out of hand, some rowdies at the *Landhaus* broke in at 11:00 a.m. and occupied themselves by breaking up the furniture.

The President of the *Landesregierung* (Provincial Government) sent a request for troops to Archduke Ludwig and other civilian authorities also began to follow suit as violence erupted. Habsburg military efficiency was up to its usual standard since few security precautions had been taken and the majority of Vienna's garrison of 14,000 troops was in barracks outside the Inner City under the command of Archduke Albrecht. The latter was the eldest son of Archduke Karl, thirty years of age and inexperienced. It took the troops about two hours to arrive and clear the area of disturbance around the *Landhaus*.[8] Imperial troops were cordially detested by the Viennese who jeered and threw whatever objects came to hand while ignoring repeated orders and requests to disperse. The

---

independent academic inquiry was virtually forbidden. Austrian professors enjoyed the protection of the State and Austrian students had no independent personality. The universities "resembled convict prisons." Lengyel, *Reformersors Metternich Ausztriájában*, pp. 24-27.

8 The gates of the Inner City were eventually closed but many workmen were left inside now cut off from their quarters in the suburbs.

*Platz-Kommandant* of Vienna was severely injured while making such a request and Archduke Albrecht himself, as he advanced on foot urging the crowd to disperse, was struck on the head with a missile. One patrol, which happened to be composed of Italian engineers, opened fire which killed four individuals and injured others. Following this example of belated, minor, and mindless repression, matters predictably went from bad to worse. There were more sporadic confrontations, more shooting, and more deaths. Shops were looted and better dressed people were molested with one excise collector even being thrown alive into a bonfire.

Amid all this, the largely ceremonial burgher Civic Guard busied itself by presenting a petition to the Court to form itself into a National Guard, while the students, for their part, were forming an "Academic Legion." The ongoing displays of social antagonisms and upheaval probably did not please the burghers any more than the aulic aristocrats. Nevertheless, the burghers took advantage of the situation to present several demands to the Court, which amounted in substance to an ultimatum. The deadline was set for nine o'clock that evening. Judging from these demands the thought of a constitution was less immediate in their minds than the fear of reprisal. Imperial troops were to be withdrawn from the Inner City, all their own actions to date, such as the forming of the Guard and the distribution of arms to the "Academics," were to be considered legalized in an *ex post facto* manner. Finally, they demanded a last Imperial concession which would "comprise all others in itself," the dismissal of Metternich.[9]

9 Metternich later stated that he had sometimes governed Europe, but never Austria, which was essentially true; but he must, nevertheless, bear a heavy responsibility for the situation in March, 1848, because he had for many years insisted on the priority of foreign over domestic policy and used his considerable influence to reassure Franz I that the "system" dedicated to immobility and political absolutism was best perpetuated. Macartney, *Habsburg Empire,* pp. 190-92, 210, 256-57. The March 13th petitioners in their simplicity did not demand the dismissal of any advisor other than Metternich. Count Franz Anton-Kolowrat-Liebsteinsky, for example, was an able bureaucrat and slightly ahead of Metternich in his economic ideas for the Monarchy, earning a reputation as a "Liberal" because he supported the *Juridisch-politischer Leseverein.* In early March, accompanied by Archduke Franz Karl, he had even attended a meeting of the Lower Austrian Trade Association (*Gewerbeverein*). His Liberalism was, however, more surface and economic than thorough. In political matters he was a centralist (hating the Hungarian Constitution) and an absolutist *au fond.* After 1836 he had been clearly

The Court remained irresolute. With a view to preserving Imperial popularity, Archduke Albrecht was recalled from his command of the troops. But early in the afternoon Prince Alfred Windisch-Graetz was called (on Metternich's suggestion) to the Palace and the Court conferences swung between the alternatives of adopting a harsh or a conciliatory policy. Metternich procrastinated and was talking interminably until almost nine o'clock. Finally, the poor retarded Emperor and King, Ferdinand, came to one of his rare emphatic decisions. He stated with determination that as Sovereign the decision was his and to tell the people he agreed to everything.

The announcement was met with a great outburst of popular enthusiasm and dynastic loyalty. However, after the initial popular delight, distrust again began to appear. The following day, Tuesday, March 14th, Metternich, ungratefully ignored by the Imperial family, left Vienna with the secret financial help of Baron Rothschild. After some reshuffling in the *Staatskonferenz* and more painful debate, the basic decision was reached. On Wednesday morning, March 15th, an Imperial rescript announced that the Emperor had decided "to assemble round Our throne representatives of the Estates of Our German-Austrian and Slavonic Realms and of . . . Our Lombardo-Venetian Kingdom with the purpose of assuring Ourselves of their advise on legislative and administrative questions."[10]

The rescript showed that the immediate and major decision to be conciliatory rather than brutally repressive had been made. It is also noteworthy as the first time in the history of the Monarchy that a single legislature for all the Western Lands — later known officially as the "Kingdoms and Lands represented in the *Reichsrat*" or more conveniently and popularly as the "Austrian *Reichsrat*" — was indicated. However, to the disturbed mood in Vienna on March 15th, the

---

in charge of the Monarchy's internal affairs. His policy of arrest and suppression in Hungary until 1839 did little to improve the internal stability of the Monarchy and it seems he could be held as responsible as Metternich for some of the immobility of the "system" in March, 1848. During the crisis he occupied himself with glee in working for Metternich's dismissal. *Ibid.,* pp. 234-39, 256 and n. 3, 259, 263, 284-85, 302-303, 304 and 325-26. See also Zarek, *Kossuth,* p. 141.

10 Macartney, *Habsburg Empire,* p. 332.

rescript was regarded as totally inadequate. Stylistically it differed from Hungarian royal rescripts by implying that sovereignty flowed from the Emperor alone and was "dispensable" by him, but what the aroused Viennese noted was the deliberate absence of the word "constitution."

Disorder continued in the suburbs, bourgeois leadership in the Inner City was in a mildly chaotic state, and by early evening menancing crowds were again gathered about the Hofburg. Little is known about the Court deliberations, but at 5 p.m. a mounted herald appeared at the gate of the Michaelerplatz and read to the crowd a proclamation containing the final crucial concession. The Emperor "had taken the necessary steps to convoke as quickly as possible, representatives of all provincial Estates and of . . . Lombardy-Venetia, with increased representation for the burghers, and for the purpose of the Constitution which We have decided to grant."[11] The magic word had been authoritatively uttered. "Austria" was to have a constitution. Houses were illuminated. Jubilation overflowed, and the first Viennese revolution of 1848 was over.

As a concluding observation to these events it is noteworthy that the previously omniscient Imperial *Staatskonferenz* did not yet include Hungary in its beneficence since it was freely admitted that the country already possessed a Constitution, and it seemed an unrealistic project to dream-up a "Constitution" for the total Monarchy which would not have to defer to Hungary's status in some manner. Therefore, March 14-15th, in Vienna may be seen in retrospect as constituting a rather recent Habsburg recognition of the traditional Hungarian view concerning the political structure of the Monarchy. The Imperial concessions to the Western Lands were obviously issued under pressure and in a pragmatic manner, but, intentionally or not, their implicit recognition of the Hungarian Constitution certainly foreshadowed the Dualism of 1867-1918, which had already been implied in Pragmatic Sanction of 1723.

---

11 *Ibid.* The text is provided in Rath, *Viennese Revolution*, pp. 84-85. See also Springer, *Geschichte Oesterreichs seit dem Wiener Frieden 1809*, pp. 193-94.

*Chapter IV*

## MARCH 14TH IN POZSONY: THE ADDRESS TO
## THE CROWN IS PASSED BY BOTH HOUSES

In Pozsony, early Tuesday morning, March 14, Archduke Ludwig's message arrived in the Diet containing the news of Metternich's fall. Many of the excited Delegates hurriedly dashed off letters to their constituents imparting this astounding fact as well as word of the resignation of Count Apponyi from his office as Hungarian Chancellor, and as much information as could be obtained concerning the events of the 13th in Vienna.[1] The conservative Magnates of the Upper House had their answer concerning the Crown's policy, and it was no longer possible to obstruct with doubtful legality the constitutionally expressed demands of the majority of the Hungarian political nation. Surprisingly enough, it was the Habsburg Archduke Stephan, recently elected Hungarian Palatine by the Diet and then resident in the city, who was one of the first to conclude that it was now necessary to pass the Address through the Upper House without modification. He was well aware that the Lower House had already completed some draft bills which were based on the points made in the Address (subsequently to receive sanction as the "April Laws"[2]), and he informed several leading political figures,

---

1 *Deák Ferencz beszédei*, II, 18-19; Macartney, *Habsburg Empire*, p. 333. Both Apponyi and Count Josef Sedlnitzky, who had been in charge of Austrian Police and Censorship since 1817, had resigned in Vienna the evening of March 13th. *Ibid.*, p. 330. Károlyi states that "the news of this event struck the Diet at Pozsony like lightning and staggered the conservative party." *Az 1848-diki Pozsonyi törvénycikkek az udvar előtt*, p. 6.

2 Macartney, *ibid.*, p. 337, n. 2. The bill for the abolition of the subject peasant's obligations had been in committee in the Lower House since March 6th. On this date, March 14th, the Diet urged the committee dealing with a bill on freedom of the press to hasten its work and organized a committee to devise a bill for a National Guard. On the next day, March 15th, the Diet declared that all *Robot* (work) and other obligations between peasant and lord were to be abolished. Irányi and Chassin, *Histoire politique*, I, 135, 138-39.

who were hastily summoned to his residence early on this morning, of his support for the national program of reform.

Among those summoned was a very surprised Count István Széchenyi, then fifty-six years of age, who was responsible more than any other single individual for having initiated the Hungarian Reform Era as early as 1825. However, by the 1840s the rapid political changes had passed him by, and compared to Kossuth and his followers he had become a "conservative." Because he feared a confrontation with Vienna, and saw Hungary's future better assured within the Habsburg Empire, he tried to steer his fellow Delegates toward a cautious course. Thus, on March 13th he had used his influence in the Upper and Lower Houses to obtain support for his own proposed amendments, which would have diluted the tone and the content of the already drafted Address to the Crown. His efforts had had virtually no effect among the Delegates. Now, before sunset on this extraordinary day of March 14th, after much painful soul searching which is revealed in his Diary, Széchenyi reached the conclusion that the opportunity provided by the Viennese upheaval required a change in his thinking and tactics. Anxiously, but nonetheless sincerely, he decided to give support to the forceful policy contained in the Address.[3] Other conservative Hungarians, though some with less complex and pure motives, also belatedly joined the existing consensus during the course of this day.

Blackwell, in his report to Lord Ponsonby which was concluded about midnight on Tuesday and posted on Wednesday, March 15th, described the situation:

> It was . . . finally decided at a private conference that both Houses should meet at 3 o'clock this afternoon (the 14th) and pass the representation with an additional paragraph by acclamation. Long before 3 the galleries of the Chamber of Magnates were taken possession of by the jurists [i.e. the Dietal Youth who accompanied and assisted the Delegates]. When the sitting commenced the House was crowded to suffocation. The representation was, of course, voted by acclamation, together with the

---

3 Spira, *Hungarian Count,* pp. 41 ff., and ns. 63-71.

additional paragraph demanding in express terms, liberty of the press, trial by jury, and annual Diets at Pest. A renuncium was immediately sent to the Delegates who also passed the representation thus amended by acclamation. The representation was then signed and sealed at a Mixed Sitting [i.e. a formal *sessio mixta* of both Houses] with the customary formalities; but instead of being transmitted in the usual manner through the Hungarian Chancery, it will be taken to Vienna tomorrow (the 15th) by a numerous deputation of Magnates and Delegates, and presented to the King (Emperor) in person.[4]

Besides the "additional paragraph" mentioned by Blackwell, the wording of the Address to the Crown on Tuesday, March 14th, was strengthened in regard to popular representation, popular education, and concerning the union of Transylvania with Hungary. In place of the original "conversion" of the collegial system of government into a responsible Hungarian government, it now called for the abolition of the entire administrative system and the appointment of "a responsible and independent Ministry." It also called for Pest to be designated as the seat of the new government.[5]

These events of March 14, 1848, in Hungary constitute a somewhat belated confirmation of reforms which had, in reality, already been voted in the Lower House on March 3rd. Achieved by a constitutional process, this milestone of March 14th stood in marked contrast to the scene of violence and bloodletting which characterized the movement of the

---

4 Mr. Blackwell to Viscount Ponsonby. Presburg, March 15, 1848. Inclosure 2 in No. 7. Continuation of the Proceedings of the Hungarian Diet, *CRAH*, p. 47. Horváth also noted that the public galleries of the Diet were packed to "suffocation" on the 14th for this sitting and further that the entrance and area around the building were "packed with people of all classes." *Huszonöt év*, III, 370. The Upper as well as the Lower House of the Hungarian Diet was traditionally open to the public, the only requirement being presentable dress. See John Paget's description of his visit to the Diet in 1832. *Hungary and Transylvania*, I, 28, 103-104, 109-111.

5 Macartney, *Habsburg Empire*, p. 333. The insertion of a specific request for the appointment of a responsible and independent Ministry was due to the success of the Vienna upheaval of the 13th, as well as to the frustration experienced by the ten day delay of the Address. Árpád Károlyi states this to be the case and notes a difference in tone between the middle of the Address which contained the additions of the 14th and the end of the Address which remained unchanged from the 3rd. *Az 1848-diki Pozsonyi törvénycikkek az udvar előtt*, pp. 6-9.

burghers, students, and working people in Vienna on the previous day. It can be observed that the crumbling of the Magnate resistance in the Hungarian Upper House probably would not have occurred had it not been for the earlier violence in Vienna. Moreover, one may also assume that the original March 3rd passage of the Address by the Lower House might not have taken place without the news of the Parisian revolution. On the other hand, it must be made clear that the Hungarian constitutional reform Address of March 3rd, as strengthened and formally approved by both Houses on the 14th, could never have occured without a reform program which had been advocated for some sixteen years by ever-increasing numbers of the Hungarian common nobility. At this point the "Hungarian Revolution of 1848" fully deserves such a designation from the point of view that significant change was being sponsored under rather extraordinary circumstances. On the other hand, the Hungarian movement was not revolutionary at all if one measures it by violence, bloodshed, class, or other forms of hatred. Class antagonisms certainly did exist in Hungary. It is also true that many conservatives (and by no means all of them aristocrats) felt that things were moving too far and too fast.[6] However, despite such tensions and misgivings, the outstanding feature of the "revolutionary" movement in Hungary through mid-March was its legal and constitutional nature. Other European revolutionary movements in 1848 eventually succumbed to class antagonisms and to a lack of inter-class accommodation.[7] But, in contrast, the Hungarian 1848 remained comparatively impervious to crippling internal social dissention.[8]

The distinctiveness of Hungarian development in 1848 undoubtedly lies in the fact that it was a comprehensive social, political, and national reform movement that had been initiated and led by members of the traditional leading classes

---

6 Macartney, *Habsburg Empire*, pp. 315-16, 324.

7 For example, see T. S. Hamerow, *Restoration Revolution, and Reaction* (Princeton: Princeton University Press, 1958), pp. 163, 172, 181 and 190-91.

8 The nationality problem as it unfolded in 1848 cannot be completely classified as a social problem, though perhaps it should be in some of its aspects to a greater degree that is realized.

imbued with a love of constitutional tradition. The influence of the Hungarian Constitution on the unfolding situation must be acknowledged if the nature of the development is to be completely understood. The Constitution was filled with precedents and patterns upon which the reformers could rely as an almost instinctive guide in their struggle vis-à-vis the Crown. The outcome of this struggle would determine the success of the proposed internal political and social reforms, and the legal manner in which they were pursued was shaped by the Constitution. For this reason intemperance and violence simply did not command the scene in mid-March, 1848.[9]

A small example of this constitutional outlook is provided by Ludwig von Wirkner, the Viennese government's secret agent in Pozsony. On Monday, the 13th, when there was great dissatisfaction in Pozsony over the failure of the Magnates to meet, he reported that one individual jumped onto a table in one of the town's coffee houses and spoke in favor of a republic. But he was promptly pulled down before he could utter much more.[10] Admittedly, Austrian agents generally wrote what the Court liked to hear. Yet there does not appear to be any evidence[11] of a popular desire in the Dietal city to use force to bring about the desired political changes. And this was true despite the fact that a bloc of conservative Magnates were then using constitutionally questionable tactics to obstruct the manifest and legally formulated views of the Lower House in favor of reform.

Still less was there any desire among the Delegates or the *jurati* to overthrow the dynasty or to separate Hungary from the Monarchy. On the contrary, as Hugessen observed,[12] one can see in the Address to the Crown[13] a conviction that there

---

9 Inclosure in No. 23. Acts passed by the Hungarian Diet, *CRAH,* p. 65.

10 Hugessen, *Political Evolution,* II, 11, n. 4.

11 The question of radical and republican sentiment in Hungary during this period is discussed below in Chapter V.

12 Hugessen, *Political Evolution,* II, 5.

13 Representation respecting the Questions before the Diet, adopted at a Circular Sitting of the Delegates, March 3, 1848, *CRAH,* p. 44. The third from the last paragraph of the Address to the Crown as it was formulated and passed by the Lower House on March 3, 1848.

was no essential divergence between the interests of Hungary and those of the Hereditary Provinces. One perceives a confidence that the establishment of responsible, parliamentary, and constitutional governance throughout the Monarchy would provide the basis to clear the clouds of misunderstanding which had been so long employed by Imperial absolutism to obscure the relations between Hungary and Austria. The Hungarian reformers expressly stated that they had no quarrel with the peoples on the other side of the Leitha, and they certainly had no desire to sever Hungary's connection with them. They again emphatically reaffirmed their traditional recognition of the existence of affairs of common interest and stated that they desired a settlement satisfactory to both parties. They believed that two constitutionally governed States could arrive more easily at an equitable solution of crucial common questions. They were also convinced that if these questions remained unsolved or were solved in the old unilateral manner, this would ultimately weaken both interested parties.[14]

This forthrightly stated the Hungarian concept of a constitutional relationship with the Habsburgs appeared at long last to be making real progress on the afternoon of Tuesday, March 14, 1848. In the House of Magnates, just after the passage of the strengthened Address, the Palatine Archduke Stephan[15] announced that "I assure the House that I shall

---

14 This belief in the desirability of having constitutional institutions established throughout the Habsburg Monarchy was not new at this time. The "Oppositional Declaration" of June, 1847, had stated this view which had been put forward by a speaker in the debates of the Diet of 1825. Macartney, *Habsburg Empire*, p. 316 and n. 2.

15 His father, the Archduke Josef, had held the office of Palatine for nearly fifty years with great success. He died on January 13, 1847. Stephan, thirty years of age in 1848, had been born and brought up in Hungary and spoke Hungarian. Though loyal to the Habsburg House, he unfortunately lacked his father's skill. His nomination by the Hungarian Diet had been opposed by the *Staatskonferenz* and by Hungarian conservatives, but went through due to Ferdinand's insistence. Macartney, *Habsburg Empire*, pp. 316-17. Because he was somewhat friendly to Hungary and at least appeared to fulfill his constitutional role in this crisis, it was not long before the Imperial circles and the Court party were accusing him of disloyalty and a desire to become King of Hungary, an accusation raised by the conservative Baron Miklós Vay in Vienna in the very beginning of March. Hugessen,

consider it my duty to join hands with the Orders in the task of promoting the Constitutional development of this country." [16] His statement was received with great applause.[17] Somewhat earlier in the day in the Lower House, when the news arrived from Vienna of the upheavals and of Metternich's dismissal, Kossuth was disturbed. He reviewed the points in the Address to the Crown and the proposed Laws to be based upon these points, which had been under consideration for nearly two weeks, and concluded "it will now be our splendid task to steer the movement wisely . . . for only so can we advance constitutionally . . . ."[18] At this juncture, Kossuth's loyalty to the House of Habsburg was as yet untroubled. This was indicated by the earlier but still valid comment of his political opponent Somssics:

> Ich weiss, dass Kossuth noch im Februar 1848 . . . welche entschieden beweisen, dass er damals noch keine Revolution wünschte, oder wenigstens an eine solche nicht glaubte. Ich fande (*sic*) ihn stets monarchisch, ja dynastisch, gesinnt.[19]

Another incident in the afternoon of this day again appeared to confirm the prospects for an evolutionary and constitutional settlement within the Monarchy. This happened at Kossuth's

---

*Political Evolution*, II, 16 and n. 2; Károlyi, *Az 1848-diki Pozsonyi törvénycikkek az udvar előtt*, p. 19. There is no question that Stephan effectively promoted Hungarian interests on several occasions, but on the other hand documentary evidence contained in his letters indicates that as early as March 24th he was advising the Court on the prospects of a counterrevolutionary policy and that he did not regard the rescript of March 31st as a firm commitment on the part of the Crown. See Spira, *Hungarian Count*, pp. 82, 93; Horváth, *Huszonöt év*, III, 447. A detailed and balanced judgment is in István Deák, "The Month of Defiance: Revolutionary Hungary in September, 1848," *East Central Europe/L'Europe du Centre-Est*, I, no. 1 (1974), 41-42, 46.

16 Hugessen, *ibid.*, p. 12.

17 Horváth, *Huszonöt év*, III, 370-71.

18 Zarek, *Kossuth*, p. 143.

19 Quoted from *Das Legitime Recht Ungarns und seines Königs* (Vienna: 1850), p. 18 by Hugessen, *Political Evolution*, II, 11, n. 2. "I know this, that as late as February 1848, Kossuth . . . decidedly showed that at that time he had no desire for a revolution, or at least I believe so. I found him consistently monarchist, yes, even dynastically-minded." This statement is all the more convincing coming from the onetime *personalis* who was very "pro-Vienna" in his political views. See Barany, *Stephen Széchenyi*, pp. 110, 345, 371, n.

quarters during a discussion concerning the selection of members of the Deputation to carry the Address to Vienna. When buttonholed by a student who suggested that "if you will make a speech, in two hours you can incite a public meeting to proclaim a republic," Kossuth made an angry reply decidedly in the negative.[20] Thus, even after the capitulation of "Vienna" and the conservative Magnates, Kossuth asked for no more than before, and stood ready to cooperate with the Habsburgs in a loyal manner as required by the Hungarian Laws implementing the Pragmatic Sanction.

Throughout the 14th, there is evidence that uncertainty concerning the course of events in Vienna prompted a certain degree of traditional and generous Hungarian sympathy for the King. The wearer of the Holy Crown might be under duress from tyrannical popular excesses only a short distance from the borders of Hungary. In reply to an inquiry from Archduke Ludwig concerning the safety of Hungary as a refuge in the event the Court should be forced to flee the Imperial city, Wirkner wrote that "Vienna being in a state of actual revolution the moment had come for Hungary once more to give proof of its centuries-old fidelity and magnanimity to its King."[21] Széchenyi made the public statement that once again Hungarians might have to prove their loyalty to the throne with the cry of Maria Theresa's time, *moriamur pro rege nostro,* which was well received. A petition inviting Ferdinand to take refuge in Hungary was even circulated though never sent, for soon word was received that Vienna had quieted.[22]

In the evening at nine o'clock, students headed a torchlight procession through the streets of Pozsony which included the city's Civic Guard in full uniform (but without their arms), as well as hundreds of the Dietal Youth bearing the national tricolor and brandishing their sabers. A band played the

---

20 Zarek, *Kossuth,* p. 144.
21 Hugessen, *Political Evolution,* II, 11, n. 4.
22 *Ibid.,* pp. 11-12.

"Rákóczi" and other national marches [23] which until recently had been forbidden by the Vienna government's orders. [24] Even the German inhabitants of Pozsony, who normally maintained a distance from their Hungarian neighbors and other nationalities, were moved to join in the general celebration as the procession treated both the Palatine at his residence and, above all, Kossuth — the "Liberator of Hungary" — to a noisy torchlight serenade. Kossuth responded by delivering a speech from the balcony of his hotel with the respected Liberal Magnate, Count Lajos Batthyány, at his side. With a typically precipitate and generous demeanor, he embraced the Magnate. Stepping aside, he announced "here stands your first responsible Prime Minister," a revelation which heightened the crowd's jubilation. [25]

Only Széchenyi with his uncanny gift of prescience had private misgivings concerning the day's events. On this night of Tuesday, March 14th, he wrote in his Diary that Hungary stood on the threshold of disaster. [26] The same evening, Mr. Blackwell, writing in his lodgings, concluded his report to Lord Ponsonby with the observation that "at the hour I write (12 o'clock), Presburg is as quiet as the greatest love of order could wish it to be." [27]

\*     \*     \*

The morning of Wednesday, March 15, 1848, dawned a glorious spring day over Pozsony. At an early informal session of the Lower House there was much talk over the resolutions passed in favor of the immediate liberation of the subject

---

23 Mr. Blackwell to Viscount Ponsonby. Presburg, March 15, 1848. Inclosure 2 in No. 7. Continuation of the Proceedings of the Hungarian Diet, *CRAH*, pp. 47-48. Blackwell stresses the Guard carried only torches. The law students' sabers were a part of the traditional Hungarian national dress.

24 The "Rákóczi March," nevertheless, had been publicly sung in Pozsony since at least 1833. László Révész, "Das Junge Ungarn 1825-1848," *Südostforschungen*, XXV (1965), p. 87.

25 Zarek, *Kossuth*, p. 144.

26 *Ibid.*, p. 145.

27 Mr. Blackwell to Viscount Ponsonby. Presburg, March 15, 1848. Inclosure 2 in No. 7. Continuation of the Proceedings of the Hungarian Diet, *CRAH*, p. 48.

peasants and the introduction of a system of general taxation. Széchenyi observed in his leavetaking speech that "the nation is finally placing its constitution upon a base wider than the one from which it has hitherto been dangling." [28]

The joint Deputation [29] chosen to carry the Address to Vienna was formally headed by the Palatine, [30] and consisted of thirteen Upper House members and fifty-two Delegates of the Lower House. However, when the steampacket finally departed Pozsony at ten o'clock in the morning, the Deputation was accompanied by a host of dignitaries and a swarm of Dietal Youth. [31] In addition to Count Lajos Batthyány and Kossuth there was Széchenyi (invited by Batthyány); [32] the noted Liberal reformer and author of *The Village Notary,* Baron József Eötvös; the young aristocrat, Prince Pál Esterházy who was then reportedly an outspoken believer in modern constitutionalism; [33] the Serbian Patriarch Rajačić; Count László Teleki; Count György Károlyi; Count Gyula Andrássy — all to be well known in future politics, as well as numerous other no less widely known figures.

During the passage, some members of the Deputation, anticipating the delay which the *Staatskonferenz* would

---

28 Spira, *Hungarian Count,* p. 46. The discussion at the early morning Dietal session on the 15th was likely a carry-over from the differences expressed at a late afternoon sitting of the 14th. According to Károlyi there was much questioning of definitions for certain phrases in the Address and many asked why this or that was not stated more plainly. There were many "neither fish nor fowl decisions which were probably meant as instructions to the Delegates going to Vienna." *Az 1848-diki Pozsonyi törvénycikkek az udvar előtt,* pp. 9-10 and n. 15.

29 Macartney, *Habsburg Empire,* p. 333.

30 Many sources leave the impression that the Palatine was aboard when actually he as well as Szemere had departed for Vienna the previous evening (Tuesday, the 14th) and were awaiting the Deputation when it arrived. Spira, *Hungarian Count,* p. 26, n. 30.

31 Zarek, *Kossuth,* p. 145; Hugessen, *Political Evolution,* II, 12; Révész, "Das Junge Ungarn 1825-1848," p. 117.

32 Despite his private misgivings, Széchenyi publicly stated: "We must support Batthyány and Kossuth; hatred, ambition, and antipathy must be silenced." Hugessen, *Political Evolution,* II, 12.

33 Esterházy was known in Vienna for having stated: "Rather a constitutional hell than an absolutist paradise," which caused some aulic wits at the Imperial Court to hopefully predict he would soon get what he requested — hell and the Constitution. Zarek, *Kossuth,* p. 145. György Spira, however, states that Esterházy by the end of March was a somewhat lukewarm supporter of the designated responsible Ministry. See *Hungarian Count,* pp. 92-94.

exercise, suggested that a memorandum be added to the Address demanding that the already requested responsible Ministry be immediately appointed and that this demand be phrased in such language that no subsequent interpretation could be read into the document. Obviously, this suggestion was generated by a noticeable anxiety to secure unequivocal consent for the central political demand contained in the Address. It was widely agreed that the demand for a responsible Ministry was the cornerstone upon which the realization of all the other points would ultimately depend. The advocates of changing the Address en route were nonetheless quickly forced to retreat. It was immediately and generally acknowledged that even a Deputation designated by the Diet had no constitutional right to alter a representation whose contents and form had been designed and passed jointly by both Houses. Nevertheless, a general uneasiness persisted due to a universal desire to ensure that the extraordinary mission upon which they were now embarked should meet with success. Then an even more disquieting question arose. Even if a Ministry were appointed, all its decisions—including those on purely domestic affairs—would still be sent to Vienna and subject to the influence of the King's Austrian councillors. [34]

It was Széchenyi, the "conservative," of all people, who provided a solution which enabled the Deputation to arrive before the Vienna Court with a strong procedural advantage concerning these crucial issues. At his suggestion, a few of them (including himself, Batthyány, Kossuth, and two or three others), [35] hurriedly assembled in the steampacket's cabin and

---

34 Spira, *Hungarian Count*, p. 22; Károlyi, *Az 1848-diki Pozsonyi törvénycikkek az udvar előtt*, pp. 10-11.

35 Spira, *ibid.*; Károlyi, *ibid.* The drafters were: Dénes Pázmándy, one of the Dietal Delegates of Komárom county who was a member of the Liberal opposition before 1848 and to be speaker of the Lower House in the July Parliament; Mór Szentkirályi, a conservative who would become *főispán* of Pest county and in August, 1848, royal commissioner in the Serbian-inhabited southern region of Hungary; and, very likely, Kálmán Ghyczy (who left his written recollections), who, it seems, was not present at the initial drafting, but whose opinion must have carried weight because he was one of the Palatine's legal councillors (*ítélőmester*, an office dating from the thirteenth century whose holders by Law I of 1608 were required to be present at Dietal sittings as non-voting members). As such he was responsible for the drafting of the Diet's bills. It was he whom Kossuth soon entrusted the drafting

simply drafted a proposed royal rescript in reply to the Address. This rescript, would be submitted to Ferdinand, ready made, for his consideration and signature! In the Hungarian draft, the King was to authorize[36] the Palatine to appoint an independent Hungarian Ministry responsible to the legislature. This provision, if it could be successfully retained, had the double advantage of neatly circumventing the eternal procrastination toward Hungarian demands in which "Vienna" habitually excelled, and also provided a simple and fast procedure for the initial designation of Ministers which would hopefully keep their selection firmly in Hungarian hands.

When the Deputation arrived at its destination the same day at two o'clock in the afternoon,[37] huge Viennese crowds received the Hungarians at the docking on the Danube meadows. The city was encouraged by the appearance of the representatives of a nation which had fought long and hard for its Constitution. There was a fraternal feeling and general

---

of the future fundamental Law III of 1848 whose 38 articles established the responsible Ministry's powers and function. d'Eszlary, *Institutions*, II, 208-9; Hóman and Szekfű, *Magyar történet*, V, 392.

36 The crucial phrase in this matter simply stated that Ferdinand recognized the Palatine as his official "alter ego" (Spira, *Hungarian Count*, p. 22; Károlyi, *Az 1848-diki Pozsonyi törvénycikkek az udvar előtt*, p. 12), which, on its face, does not appear especially effective when one notes that few Hungarians entertained illusions about any Habsburg and that even Széchenyi had his reservations about the Archduke Stephan at his 1847 election. Spira, *ibid.*, p. 91. However, the virtually unanimous support for this devolution of royal powers to the Palatine becomes understandable in view of the fact that the exercise of executive power by the Palatine was constitutionally and very precisely limited by several old Laws (the cardinal "Palatinal" Law X of 1485; article 4 of Law XXVI of 1567; Law XVIII of 1608; Law LXVI of 1609, d'Eszlary, *Institutions*, II, 122-25). Though generally ignored by the Habsburgs, these Laws were still valid in the *Corpus Juris Hungarici*. More importantly, the Deputation was confident in the Diet's ability to soon devise a bill which, once it received royal sanction as a Law, would forever prohibit the arbitrary and unilateral exercise of monarchic power by either King or Palatine. This was precisely what became embodied in Law III of 1848, defining the operation of the responsible Ministry and its relationship with the Crown. The lines of ministerial accountability, financial control, and the power of impeachment were to be so firmly grounded in the legislature by this Law that it was legally impossible for the King to govern Hungary for long with Ministers who did not enjoy the support of the Parliament. On articles 4, 6, 10, 12, 29, 30, 32, 33, and 37 of Law III of 1848, see d'Eszlary, *Institutions*, III, 142-44; Hugessen, *Political Evolution*, II, 26-29; Horváth, *Huszönöt év*, III, 506.

37 Spira, *Hungarian Count*, p. 26.

rejoicing because Vienna itself was coming to realize that on this very day the Court was acceding to popular demands with an Imperial promise of a constitution for the Hereditary Lands.[38]

38 Zarek, *Kossuth,* p. 146. Thus, Vienna received the Emperor's definitive promise to establish a constitution three hours after the arrival of the Hungarian Deputation, i.e., at 5:00 p.m. See Rath, *Viennese Revolution,* pp. 84-85; Macartney, *Habsburg Empire,* pp. 332-33; Springer, *Geschichte Öesterreichs seit dem Wiener Frieden 1809,* II, 194, all of which establish the Imperial announcement at five in the afternoon. However, most authorities state that the Hungarian Deputation arrived in the late afternoon or early evening immediately after the Imperial announcement of an Austrian constitution. See for example, Károlyi, *Az 1848-diki Pozsonyi törvénycikkek az udvar előtt,* p. 13; William H. Stiles, *Austria in 1848-49* (2 vols.; New York: Harper and Brothers, 1852), I, 111. Springer avoids the problem by stating that the Hungarians arrived "about the same time" as the Imperial announcement. *Ibid.,* p. 204. This discrepancy, though vexing, is not terribly important and is probably explained by the excitement of the day. Also, on the afternoon of the 15th a second steampacket filled with Dietal Youth had departed Pozsony and followed the first to Vienna; its later arrival would well explain the confusion. Irányi and Chassin, *Histoire politique,* I, 155.

*Chapter V*

# THE SITUATION IN PEST
# UP TO MARCH 15TH

In March, 1848, Hungary's cities were under represented in the national Diet. This was due to the fact that in past centuries they had often been inward-looking and frequently perceived as anti-national extensions of Habsburg power. But the continuation of their situation became increasingly intolerable under nineteenth century conditions. Moreover, their internal class structures reflected great political, social, and economic inequalities which no longer corresponded to the needs and opportunities of that age of economic liberalism and political change. Since virtually the largest city, Pest, was already the economic and intellectual center of Hungary, one would except the pressures of March, 1848, to unleash a sequence of events there similar to the class violence and urban bloodshed which became almost commonplace in many Western capitals. This appeared all the more likely because Pest was expanding. Not counting adjacent Buda's 35,000, by 1848, Pest's heterogeneous population stood at some 110,000 inhabitants. Most of these, however, lacked political rights for, as Baron Emile Langsdorff observed, such rights were reserved to the privileged, many of them bankers, who composed an extremely small proportion of the total population. He also noted that a council of 110 members in association with fifty lifetime electors nominated two Delegates to the Diet, while many writers, the richest merchants, and the artisans, all remained excluded from legal status.[1] Notwith-

---

1 "La Hongrie: La Diète et les Réformes sociales," *Revue des deux mondes,* XXIV (1848), 751. The author was attached to the French embassy in Vienna.

standing this essentially medieval governmental structure, in the course of the 1830s and 1840s Pest had become a center of political agitation.[2]

The city's increasing political importance could be attributed to its growth as the country's natural agricultural market center and to the gradual but steady promotion of small and large manufacturing concerns. Commercially (excepting certain periods of conquest and destruction), Pest had generally been a natural funnel between the West and the eastern two-thirds of the Carpathian Basin,[3] and this advantage was further enhanced in the late 1830s by the inauguration of steamboat traffic on the Danube.[4]

2 Much of the information in the following paragraphs is found in Révész, "Das Junge Ungarn 1825-1848," pp. 72, 97-98.

3 Burghardt, *Borderland*, pp. 137-43.

4 The first company was formed with Austrian capital in 1830 and the first steampacket, *Franz I*, began a Vienna, Győr (Raab), Pest, Zimony (Semlin) run in 1831. The economic effects, while gradually improving, were not as spectacular as one unfamiliar with the Austrian bureaucracy, Hungarian economic conditions, the national psychology, and the preponderance of internal, political, and diplomatic considerations over economic interests in Central Europe might expect.

The idea of the improvement of Hungary's rivers for commercial purposes was not at all new. Josef II had envisioned such projects for the Monarchy and they had been discussed in the Diet. The Palatine Archduke Josef had strongly recommended in his reports a project connecting the Danube and the Tisza Rivers. But it was due to the energy, persistence, and practical hard work of Count István Széchenyi that a beginning was made in this direction. He devoted his time, money, and utilized every domestic and foreign contact and device to proceed toward his vision of free navigation from Vienna to the Black Sea and Istanbul which would ultimately benefit all Danubian peoples. See Barany, *Stephen Széchenyi*, pp. 246-67 which is especially interesting for Széchenyi's efforts to influence foreign Powers. For comments on the Danube trade in the 1830s and frustrated observations concerning bureaucratic obscurantism and political concerns which hindered its otherwise promising growth in Hungary, see comments of John George Schwarz, acting U.S. Consul in Vienna from 1830 to 1850. He noted with impatience in 1833 that finally a second steampacket was in operation on the Danube, complained about the inwardness of Austrian trade and upper class views toward it, and speculated that direct trade between Hungary and the U.S. would be advantageous if restrictions were changed. Mr. Schwarz to the Honorable Louis McLane, Vienna, August 15, 1833. *House Executive Document No. 71, 31st Congress, 1st Session,* p. 16. In April, 1834, he reported work on the "Iron Gates" (narrows) and that a steampacket was in operation from Zimony to Orsova, and in March, 1835, that it was possible to navigate the Danube to the Black Sea. Mr. Schwarz to the Honorable Louis McLane, Vienna, April 10, 1834, and Vienna, March 10, 1835, *ibid.*, pp. 21, 26. On June 16, 1836, Schwarz reported a considerable increase of trade and navigation on the Danube centered on Pest and advised on economic grounds the appointment of a U.S. Consul there, but hesitated to recommend it on political grounds. Mr. Schwarz to the Honorable John Forsyth, Vienna, *ibid.*, p. 33. Further comments on the economic situation, pp. 39, 44, 45, and *passim.* In this twenty

However, in this pre-industrial age of March, 1848, it was much more politically significant that Pest was the seat of the nation's central administrative institution—the *Consilium*—and of the highest courts. The city was also the site of the Academy of Sciences, the National Theater, the Museum, the Casino, the race track, and the Royal University—all of which played their part in drawing various generations from all parts of the Kingdom. Finally, it was of greatest political significance that the City of Pest was the seat of the administration of Pest county whose increasing and sometimes pivotal importance during this era was obvious to all. For this reason Kossuth together with other reform-minded nobles[5] had made his headquarters there and obtained a small estate in order to possess the right to participate in the debates of the assembly of Hungary's "leading county."[6]

At this time the coffee houses of Pest, which had been in-

years' service Mr. Schwarz appears never to have visited Hungary and his comments make it obvious he took the word and followed the policy of the Austrian government on virtually all matters, including the 1848 revolution. His embittered comments reveal his reports were generally ignored by the U.S. government.

For a better impression of the economic aspirations and conditions of Hungary in the 1840s, see the personal account of the 1842 trip to Hungary by Daniel Jenifer, second U.S. Minister Plenipotentiary to the Austrian Court in G. Barany, "The Opening of the Hungarian Diet in 1843," *Journal of Central European Affairs,* XXII, n. 2 (July, 1962), 153-60.

5 Despite the very real legal equality of all nobles which made a singular contribution to the quality of public life in Hungary, custom had come to generally require a noble to possess land in a county before he could participate in debates, stand for office in the county administration, or be nominated as county Delegate to the national Diet. Hóman and Szekfű, *Magyar történet,* V, 385.

6 Professor Taylor states that Kossuth was elected to the Diet of 1847 though not qualified since he held no land which is inaccurate. He further indicates that it was Kossuth's personal desire to do away with land qualifications which made him a radical nationalist since he was "trying to be accepted as a Hungarian gentleman." *The Habsburg Monarchy 1809-1918,* pp. 51-52. In reality there was nothing unusual about Kossuth's actions in this regard. For example, in 1835 a Delegate of Arad county named Török purchased a small holding in Pest county for the same purpose. Révész, "Das Junge Ungarn 1825-1848,", p. 92 and n. 75. In 1830 Baron Miklós Wesselényi, a Transylvanian Magnate entitled by birth to a royal invitation to the Transylvanian Diet, secured estates in Inner Hungary in order to participate in the Hungarian Diet. Horváth, *Huszonöt év,* I, 224-31, 253; Barany, *Stephen Széchenyi,* p. 271 and n. 91. At the Diet beginning in 1847, Széchenyi, a Magnate and entitled to a seat in the Upper House, sat in the Lower House as a Delegate of Moson county on the technical basis of family holdings there in order to offset Kossuth's influence. Mr. Blackwell to Viscount Ponsonby. Presburg, December 22, 1847. Inclosure 2 in No. 3. Summary of the Proceedings of the Hungarian Diet of 1847-48, *CRAH,* p. 7.

troduced in the eighteenth century, existed in great numbers and possessed recognized social and political connotations. Each social group tended to center on a particular coffee house. The most "radical" was the well-known Cafe Pilvax [7] where the law students, the younger politicians, and many literary figures gathered. Here, Kossuth, in 1843, had nominated Count Lajos Batthyány as President of the *Vedegylet,* an organization for the protection of Hungarian manufacturing industry. Here, in private discussions, it was often decided which candidate the Youth would support as Delegate from Pest county, what position should be taken concerning county affairs or how some matter before the Pest City Council should be decided. Here, the current writers and literary figures (some of non-noble origin) exchanged views and spoke on political, social, and literary topics. In this setting conservative writings and Vienna-inspired articles were religiously burned, and torchlight demonstrations of approval or dissent were organized. One Hungarian observer, after reading a contemporary newspaper description, wrote with a tongue-in-cheek sense of amused selfcriticism that "it is ironic but not too inaccurate that the coffee houses of our law students are a factory of public opinion . . . here are decided the actions of our national and social life."[8] This was clearly a somewhat sarcastic and intended over-statement of the situation, but it is true that the "Pilvax" by the 1840s had become a concept in the terminology of the Hungarian Liberal politics.[9] The opinions "manufactured" there and in other coffee houses did exercise some influence on the thinking of the Diet.

The Habsburg Imperial government, however, had never really been known for either its tolerance or its sense of humor in matters of political criticism. The Austrian Secret Police reports despaired of the fact that the public was looking to the coffee houses in order to read the otherwise hard-to-obtain

---

7 Various sources (e.g. Horváth, *Huszonöt év,* III, 372) refer to it by various names because over the years it had three proprietors, Pächter, Privorsky, and Fierlinger besides Pilvax. Révész, "Das Junge Ungarn 1825-1848," p. 97.

8 Révész, *ibid.,* p. 95 and n. 5.

9 *Ibid.*

newspapers. In the summer of 1846, the King had ordered the Hungarian Chancellor, at that time Count Majláth, to see that the "disturbances" in the Cafe Pilvax should be countered by all means possible. In 1847, the same directive had been extended to the coffee houses "in the provinces."[10]

Since the Diet of 1843, the Youth of the Cafe Pilvax had decided to support the opposition Delegates at the Diet in Pozsony.[11] By the early days of March, 1848, the "Pilvax," as well as all of Hungary which could do so, was following with tremendous interest the conflict between the Vienna-backed conservatives in the Upper House and the reform-minded Lower House.[12] The city of Pest, as a whole, was kept well informed on the progress of the Dietal discussions taking place in Pozsony by the daily and punctual arrival of steampackets, and probably in no other city in Hungary was greater or louder enthusiasm expressed for the great reform proposals in Kossuth's March 3rd speech and for the resulting Address to the Crown. Conversely, the Dietal opposition found encouragement in the warm support emanating from Pest. During the ten-day period in which the Magnates obstructed the recommended Address, furious political debates continued daily in Pest, their tone becoming more and more impatient as time passed. Nowhere was the impatience more pronounced and sharply expressed than in the Cafe Pilvax.[13]

Just how extreme was radical feeling in Pest at this juncture? It is certain that at least a minority fringe of the legally powerless group at the Cafe Pilvax (such as Petőfi, and his followers)[14] were republican-minded, as were some of ardent spirits among the Youth assisting the Dietal Delegates

---

10 *Ibid.*

11 A support organized by Pál Vasvári, a history teacher (*Ibid.*, p. 98 and n. 99), among others, such as József Irinyi, a lawyer, who was a member of both the Pilvax group and the so-called Pest "Opposition Circle," which was composed largely of nobles and had contacts with the Diet.

12 The contemporary historian, Horváth, stated that "the great spiritual movement which since the beginning of March ruled in the Pozsony Diet was followed with acute interest by the whole country." *Huszonöt év*, III, 371.

13 *Ibid.*, p. 372.

14 D. Mervyn Jones, *Five Hungarian Writers* (London: Oxford University Press, 1966), pp. 279-80.

in Pozsony. Their republicanism was derived from abstract concepts and a doctrinaire sort of tradition rooted in the Enlightenment, the French Revolution, and the experience of the Hungarian "Jacobin Conspiracy."[15] These somewhat imaginative souls were evidently entirely capable at various junctures of ignoring the realities which surrounded them. Constituting a small and by no means constant group, they appear to have been representative of very few in Hungary except themselves. Given the circumstances it appears fortunate that less impetuous and wiser reformers (Kossuth included) held actual legal power as Delegates in the Lower House in Pozsony. The open adoption of a republican stance at this juncture was unthinkable and would have immediately and irreversibly placed Hungary in an unconstitutional position vis-à-vis the Habsburgs. More than this, it was simply not a serious proposition in the Hungary of 1848. Subsequent events were to prove that Kossuth and many Hungarian reformers possessed the courage and political ability to lead Hungary on an independent course when the Habsburg camarilla drove them to it. But their prudent reluctance and disinclination to do so, quite apart from the nation's moral

---

15 József Pruzsinsky, the young Eötvös' tutor, is an example of the origins of the frustration which could lead to a republican stance. He had been sentenced in 1795 to a long prison term as a Jacobin "conspirator" and nursed a resentment against Imperial Vienna, the Hungarian conservatives who supported it, and the whole privileged social order which denied his convictions. With the fierceness of the academic intellectual, he remarked to his young charge upon their walking past the site of the 1795 executions in Buda that someday a gallows would be erected as a monument upon which would be hanged "such men as you are going to be." Paul Bödy, *Joseph Eötvös and the Modernization of Hungary, 1840-1870: A Study of Ideas of Individuality and Social Pluralism in Modern Politics*, in *Transactions of the American Philosophical Society*, new series, Vol. LXII, Pt. 2 (Philadelphia: The American Philosophical Society, 1972), p. 11.

Révész's information-filled study indicates that republican sentiment among the radical Youth in the 1830s and 40s rose and fell according to the strength of the obstruction by the Habsburg Vienna government toward Hungary's national and reform demands. Thus, prior to 1835, a great majority of the Youth were loyal to the dynasty and were attracted toward republicanism only in 1836. During the Diets of 1839-40 and 1843-44 they were less attracted to republican ideas and less anti-monarchical in feeling since the prospects of reform appeared brighter. "Das Junge Ungarn 1825-1848," pp. 80 and 84.

For examples of youthful expressions of republican sentiment in this period by Tormassy, Palóczy, and Majthényi, see pp. 78, 80 in "Das Junge Ungarn 1825-1848."

and legal obligation under the Pragmatic Sanction, was grounded in their sound estimate of their nation's lack of material preparedness for such a policy coupled with the dangerous possibility of threats from foreign powers. Even in extreme circumstances, in September, 1848, during the *de facto* break with the dynasty and in April, 1849, when Hungary declared itself independent, a republican form of government was not, as is sometimes stated, adopted.[16] Hungary remained a monarchy showing that the abolition of this governmental form was not a primary concern or objective of any sizeable number of reformers, the occasional hot-headed exhortations coming from frustrated groups of radical Youth such as gathered at the Pilvax notwithstanding. It is paradoxical in one respect, however, that the agitation of the radical Youth in the early March days was underestimated by the Austrian Secret Police. As Révész notes, these radicals subsequently became some of Hungary's leading political figures.[17]

In any event, during the first two weeks of March, 1848, the fury mounted higher and higher among all the Pest Youth as the Magnates in Pozsony continued to obstruct the Address to the Crown after it had been passed by the Lower House. It seems that a majority of the Pest Youth regarded the propositions in the Address as just a beginning. In Horváth's words:

> Their hopes far over-flew the reform plans that were prepared at the Pozsony Diet. They were not satisfied that the rights of the country were to be guaranteed, that its developmental abilities were to be freed from the Viennese government's handcuffs, they wished to use the favorable times to change things from the roots. They felt it necessary to assist in the social law changes . . . .[18]

This impatience on the part of the Pest Youth had been in-

16 On the September, 1848 break with the dynasty, see the excellent account by István Deák, "The Month of Defiance: Revolutionary Hungary in September, 1848," especially pp. 43-44. On the April 14, 1849 declaration, see Stiles, *Austria in 1848-49*, II, 218-21; Macartney, *Habsburg Empire*, p. 428 and n. 1.

17 Révész, "Das Junge Ungarn 1824-1848," pp. 74, 118 and 119.

18 Horváth, *Huszonöt év*, III, 372.

creasing immeasurably ever since February. During the first days of March Kossuth had sent word down to his associates in Pest, the "Opposition Circle" as they were known, to get up a petition in order to apply some pressure upon the Diet. [19] Upon hearing this, the Youth of the Cafe Pilvax, led by Petőfi, József Irinyi, Mór Jókai, Pál Vasvári, Gyula Bulyovszky and others, had thrown themselves into the project with a passion. Consciously following the practice of the Parisian reform banquets, they had nailed up a set of points for signatures at the meeting hall of the Opposition Circle. On Sunday, March 12th, in an open public meeting, Irinyi read them for public approval as a petition to be sent to the Diet in Pozsony. These "Twelve Points" were presented as follows:

What Does the Hungarian Nation Desire?

Peace, Freedom, and Mutual Understanding

1. Abolition of censorship and freedom of the press.
2. A responsible Ministry seated in Buda-Pest.
3. Annual meetings of the Diet held in Pest.
4. Equal civil and religious rights for all.
5. A National Guard of defense.
6. Equitable distribution of the burden of taxation.
7. The termination of the urbarial relationship.
8. Popular representation and jury trial.
9. A national bank.
10. Hungarian troops to take an oath to the Constitution; Hungarian soldiers not to be ordered out of Hungary; foreign troops to be removed from Hungary.
11. Political prisoners to be freed.
12. Union of Transylvania.

Fraternity, Liberty, Equality [20]

---

19 Macartney, *Habsburg Empire*, p. 337. Kossuth's request was, in fact, carried down to the Opposition Circle by Dániel Irányi. The President of the Pest Opposition Circle was the respected statistician, Elek Fényes. Irányi and Chassin, *Histoire politique*, I, 142.

20 Although Horváth does not hyphenate "Budapest," the original printing of the "Points" did so. *Huszonöt év*, III, 372-73. See also, Hugessen, *Political Evolution*, II, 13. Actual authorship of the final version of the "Twelve Points" is not entirely certain. See Irányi and Chassin, *Histoire politique*, II, 142-43, who attribute them principally to József Irinyi as well as, more recently, György Spira,

However, at this time the social and political demands in the petition were already commonplace among the Dietal opposition (since at least June, 1847).[21] All the "points" excepting the bank, the National Guard, the relocation of the seat of the Ministry and the convocation of *annual* Diets *in Pest,* were already contained in the Dietal Address to the Crown as previously adopted by the Lower House on March 3rd. Also, as Hugessen observed,[22] there is nothing in these "Twelve Points" which was not already well-grounded in the Hungarian Constitution.[23] The "Twelve Points" in this context then can hardly be considered an original nor even an especially divisive document.

Irinyi's reading of the "Twelve Points" in Pest on Sunday, March 12th, did not raise any tremendous upsurge of popular support.[24] Some of the older and more cautious patriotic reformers at the Opposition Circle began to argue that it would be bad political tactics to press these points on the Diet

---

*Hungarian Count,* p. 50. József Irinyi was then twenty-six years of age and worked on the newspaper *Pesti Hírlap.* He was an ardent Francophile which would explain the choice of phrase and general tone. This agrees with the facts that the never-shy Petőfi did not claim authorship and that Jókai attributed it to Irinyi, though he did state that he helped with some of the language and that *he* supplied the heading. See László Deme, "The Radical Left in the Hungarian Revolution of 1848" (unpublished Ph.D. dissertation, Dept. of Political Science, Columbia University, 1969), pp. 36-39.

21 Macartney, *Habsburg Empire,* p. 316, 337 and n. 1. The only minor differences between the 1847 Dietal "Oppositional Declaration" and the "Twelve Points" are that point seven of the latter ignores the question of compensation to landlords and point twelve makes no mention of the Union being dependent upon a vote of the Transylvanian Diet.

22 *Political Evolution,* II, 13.

23 For example, in regard to the tenth point, Law XVIII of 1791 required all Hungarian officials to take an oath to the Constitution as a condition of assuming office, while it was extremely old Hungarian constitutional principle that consent was required for military service outside the frontiers of Hungary. See W. Sólyom-Fekete, "The Golden Bull of Hungary 1222-1972," *The Quarterly Journal of the Library of Congress,* XXIV, no. 4 (October, 1967), 366, 367, 368, 371, explaining Article 7 of the Golden Bull. Law VIII of 1715, which had established a Hungarian armed force to be a part of the Imperial Army was silent on the question of command. d'Eszlary, *Institutions,* III, 166.

24 Professor Macartney observes that the Petition would likely have gone up to Pozsony with only a few signitures on it. *Habsburg Empire,* p. 337. The "points" were first discussed in the Opposition Circle on this date and were still under discussion on Tuesday, March 14th. Deme, "The Radical Left in the Hungarian Revolution of 1848," p. 42.

at this delicate stage of negotiations between the Lower House and the conservative Magnates in the Upper House. In the end, it was decided at a second public meeting on Tuesday, March 14th, as the actual public signing of the petition began, to submit the "Twelve Points" personally to the Dietal opposition Delegates rather than formally to the Diet as a whole. [25] As has been shown, on that very afternoon, unknown to Pest, both Houses of the Hungarian Diet had voted final approval of the Address to the Crown with its wording considerably strengthened to include the demands for a free press, jury trials, a guarantee of *annual* national Diets *in Pest,* and a responsible Ministry. Therefore, as of March 14, 1848, the legally constituted national Diet of nobles in Pozsony was still leading, or at least very much abreast of, the Pest "radicals" in the general and increasingly precipitate movement toward reform. [26]

---

25 Horváth, *Huszonöt év,* III, 373.

26 Irányi and Chassin, *Histoire politique,* I, 138.

*Chapter VI*

## MARCH 15TH IN PEST

The morning of Wednesday, March 15, 1848, dawned a pleasant spring day over the adjacent cities of Pest and Buda some 130 English miles down the Danube from the Dietal city of Pozsony. The extraordinary events of this day were to transform a simple political petition to oppositional members of the Diet into a national manifestation. The day itself was to become symbolic in retrospect and it is this date rather than March 3rd or 14th upon which the popular national tradition fixed and established as commemorating the Revolution of 1848.[1] On this day in Pest the privileged and the non-privileged of the various classes and nationalities of the outwardly heterogeneous Hungarian State assimilated the long-standing and long-advocated reform ideas in a manner which was not overly hostile or suspicious. The people as a whole seemed to accept them as their own, and to throw down the gauntlet, as it were, to the immobility and obscurantism of "Vienna."

Word of the Viennese events of Monday (the 13th) including Metternich's dismissal had arrived in Pest via steampacket late Tuesday evening:[2] On Wednesday morning the inconceivable news was made generally known to an astonished and already restless public via the city newspapers. [3]

The youthful circle in the Cafe Pilvax had learned of it late in the night and as a result few had slept. When the Youth met at the cafe in the morning, Petőfi carried in his pocket a poem

---

1 Zarek, *Kossuth*, p. 151.

2 Horváth, *Huszonöt év*, III, 373.

3 Zarek, *Kossuth*, p. 153; Macartney, *Habsburg Empire*, p. 337. Professor Macartney states that the news was brought on the 15th of March but the difference with Horváth is slight since the boat obviously did not arrive until very late. In any case, the news was not public knowledge until March 15th.

which he had polished to his satisfaction during the night. As the streets began to fill, a small crowd gathered around the cafe. The general feeling was one of ill-defined expectancy. Negotiations with Vienna had been going on too long; should not Hungary's ancient capital take on a role of leadership in a fitting manner?[4]

The little band of Youth (fifteen young men) came out of the cafe and grouped itself under the tri-colored Hungarian banner. Led by the great poet Petőfi and the noted novelist Jókai, they began a procession soon joined by students from the University and by "many men from all stations of life and of various age groups."[5] They proceeded to the National Museum from the steps of which Petőfi spoke rather haltingly. But, nevertheless, his fame and the sincere fire of his words inspired his listeners[6] who now numbered about 2,000 souls. Next, the growing procession, perhaps at Jókai's suggestion, went in good spirits to Landerer's printing house on Hatvani street (present-day Kossuth street) where Petőfi virtually hurled his poem[7] at an astonished audience of 5,000 people who in turn loudly demanded that the poem as well as the "Twelve Points" be printed. Landerer protested that this was illegal according to the censorship regulations. But, if someone would first "lay hands" on the presses, his people (the printers themselves were enthusiastic) would be "constrained" to work them. Thus, the "Twelve Points" and the National Song, the first uncensored and publicly printed documents in modern Hungarian history, were distributed on the streets within a few

---

4 Zarek, *Kossuth*, pp. 153-54.
5 Horváth, *Huszonöt év*, III, 344.
6 Zarek, *Kossuth*, p. 153.
7 The first verse of the *Nemzeti dal* (National Song):

| | |
|---|---|
| *Talpra magyar, hí a haza!* | Up Hungarian, your country is calling! |
| *Itt az idő, most vagy soha!* | Here is the time, now or never |
| *Rabok legyünk, vagy szabadok?* | Slaves shall we be, or free? |
| *Ez a kérdés, válasszatok!* — | This is the question, answer! — |
| *A magyarok istenére* | By the God of the Hungarians |
| *Esküszünk,* | We swear, |
| *Esküszünk, hogy rabok tovább* | We swear, that slaves no more |
| *Nem leszünk!* | Shall we be! |

hours, in copies by the thousands, still wet with ink.[8] At noon the church bells of Pest rang in memory of a Hungarian triumph over the Turks and doubly again to mark this extraordinary event.

In the early afternoon the March Youth debated the next steps. Despite frequent and vigorous rain showers, large crowds from every class of the city's population filled the streets.[9] Also visible here and there were the ample-sleeved shirts of the peasants who came regularly to sell their produce in the market located in the field just outside the city walls.[10]

Finally, from the steps of the National Museum, Pál Vasvári, an upcoming historian and one of the leaders of the March Youth, opened a public meeting before an enthusiastic crowd. József Irinyi, a young lawyer and journalist, spoke on the importance of the "Twelve Points." Then he ceded his place to Dániel Irányi, a future historian of the revolution, who proposed to carry the "points" to the City Hall, "not to overthrow the City Council, but to induce it to rally behind these demands."[11] He stated that these demands should then be carried to Buda, the seat of the Hungarian *Consilium* and central administration. Pest, he observed, could do little at this time about such things as the abolition of the peasant's subject status or the Transylvanian Union. But something could be done to realize the demand for press freedom by effecting the release of a certain unfortunate, Mihály Táncsics, a onetime artisan turned propagandist, who had been a

---

8 Zarek, *Kossuth,* p. 153; G. Spira, "A vezérmegye forradalmi választmánya 1848 tavaszán" (The Revolutionary Executive Committee of the Leading County in the Spring of 1848), *Századok* XCVIII, no. 4 (1964), 712; G. Spira, "Le grand jour: Le 15 mars 1848," *Études Historiques 1970 publiées à l'occasion, du XIII Congrès International des Sciences Historiques par la Commission Nationale des Historiens Hongrois* (2 vols.; Budapest: Akadémiai Kiadó, 1970), I. The first copies of the National Song and the "Twelve Points" came off the press at about 11:30 in the morning. The Hungarian language versions were soon followed by German translations which were hastily composed by two printers, Ludwig Giersch and Johann Weiss, 342-43. Spira's work is an outstanding source for eye witness accounts and quotes from Zichy, Klauzál, Nyáry, Petőfi, Landerer and others as well as from the official records of the Buda and Pest Councils and the *Consilium.*

9 Horváth, *Huszonöt év,* III, 373.

10 Spira, "Le grand jour," p. 347.

11 *Ibid.,* p. 348.

prisoner for some months because of a "libelous" publication. The crowd greeted these proposals with acclamation and without discussion.[12]

From this point, matters could have gotten ugly. The demand for the release of a prisoner was easy to construe as a direct challenge to all constituted authority. The situation was made all the more explosive as the demand for the formation of a National Guard was also one of the "Twelve Points."

The fact that the constantly growing, eventually huge and noisy crowd did not become a threat to life and property can be attributed to two men. One of these men was Gábor Klauzál, formerly a Delegate from Csongrád county who was a figure of note in the reform opposition and who had played a fine part in several previous Diets. Due to "Vienna's" bribes and influence he had not been reelected in 1847.[13] Because of this turn of events he was in the capital at this time as an emissary of Kossuth working with the Youth in organizing the drive for signatures on the petition.[14] The other man was Pál Nyáry, the acting administrator (sub-*alispán*) of Pest county. Seeing the importance of the moment, these men "seized the reins"[15] of the movement, a development which Petőfi and other non-nobles among the Youth were willing to accept because they wished to enlarge the circle of support for the actions they had taken up to this moment.[16] At four o'clock Klauzál, Nyáry, and the Pest Youth, a noble and non-noble leadership, arrived at the City Hall followed by a crowd

---

12 *Ibid.*; Horváth, *Huszonöt év,* III, 374. Táncsics, an elderly man, had earned his living for years as a weaver before he became an itinerant school teacher. In March, 1848, he had been in prison for several months because in writings and speeches on many occasions he had attacked the privileges of the Hungarian nobility, the burghers, and the entire structure of society. His lack of moderation and judgment can be seen from the fact that he was habitually against everything — the construction of railroads, Széchenyi's beneficial "two penny" direct tax, and the creation of the Academy of Sciences. Nevertheless, he was something of a *cause célèbre* among the Pest Youth — a symbol of freedom of the press and human rights which they felt should be sacrosanct. Hóman and Szekfű, *Magyar történet,* V, 348.

13 Horváth, *Huszonöt év,* III, 374.

14 Spira, "Le grand jour," p. 349.

15 Horváth's phrase repeated by other writers. *Huszonöt év,* III, 374.

16 Spira, "Le grand jour," p. 349.

estimated at 15,000 to 16,000 persons. At this juncture the City Council — a full general assembly totalling just over 100 individuals — had just adjourned, but it now quickly reconvened with whatever composure its members could muster. Soon the council chamber was filled with people for the first time since the building was constructed. They surrounded the seated deliberative body whose members, as Petőfi and others later recalled in their writings, were obviously ill at ease. [17]

The Pest City Council as it was then constituted represented the end-product of a highly restrictive political system inherited from the Middle Ages and characteristic of the charters of Hungarian cities. The hierarchy did contain some reform-minded members, but very few. When elections had been held on October 19, 1847, to send two Pest Delegates to the national Diet, conservatives had been returned and the two Liberal candidates had received only twenty votes out of 140 cast. [18]

Thus, on this late afternoon of March 15th, after Irinyi spoke first in favor of the City's formal adoption of the "Twelve Points" — a dead silence followed. Nyáry then spoke briefly. Then Klauzál, whose words carried great weight, submitted his views skillfully for the Council's consideration. He spoke of the timeliness, justice, and necessity of the "Twelve Points" and the danger of a popular explosion. He concluded with the observation that the Council members could see for themselves how political leaders coming from the ranks of the Liberal nobility were monopolizing the confidence of the people. [19]

After Klauzál's speech the Council's reaction was equivocal. Petőfi later wrote with typical impatience that every other word the members uttered was "order." [20] A Council member

---

17 *Ibid.*, p. 350 and ns. 70-73.

18 *Ibid.*, p. 350, n. 74.

19 *Ibid.*, p. 350. Klauzál was in effect telling the Council, most of whose members were non-nobles, that even though they were privileged burghers, popular opinion was behind the reform party of the nobles and that they (the burghers) would do best to support the movement for reform or run the risk of being left behind and incurring popular displeasure. To be exact, a full general assembly of the Pest City Council consisted of nineteen lifetime members of the inner council, several of whom were nobles, and ninety-six commoners elected on a burgher franchise of 2,798 souls. *Ibid.*, pp. 339-40, 334.

20 *Ibid.*, p. 350 and n. 77.

named Boldizsár Holovich held the floor, stating that it was necessary to examine the "Twelve Points" in detail and that such a discussion was impossible under the present circumstances.[21] He continued speaking in this vein while his listeners grew more and more restless and outside the crowd repeatedly shouted the *Nemzeti dal* — "Now or Never." Within the room an indignant voice cried that "the nation has already deliberated these points for fifty years" and a more anxious voice, speaking in German, broke in with the odd exhortation, "secure the windows."[22] Nevertheless, Holovich, the former Liberal, persisted.

This dangerous impasse was broken by Leopold von Rottenbiller, the assistant Mayor of Pest and a leading Liberal, who spoke of the obvious necessity for swift and positive action. He stated that "Pest must not remain behind the other European movements so that history may not later blame us."[23] He urged the Council to endorse the "Twelve Points" and, turning to the March Youth, stated:"You have brought us the hope of full liberty, it is you who have broken the chains from the press and I am deeply convinced that under your aegis our city will avoid disruptions of public order."[24] The radical Youth were flattered at this attention and the more moderate Liberals were pleased; the two groups who had entered as allies now drew even closer. Most importantly, Rottenbiller's influence won over the more conservative members of the Council.

All the members of the Council signed a copy of the newly printed "Twelve Points," the city seal was affixed, and it was taken to the window eliciting from the crowd in Petőfi's words "a gigantic explosion of enthusiasm."[25] According to the

---

21 *Ibid.*, pp. 350-51. The Austrian Secret Police records of 1846 and 1847 show that Holovich was under surveillance for his Liberal tendencies, p. 51, n. 78.

22 The latter remark, amusing in retrospect, struck at least one of those present forcefully enough for him to record it later. It seems reasonable to assume that the man who shouted this precaution was one of the workers from Bohemia (many of whom were engaged in Pest at the time) because it was in their country "above all that defenestration is a popular and very appreciated custom." *Ibid.*, p. 353.

23 *Ibid.*

24 *Ibid.*

25 *Ibid.*, p. 355 and n. 96.

Mayor Ferenc Szepessy, this signified that the Council "united itself with all the people of Pest in desires and sentiment" and "offered its fraternal hand in order to successfully realize all the points . . . in peace, order, and legality." [26]

Under this authority from the city's legally constituted Council and in cooperation with it, a security committee of nobles and non-nobles, totalling fourteen individuals, was selected to be responsible for the maintenance of order. Then a delegation was quickly chosen to carry the endorsed "Twelve Points" to both the King and the Diet, and it was also agreed that emphasis be placed on the point that the Diet should be transferred to Pest as soon as possible. [27] The Youth, many of whom as non-nobles did not have the right to vote, were particularly satisfied at the opportunity which now arose for them via this delegation to exercise some influence in person on the national assembly. [28] Lastly, it was resolved that a second delegation be selected to address the *Consilium* located across the river in Buda. It was to demand that freedom of the press be announced by the central Hungarian government, that Táncsics be released, and that the formation of a National Guard be authorized. When selected, the delegation charged with this task consisted of members from both the City Council and the new *ad hoc* security committee. It was to be led by Nyáry, the acting *alispán* of Pest county. [29]

Although these arrangements were made with considerable rapidity, the crowd waiting outside in the rain (which obstinately continued to fall) found the delay inexplicable once it had been learned the Council had endorsed the "points." Cries of "To Buda!," "To the *Consilium!*," and "Let us open Táncsics's cell!" showed that many were anxious to go on to the next objective which had been outlined on the steps of the National Museum. [30]

26 *Ibid.*, p. 355.
27 Horváth, *Huszonöt év,* III, 373-74.
28 Spira, "Le grand jour," p. 356.
29 *Ibid.*; Horváth, *Huszonöt év,* III, 374.
30 Spira, "Le grand jour," 356.

During this interval, news circulated in the crowd concerning the approach of Imperial troops. This caused the young poet, János Vajda, to issue a call to arms while waving his umbrella about, a situation not without its humor. He challenged the crowd to follow him in an assault on the arsenal in Buda observing that it was not with an umbrella in hand that they would "conquer liberty." However, the "Imperial troops" were soon seen to be the police who were making their regular early evening rounds. Thus, the incident was over as quickly as it had begun.[31]

Yet, just at the moment the delegation headed by Nyáry was preparing to set out, news of an accurate and significant nature did arrive at the Hall. Count Móric Almásy, one of the presiding officers of the Upper House of Magnates, arrived on the outskirts of the crowd. He stated that he had just come down from Pozsony under the authorization of the Palatine and that he brought good news concerning what had happened in the Diet. He was received with ". . . no hostility, still less hate, but was cheered and admitted quickly into the Council Chamber . . . ."[32] After a brief consultation with the leadership in which he learned of the actions just taken, he appeared at a window and delivered an improvised address to the crowd summarizing the important steps taken by the Diet in the last few days. He announced that "the Address to the Crown has been adopted without modification by their Excellencies, the members of the Upper House,"[33] and it was being carried this very day to His Majesty by a distinguished national Deputation. He concluded by urging his listeners to have patience. The crowd received the news with general satisfaction and some cheering but it was not at this point to be dissuaded from placing its demands before the central administrative authorities of Hungary.

The delegation, headed by the acting *alispán*, Nyáry, and including Klauzál, Rottenbiller, Petőfi, Almásy, and others, began the march. They went down Váci street (where the

---

31 *Ibid.*, pp. 355-56.
32 *Ibid.*, p. 357.
33 *Ibid.*

merchants closed their elegant shops with alacrity), by the National Theater, turned into the Grand Avenue of the Bridge and then by the boat-bridge across the Danube to Buda. The crowd which followed the delegation was estimated at 20,000 individuals and was described by one observer as an interminable line of umbrellas crossing the Danube in the rain; "thousands and thousands" with occasional shotguns and sabers visible among them.[34]

As the column passed into Buda, the members of the Imperial Ceccopieri regiment greeted them with cries of "*Evviva l'Ungheria!.*" It was recorded that as the Hungarian tricolor mounted the Avenue of the Lords, the windows rattled with the cheers for liberty and equality as well as for the King and the Palatine.[35]

The crowd filled the grounds of the *Consilium* and waited, since only the delegation was admitted. Count Ferenc Zichy, the *Consilium's* temporary president, had been in session with the other members most of the afternoon. They were well aware of the day's events in Pest and it took only about five minutes before they agreed to the delegation's requests.[36] Censorship was to be discontinued,[37] a National Guard authorized, and Táncsics released.[38] Count Zichy also promised that the government would call for Imperial troops only if and when the officials of Pest county requested it.[39]

Nyáry went to a window of the *Consilium* which was lighted due to the early dusk and announced to the expectant people below that all the requests had been granted.[40] It was

---

34 *Ibid.*, p. 359. Horváth states the crowd was prepared to back up its demands with force if necessary. *Huszonöt év,* III, 374.

35 Spira, "Le grand jour," p. 359.

36 According to Petőfi's description quoted in *ibid.*, pp. 357, 360 and n. 120.

37 Klauzál, whose words carried weight before the *Consilium* because of his experience in the Diet and his knowledge of the Oppositional Program, was instrumental in winning agreement to all demands. On the matter of the abolition of censorship, he assured the Council in writing that the reformers would devise an equitable bill to prevent irresponsible abuse of this freedom. *Ibid.*, p. 361.

38 His release was provisional pending the "outcome of the judicial procedure begun against him." *Ibid.*, p. 361.

39 Horváth, *Huszonöt év,* III, 374-75.

40 Spira, "Le grand jour," p. 361.

5:30 p.m. The crucial afternoon events of the Pest March 15th had taken place within the brief space of an hour and a half. Happily, the crowd went to Táncsics's cell in the Josef Barracks. He was released, and the same evening, lighting the way with torches, the crowd escorted him back across the river to Pest where they found quarters for him and his family.[41]

Further celebrations were held at the National Theater in recognition of the amazingly fast realization of the reform demands. By evening the Youth's ordinance committee had enrolled 1,500 men in the National Guard, which had perforce been authorized by the *Consilium*. The Pest-Buda Imperial Habsburg garrison, numbering only 7,500 troops, did not interfere[42] since it had no prior orders from Vienna for such an eventuality. Nor had it received any directives from the Hungarian *Consilium*, or requests from the administration of Pest county. It was only now that the habitually cautious German burghers of Pest, particularly the wealthiest among them who had hung back since the beginning of March, sided openly with the reform movement.[43] The next morning, Thursday, March 16th, posters appeared in both Hungarian and German recruiting for the Guard. By evening several units were formed, including a battalion of Jewish volunteers. Five hundred muskets had also been obtained[44] and a patrol was established. All of these actions took place without the knowledge of the national Diet in Pozsony. The slogan

---

41 Horváth, *Huszonöt év*, III, 375.

42 A. Urbán, "Die Organisierung des Heeres des ungarischen Revolution vom Jahre 1848," *Annales Universitatis Scientiarum Budapestinensis de Roland Eötvös Nominatae*. Sectio Historica. IX (1967), 106-7.

43 Horváth, *Huszonöt év*, III, 376.

44 On March 18th a thousand more muskets were obtained. On March 20th a request to the Palatine and the Diet brought no result. On the 23rd the arsenals at Komárom and Vienna sent another thousand, all of which were heavy and obsolescent, dating from the Napoleonic Wars. By March 24th about 4,200 private arms were donated and on March 27th another thousand were obtained, bringing the total to over 7,000 pieces of dubious quality. Nevertheless, the Pest Guard of some 7,000 plus men was one of the best equipped in Hungary. By mid-April the total Hungarian National Guard numbered 50,000 to 55,000 men. But of these only twenty per cent, that is some 10,000 men were well-armed. One-half or 25,000 had only sabres, battle axes, etc. Urbán, "Die Organisierung des Heeres der ungarischen Revolution vom Jahre 1848," pp. 107, 108, 110-12; Irányi and Chassin, *Histoire politique*, I, 153.

adopted by the Guard in Pest on the 16th was "King, Country, Constitutional Reforms, Freedom, Equality, Peace, and Order."[45]

\* \* \*

As noted above, for several years Pest county[46] had been the coordinating and focal point of Hungary's Liberal opposition against Habsburg bureaucratic absolutism. When March 13th had occurred in Vienna, the county assembly of nobles, which included some of the most advanced and most convinced Liberals among Hungary's untitled nobility, had nominated a committee of forty-seven members, to decide what policy should be adopted. Then the extraordinary events and conditions in Pest on March 15th caused the assembly to throw open its meetings to the public, a decision formalized on March 21st. Thereafter, about sixty non-nobles regularly took part in its discussions and the traditional county assembly, thus enlarged, may be referred to as the "Pest county executive committee."

One of these original non-noble members came from the large peasant town of Kecskemét and two from Buda, but the majority were from the city of Pest itself. Some of them, such as the assistant Mayor, Rottenbiller, were leading figures in the city's security committee so that membership in the Pest city *ad hoc* representative committee and the Pest county executive committee overlapped. Soon, non-nobles made up approximately one-half of the membership of the Pest county executive committee. They were principally merchants, writers, doctors, and other professional people from Pest. The radical March Youth group of political activists from the Cafe Pilvax contributed five members headed by Petőfi.[47] The nobles, who made up roughly the other half of the Pest county executive committee, included some of the most politically ex-

---

45 Horváth, *Huszonöt év*, III, 375; Hugessen, *Political Evolution*, II, 14.

46 Information in this and the next two paragraphs is found in even greater detail in Spira, "A vezérmegye forradalmi választmánya 1848 tavaszán," pp. 713-19, 724.

47 Mór Jókai, Pál Vasvári, József Irínyi, and Alajos Degré. *Ibid.*, p. 716.

113

perienced and best minds in Hungary.[48] In addition to the large landlords of the county, the executive committee was composed of virtually all the officials of the Pest county administration and many judges of the nation's higher appellate courts.[49] The meetings of the Pest county executive committee remained open to the public and were regularly attended by the Youth as well as artisans and working people from the city of Pest. Other non-nobles from the towns and villages of Pest county were also attracted to the debates rather quickly.[50]

The Pest county executive committee worked in harmony with the city security committee, but quickly came to overshadow it due to the superior quality of its membership. The numerous peasantry was not represented on the Pest county executive committee beyond a few individuals of peasant origin. This was not by design, but simply because of the precipitate nature of events and inherent social patterns. In addition, at this time many peasants who were normally not at all reluctant to defend their accustomed rights, showed little interest in what was traditionally regarded as a gentleman's game. Yet, aside from this absence, the composition of the committee was recommended by the fact that it was a natural and unstructured reflection of the articulate classes, forces, and influences at work in Hungarian society in 1848. Its example was followed independently in other Hungarian counties and towns, and in Pest the radical viewpoint was ably represented on the committee by Petőfi and Irinyi. In the remainder of March and in the first weeks of April, constant and open controversy continued between these radicals and their moderate or conservative opponents. But neither the differences on issues, nor the social differences between nobles and non-nobles caused one single split in the committee.

---

48 Literary figures such as Baron József Eötvös, Mihály Vörösmarty, Imre Vahót, Antal Csengery, Ágoston Trefort and Baron Zsigmond Kemény. Lawyers such as Pál Hajnik, József Ágoston, and János Fejes. Liberal politicans of note such as Pál Nyáry and Gábor Klauzál. *Ibid.*

49 Péter Kecse, József Patay, Károly Kendelényi and Sándor Reső Ensel. *Ibid.*

50 News of the events in Pest on the 15th spread out from the city "by the hour" and soon copies of the "Twelve Points" were circulated in the "humblest villages" of the county. Irányi and Chassin, *Histoire politique*, I, 154-55.

Despite disagreements about the degrees of actual application of Liberal principles and tactics to be pursued, these two broad social categories (noble and non-noble) cooperated against their mutual enemies, the Vienna bureaucracy and the Habsburg absolutism. Representatives from this common political force were eventually sent to the Diet in Pozsony where they were to exert pressure upon the conservative-minded in the Diet in support of a strengthened Dietal oppositional reform program.

To avoid assigning too great an immediate importance or even an exaggerated impression of the weight of the events of March 15th in Pest, it may be well to leave this subject for the moment with this analysis of the Pest county executive committee provided by György Spira:

> We should not overestimate its importance. They [the radicals in the committee] did not have the entire political power . . . . Their objective was not to overthrow Habsburg power, but rather to bring it under control. Nor did they wish to take away political leadership from the nobility. They only wished to get rid of some remnants of feudalism and, as far as Habsburg absolutism was concerned, they fought together with the nobility against it.[51]

By March 22nd the new Batthyány Ministry, established on the basis of ministerial responsibility to the parliament, had legalized the Pest county and city National Guard, as well as the formation of the Guard in other Hungarian counties and cities.[52] By March 27th the life of Pest, particularly its artisan

---

51 "A vezérmegye forradalmi választmánya 1848 tavaszán," p. 713.

52 Székesfehérvár (Stuhlweissenburg) received authorization on March 17th; Szeged, Esztergom (Gran), and Szabadka (Maria Theresiopol) on the 18th; Debrecen, Eger (Erlau), and Pécs (Fünfkirchen) on the 19th; Győr (Raab) and the towns in counties Borsod, Csongrád, and Bihar on March 20th. By April, eighty per cent of the Hungarian National Guard was drawn from the sixty largest towns and of the total about twenty per cent were the former burgher Civic Guards. At this time the Guard was almost entirely an urban affair and the peasants, who distrusted it, were hardly represented. In the towns themselves arms were held rather exclusively by propertied individuals. In Pest only "reliable, trustworthy and peaceful" individuals were in the Guard, and with the exception of the "Company of Equality" very few from the lower classes were participants. Urbán, "Die Organisierung des Heeres der ungarischen Revolution vom Jahre 1848," pp. 107, 108, 112.

activity, had settled back into a normal pattern.[53] There had been much excitement, but in marked contrast to Vienna on the 13th, no excesses or flagrant illegalities had occurred. Above all, no blood had been shed;[54] it had been a peaceful revolution justifying the comment, "never at one moment was law and order upset."[55] Unquestionably, many had doubts and reservations concerning the actions which had been taken. When the euphoria which surrounded March 15th in Pest quickly subsided, as Zarek records, sober, even anxious faces began to appear. The citizens of Pest and the Pest county executive committee looked to the constitutional structure and processes of the Hungarian State for support in the stance which had been taken. They awaited word from Pozsony about the outcome of the national Address to the Crown which, as they had discovered, was carried to Vienna by a Dietal Deputation on March 15th.[56]

53 Spira, "A vezérmegye forradalmi választmánya 1848 tavaszán," pp. 107, 108, 109.

54 Hugessen, *Politican Evolution*, II, 14.

55 Horváth, *Huszonöt év*, III, 375.

56 *Kossuth*, p. 154.

## Chapter VII

## THE CROWN ACCEPTS THE ADDRESS: MARCH 17TH

The Hungarian Dietal Deputation, which met a joyous popular reception upon its arrival in Vienna at two o'clock in the afternoon of Wednesday, March 15th, had not been received that afternoon or evening. The official reason given was that Ferdinand was ill, which—given his general condition—may very well have been true.[1] This announced condition of His Imperial and Royal Apostolic Majesty was the understandable result of being subjected for over two days to an endless stream of petitions, demands, and requests, as well as to conflicting and inconclusive advice. All of this culminated, at the time of the Hungarians' arrival, in the decision of the *Staatskonferenz* to issue the promise of a constitution in the Emperor's name for the Western Lands; an ultimate concession which considerably relieved the mounting tension as was duly recorded by many contemporaries.[2] Upon entering this milieu, the Hungarians immediately perceived to their considerable surprise that previous reports were not exaggerated. They quickly resolved to wring every possible advantage out of the situation by adding to the projected royal rescript which had been drafted aboard the steampacket the name of the Prime Minister to be appointed (Batthyány), as well as a commitment that royal sanction would be extended with a minimum of delay to those bills which were even then being finalized by the Diet, namely, the abolition of the

---

1 Macartney, *Habsburg Empire*, p. 333; Spira, *Hungarian Count*, p. 24.

2 See information in Rath, *Viennese Revolution*, pp. 82-84, and especially his chapter, "The Literature of the Revolution." See also William H. Stiles, *Austria in 1848-49*, I, 109-10.

Hungarian peasant subject status and the creation of a system of general taxation in Hungary.[3]

Széchenyi, who inspired the draft rescript, and who impatiently hoped to do something constructive in this crisis, was the first ashore at the Danube docking.[4] He remained firm in his recent conversion to a forceful policy and in his support for Batthyány as the best possible choice for Prime Minister. Nevertheless, he disapproved of the two points just added to the draft rescript, because in his estimation they intruded too far into a Hungarian King's constitutional right to exercise a reflective judgement and to make counter proposals concerning appointments and legislation. Also, as he recorded in his Diary on this day, they constituted a "direct humiliation" which might push the Habsburgs over the brink and "even lead to a break . . . if they [the Habsburgs] possess any vigour."[5]

However, the other members of the Hungarian Deputation recognized the incredibly favorable situation which then existed in Vienna. Thus they were more than ever determined to present their demand for the establishment of an independent and responsible national Ministry in the strongest possible terms. On this point it may be observed that they apparently knew the Habsburgs better than the cosmopolitan Count. They refused to retract one syllable in the additions to the rescript. Széchenyi was secretly filled with foreboding, but he bowed before the will of the majority (without, however, conceding his point) and maintained his resolve to do everything in his power to achieve the common objective.

He and Batthyány called directly on the Palatine Archduke Stephan who was somewhat surprised at first that Széchenyi was spokesman for the pair on behalf of the draft rescript which they presented. The Palatine was soon convinced by Széchenyi's words that the Hungarian demands

---

3 Spira, *Hungarian Count,* pp. 25, 29, 46.

4 Just before his departure Széchenyi, in his morning address before the Circular Sitting of the Lower House on March 15th, had commented with irritation on the "slowness" of the steampacket which was to carry the Deputation. *Ibid.,* p. 24, n. 23.

5 *Ibid.,* p. 25. The information in the following four paragraphs is also found in this source, pp. 24-28.

required attention even more urgently (if possible) than had been the case when he had been present at the afternoon session of the Diet in Pozsony on the previous day. According to Árpád Károlyi, the Palatine well understood the key role which he was assigned by the draft rescript.[6] Stephan again stated that he placed the honor of his office upon obtaining a favorable royal response. He requested them to act as intermediaries at Court and sent them to Count Kolowrat whose influence in the *Staatskonferenz* was on the increase. Széchenyi returned alone to the Palatine on this evening of the 15th encouraged by an "excellent" reception. The Palatine agreed with Széchenyi that the latter should forthwith call on the King's sixty-four year old uncle, Archduke Ludwig, who in view of Ferdinand's limitations, was generally regarded as the *de facto* head of the royal household and the power behind the throne.

Early the next morning, Thursday, March 16th, Széchenyi was received by Ludwig. The Archduke stated that he would agree to fill the vacant office of Hungarian Chancellor with Baron Miklós Vay (a conservative[7]), with Széchenyi himself, or, if necessary, with Count Batthyány. However, as the King's uncle he would not even consider the devolution of powers to the Palatine, nor the establishment of an independent and responsible Hungarian Ministry.[8] Withdrawing from this forthright experience, Széchenyi next called upon Prince Windisch-Graetz whose consistent advice over the past few days in favor of repression had raised him considerably in Court esteem. To Széchenyi's presentation of the Hungarian demands, this soldier, who within the year was to take the field against Hungarian troops, replied with a sincerity equalled by its inaccuracy. He declared that it was impossible to grant the demands of the "Hungarian nobility" because this would cause

---

6 *Az 1848-diki Pozsonyi törvénycikkek az udvar előtt*, p. 17.

7 The Archduke misjudged somewhat this conservative's submissiveness, since his man subsequently sided with the Hungarian national cause in Transylvania and was imprisoned for "sedition." Macartney, *Habsburg Empire*, pp. 414, 507, 525.

8 The Archduke Ludwig was consistently determined to keep all concessions to a minimum. *Ibid.*, p. 330. See also Stiles's estimate of him in *Austria in 1848-49*, I, 102-103.

the "upsetting of the constitution and the monarchy."[9] Széchenyi reportedly replied with some anger that the disruption of the Monarchy would very likely be the result if the demands were not granted.

Lastly, Széchenyi visited his two older brothers, Pál and Lajos, who resided in Vienna. He attempted to gain their support, especially that of Lajos who was an experienced courtier and household steward to the Archduchess Sophie, wife of the heir to the throne. Lajos responded by composing a memorandum in which he tactfully argued for a favorable consideration of the Hungarian demands. It was not, however, presented to the Archduchess until the following day. Wittingly or not, within the space of a few hours on this morning of the 16th, Széchenyi had managed to approach three of the most determined absolutists[10] in the entire Monarchy and for the moment his efforts appeared entirely unsuccessful.

Meanwhile, as Széchenyi was making his calls, the Palatine undertook what proved to be an effective personal initiative.[11] He hurriedly sought out László Szőgyény who was the acting Hungarian Chancellor since Apponyi's resignation, and showed him a copy of the draft rescript. They agreed to try to offset the certain opposition of the Austrian *Staatskonferenz* by sending it directly to the King accompanied by a letter from the Palatine. In his letter Archduke Stephan emphasized the critical situation in Pozsony and Pest and reminded the King that insufficient military forces were available to crush the explosion which was inevitable if the Hungarian demands were

---

9 Spira, *Hungarian Count,* p. 27. The Prince's confirmed absolutist views are apparent in his letter to Czar Nicholas I, written from Prague on June 8, 1848, in which he deplored the establishment of an Austrian Ministry and the Liberal attitude of the Archduke Johann. See Erzsébet Andics, *A Habsburgok és Romanovok Szövetsége: Az 1849. évi magyarországi cári intervenció diplomáciai előtörténete* (The Habsburg and Romanov Alliance: The Diplomatic Background to the 1849 Czarist Intervention in Hungary), (Budapest: Akadémiai Kiadó, 1961), pp. 246-47.

10 Professor Macartney notes that a popular belief existed at this time that the Archduchess and her husband, Franz Karl, were in favor of Liberal principles and the establishment of a constitution, and that although this view has been repeated by various historians, there is no conclusive evidence to support it. *Habsburg Empire,* pp. 325 and n. 1, 332 and n. 3.

11 Károlyi, *Az 1848-diki Pozsonyi törvénycikkek az udvar előtt,* pp. 17-18.

categorically refused. He stated that he had pledged his word and his office on an acceptable royal reply. If he had made a mistake, his overriding objective was to retain Hungary's loyalty to the dynasty. The situation in Hungary had developed to the point that His Majesty had no choice but to give favorable consideration to the Hungarian draft. He concluded by stating that the Hungarian movement was definitely not directed against His Majesty, but if the answer were not favorable, he could not return to Pozsony.[12] With the letter completed and sent off, Szögyény promised to do all in his power to see that the King should issue a favorable reply to the Diet's Address while the Hungarian Deputation was still in Vienna. Then, with mutual understanding and resolve, these two highest officeholders of the Royal Hungarian Government prepared to trek to the Hofburg where it was announced that the King would receive the Hungarian Deputation in formal audience.

There, just after noon on this Thursday, March 16th, the Palatine, and then shortly thereafter the entire Hungarian Deputation was admitted to the royal presence. Emphasizing that he acted in his capacity as King of Hungary, Ferdinand greeted the group courteously in Hungarian. He spoke in rather vague terms and then received the Dietal Address without undertaking any definite commitment.[13] Following this introductory speech, the ceremonial nature of the occasion was suddenly and utterly disrupted by Ferdinand himself. As if succumbing to a hitherto successfully concealed anxiety, he turned to the Palatine. His pleading hands clasped together in a childlike gesture, he blurted out in his customary Viennese dialect: "I' pitt di,' nimm mir meinen Thron nit! . . . ."[14] (I beg you, please don't take my Throne away! . . . .) The profound silence which followed the anguished plea of this poor simple-minded man was broken, as Kossuth later recorded, only by the acutely embarrassed Palatine's hastily murmured assurances of "unfaltering loyalty." Széchenyi noted in his

12 *Ibid.*, p. 18.
13 Spira, *Hungarian Count*, p. 28; Zarek, *Kossuth*, p. 148.
14 Spira, *Hungarian Count*, p. 28.

Diary entry for the day that this was "a painful scene."[15] In an instant it was revealed to the astounded and respectfully silent Hungarians:

How the bearer of the crown, the highest authority under the law, with whom the destiny of the Empire rested, was being fed on silly threats and unworthy fairy tales by those surrounding him, whose advice that incompetent man automatically followed.[16]

After this unsettling and completely unexpected experience, the members of the Deputation formally withdrew as quickly as possible. They waited in anxious anticipation throughout the remainder of the 16th without receiving an answer. While they waited, the real masters of the Imperial government, the members of the *Staatskonferenz*, assisted by advice from Windisch-Graetz and the Archduchess Sophie (both of whom urged rejection of the Address[17]), conducted a series of behind-the-scenes negotiations. These negotiations seemed dedicated to further perfect the traditional Imperial art of obscurantism. Their aim was to avoid the horrible prospect of again recognizing[18] the historic Hungarian Constitution with its now modernized political and social demands. The absence of Metternich did not change the general outlook. In fact, his influence was being replaced by that of Kolowrat whose Liberalism has been defined as "anti-Metternichism" on a personal level.[19]

The *Staatskonferenz* began its first meeting of the 16th shortly after noon, on the heels of Ferdinand's reception of the Dietal Deputation. As was customary, it was under the chair-

---

15 "Peinlicher Anblick," Károlyi, *Az 1848-diki Pozsonyi törvénycikkek az udvar előtt*, p. 12.

16 Spira, *Hungarian Count*, p. 29.

17 Macartney, *Habsburg Empire*, p. 335.

18 The Habsburgs had been forced to reaffirm the Hungarian Constitution in 1681, 1723, 1741, and 1791, after various campaigns to ignore, subvert, or overthrow it by force failed. For convenience see Macartney, *Hungary: A Short History*, pp. 86-90, 102, 122-24. English translations of the relevant Hungarian Laws for 1687-1723, 1741, and 1790 are found in Macartney (ed.), *Habsburg and Hohenzollern Dynasties*, pp. 82-94, 132-45. See also, d'Eszlary, *Institutions*, III, 98-99, 140-44, *passim*.

19 Macartney, *Habsburg Empire*, p. 335.

manship[20] of Archduke Ludwig, whom the previous Emperor, Franz I, had appointed as Ferdinand's guardian.[21] In addition to old Prince Windisch-Graetz, those present included the King's younger brother, Archduke Franz Karl, and Count Franz Hartig, an experienced sixty-four year old councillor. Despite his strong centralist and conservative feelings, the latter was in favor of some reform. Also present were: Count Münch-Bellinghausen, the President of the German Bundestag; Count Antal Majláth, Apponyi's predecessor; Baron Samuel Jósika, Transylvanian Chancellor; Lajos Rosenfeld, Jósika's colleague; Acting Chancellor Szőgyény, who arrived late, and a few others. The minutes were taken by Apponyi's assistant, Czillich.[22]

By now everyone was generally aware of the urgently worded extraordinary Hungarian Address to the Crown. Yet, the *Staatskonferenz* very typically began its deliberations with the first scheduled subject on its agenda—the acceptance of Apponyi's resignation and the appointment of a new Hungarian Chancellor—which was to be freely discussed in the best collegial fashion with the utmost secrecy. Szőgyény very shortly interrupted this discussion with a reading of the German translation of the proposed rescript drafted by the Hungarian Deputation. This fell on the group with something akin to the effect of a bombshell. The proposed recognition of the ancient viceregal powers of the Palatine, who would in turn use them to appoint Batthyány as a responsible Prime Minister, was an unexpected blow. It neatly circumvented the *Staatskonferenz's* accustomed power to exercise a decisive influence on the King's decisions concerning Hungary. More accurately, its acceptance would virtually eliminate this relatively small council's power to make and unmake Hungarian policy unilaterally by means of collective and secret decision. No

---

20 Károlyi, *Az 1848-diki Pozsonyi törvénycikkek az udvar előtt*, p. 19. In contrast to other authorities, Macartney states that Ludwig was induced to turn over the direction of the *Staatskonferenz* to his nephew, Franz Karl, sometime during the evening of March 14th and that it was Franz Karl who presided over all subsequent meetings. *Habsburg Empire*, p. 331 and n. 1.

21 Károlyi, *Az 1848-diki Pozsonyi törvénycikkek az udvar előtt*, p. 19.

22 *Ibid.*, pp. 19-20.

longer would it be possible for the Emperor's non-Hungarian advisors to sacrifice Hungarian interests illegally and unilaterally to those of the Western Lands. Immediately, almost every member present heatedly declared opposition to the draft. Jósika and his colleague, Rosenfeld, were especially outspoken, even though the latter as Court advisor on the affairs of Transylvanian Saxons technically had no right to speak on the affairs of Hungary proper. Following this initial and instinctive reaction to the Hungarian Dietal Deputation's surprise "chess move,"[23] the *Konferenz* could come to no agreement on an appropriate policy. The members, therefore, decided to adjourn for a short time.

Szőgyény used the interval to collar some members and argue cogently point by point in favor of a royal acceptance of the Hungarian draft. Eduárd Zsedényi for example, was told that the Diet's demand for an independent national government was new in name only. This, Szőgyény stated, was something guaranteed to Hungary by numerous Laws. As an example he singled out the tenth article of the fundamental Law of 1608. Concerning the principle of ministerial responsibility, he called attention to article seven of King Wladislaw (Ulászló) II"'s sixth decree, itself a reflection of several contemporary Laws, which had established the accountability of the King and his Royal Council to the Diet. Finally, Szőgyény noted that the devolution of royal powers to the Palatine during the King's absence from Hungary was spelled out with thoughtful detail in the fundamental Palatinal Law X of 1485, as well as Law XVIII of 1608.[24]

Despite the hostility expressed by the *Staatskonferenz* on this Thursday, March 16th, and notwithstanding the views of subsequent centralist-minded Austrian historians,[25] Sző-

---

23 *Ibid.,* p. 21.

24 *Ibid.,* p. 22.

25 Rudolph Springer (Karl Renner), *Grundlagen und Entwicklungsziele der österreichisch-ungarischen Monarchie* (Vienna: 1906), pp. 8, 11, 12; Friedrich Tezner, *Die Wandlungen der österreichisch-ungarischen Reichsidee* (Vienna: Manz, 1905), p. 2; *Der österreichische Kaisertitel* (Vienna: A. Holder, 1899), pp. 45, 18, 106. All these citations provide examples of the extreme Austrian centralist position which maintained that Hungary was integrated into the Monarchy in a Real Union since the Turkish era.

gyény's examples of constitutional precedents in support of the Hungarian Address and draft rescript were correct.[26] Neither election of the Habsburgs as hereditary Kings, nor adherence to the Pragmatic Sanction by the Hungarian Diet had in any way affected the legality of these precedents. Thanks to the Hungarian nobility's alert guardianship of the Constitution over many long and difficult decades, the 1848 demand for an independent and responsible Ministry under the Palatine was

---

26 The tenth article of the fundamental Law of 1608 stated that: Hungary with its annexed parts was to be governed by Hungarians only; appointments were to be made without regard to religious belief; and His Majesty was to take care that no foreigners would ever interfere in any Hungarian governmental institution. The numerous law articles of 1608 were negotiated with the Crown in pursuance of the 1606 Peace of Vienna and have sometimes been referred to as the first "Compromise" between Austria and Hungary. Hugessen, *Political Evolution*, I, 142, and n. 3, 145; Hóman and Szekfű, *Magyar történet*, III, 386. The seventh article of Ulászló (Wladislaw II of the Jagiellon dynasty) II's decree of 1507 stated that if a member of the King's Council conducted himself in his official capacity in a manner injurious to the public welfare, the other councillors were obliged to report this to the Diet which was authorized to punish him as a traitor to the liberty of the nation and a corrupter of public peace. The penalties ranged from decapitation to confiscation of the offender's property depending on the gravity of his offense. According to the first article of the decree, major decisions taken by the King without the agreement of the Royal Council were abrogated and the councillors were in turn accountable to the Diet. d'Eszlary states that the use of the terms "*libertas*" and "*commune bonum*" denote the national and political responsibility of the councillors as they carried out governmental activities and furthermore that this development marked the first emergence of a modern Hungarian parliamentary government. At the beginning of Ulászló's reign (1490-1516), Law VIII of 1495 stated that the King must choose three prelates, three barons, and fourteen lesser nobles to constitute the Royal Council, a structure favoring the smaller nobility. Law II of 1498 stated that in addition to the great office holders, the King was to nominate two prelates, two barons, and sixteen small nobles for the Royal Council and that the Diet's agreement was necessary for their instatement; in addition, the Council needed a minimum of eight of the small nobles in attendance to function. By Law X of 1500 the term of a royal councillor was set at three years; refusal to serve was illegal, reelection permitted, and a further Law established salaries. Despite several setbacks and inconsistencies, the elements of a limited monarchy with a constitutional and parliamentary exercise of political power had emerged in Hungary just prior to the Turkish onslaught. d'Eszlary, *Institutions*, II, 111, 114-15 and ns., *passim*. According to Law X of 1485 the Palatine was: empowered to receive foreign emissaries and make reply to them if the King were unable to do so (article seven); *ex officio* governor when the King was outside Hungary, and the King's will could be executed only through him (article ten); the representative of the King during his minority and could require all the obedience due the King from all inhabitants of Hungary (articles two and three). By this Law the Palatine was empowered during the King's absence or minority to convoke the Diet, sponsor and sanction legislation, and held supreme command of the Army. The only royal powers denied him were; supreme patronage of the Church, the right to confer titles, and the right to grant pardon — to which was prudently added by subsequent legislation a prohibition against granting any property rights above thirty-two urbarial holdings. d'Eszlary, *Institutions*, II, 122-25.

solidly based in law. It also opened up new possibilities which were entirely legal. Judging by the subsequent Austrian interpretation of 1848, the *Staatskonferenz*'s objection to the *de facto* implementation of these precedents was not based on the practical argument that these laws had lain largely dormant and inoperative since the Turkish conquest. Rather, it was based on their belief that implementation would undermine the long-standing Habsburg policy of centralism. Thus, they had to be made into "innovations" which would consequently appear "unconstitutional" or "illegal." However, Hungarian legal usage provided an explicit answer even on this point. Werbőczy's *Tripartitum* as early as 1517, had gone to considerable pains in defining custom and limiting its weight in law. Written Laws as passed by the Diet, sanctioned by the King, and entered in the *Corpus Juris Hungarici* were the highest expression of sovereignty. They always superseded customary practice (e.g. Habsburg centralism) no matter how long it might have been in effect.[27] Hence, it was legally irrelevant how long the Habsburgs had managed to divert Hungarian revenues by assigning Hungarian duty stations to the Austrian Lands,[28] or how long they had subordinated the Hungarian policy-making and administrative institutions to the Imperial government. Regardless of the circumstances, the Hungarians had always maintained that such *de facto* practices, conducted without Dietal consent, were illegal.

However, initially, on the afternoon of this Thursday, March 16th, the *Staatskonferenz* members and the Court were less concerned with arguing constitutional legalities than with trying to maintain their *de facto* power in its accustomed channels. The dominant desire was, in Wirkner's phrase, that "everything might be recovered in a roundabout way."[29] Eötvös, still a relatively young man at thirty-five, was offered a

---

27 d'Eszlary, *Institutions*, II, 20-21; III, 14-16.

28 Not long after Mohács the Habsburgs assigned the revenues of two major Hungarian custom houses, Pozsony and Magyaróvár, to the Lower Austrian *Kammer*, a tactic which had the effect of concealing Hungary's real contribution to the Monarchy's budget. The same tactic was applied to the highly lucrative estates which supported five fortresses in western Hungary. Hóman and Szekfű, *Magyar történet*, III, 83-87.

29 Quoted by Hugessen, *Political Evolution*, II, 15.

position in the Imperial government.[30] Count Batthyány was presented with the dazzling opportunity of filling Metternich's vacated position with the title of State Chancellor.[31] Simultaneously, Széchenyi and Prince Pál Esterházy both continued to use their personal connections on behalf of Hungary's constitutional requests. Esterházy saw Archduke Ludwig late in the afternoon and employed essentially the same arguments which Széchenyi had presented to him in the morning, apparently with a similar negative result.[32]

As evening approached, the atmosphere became more tense. Széchenyi wrote in his Diary at this time, very likely with considerable jealousy and revulsion, that the Viennese temper and the popular idolization of Kossuth was such that if Kossuth had given the word, the people would have stormed the palace and utterly destroyed it. Dániel Irányi made the same observation and praised Kossuth's "moderation" and "good council" to the Deputation at this time.[33] The Archduke Franz Karl granted an interview to Kossuth in which, according to Kossuth, he was told that Ferdinand had decided to meet the Hungarian demands and wished to do justice to "his true Hungarian nation," but not under the appearance of the pressure of violence. Kossuth replied that "if your Imperial Highness will give me your word . . . that you will do what equity and justice bind you to do for my country," he would ensure quiet in Vienna. Franz Karl replied that "the House of Austria will be everlastingly grateful to you for your action,"[34] following which Kossuth withdrew.

---

30 The young Baron's fame as a reforming writer would have made him a valuable asset and in addition someone may have thought there was a good prospect here since both József's father and grandfather were conservative Magnate pillars of Austrian rule, who had made the family name odious in Hungary. Jones, *Five Hungarian Writers*, p. 160.

31 Zarek, *Kossuth*, p. 148. The subsequent barbaric circumstances of his execution may well be an indication that the Habsburgs could never tolerate the rejection of such an offer.

32 *Ibid.*; Spira, *Hungarian Count*, p. 29.

33 Hugessen, *Political Evolution*, II, 14; Irányi and Chassin, *Histoire politique*, I, 158. Kossuth in later life stated that he had held the dynasty "in the hollow of his hand." This observation is supported by Lázár Mészáros *Élettörténete*, (Autobiography) I, 41 and Ferencz Pulszky, *Életem és Korom* (My Life and Times), I, 285 as cited by Hugessen, *ibid.*, n. 1.

34 Quoted by Hugessen, *Political Evolution*, II, 15 and n. 1. from Kossuth, *Schriften aus der Emigration*, II, 207.

After nightfall, the *Staatskonferenz* resumed its delibera-tions. According to the account left by Szőgyény,[35] hardly anyone present was favorably disposed toward the Hungarian Address. Most members fervently desired to retain collegial procedures and royal absolutism as a means of governing Hun-gary. This time Archduke Ludwig held in his hands the letter which the Palatine had sent to the King that morning.[36] Visibly upset, he turned on the Palatine and reproached him for having agreed to the draft rescript. He felt that now it would be impossible to use the independent Ministry promised to Vienna on the previous day as a means for centralizing monarchical affairs. The Palatine thereupon expressed regret that his action was the cause of displeasure, but stated emphatically that he had given his word to support the draft rescript and could not in good conscience withdraw it. Count Hartig spoke up in favor of a lenient policy in view of the Vien-nese people's enthusiastic reception of the Hungarian Deputation. He said that the King should express a willingness to meet the Hungarian wishes, but then require detailed reports and recommendations from the Hungarian Diet. He expressed the fear that if Hungary got everything in the proposed rescript, this would prompt similar demands from other Lands and invite the disintegration of the Monarchy.

As the debate continued with negative comments predomi-nating, it was all too clear that the House of Habsburg was more devoid than usual of a member with innovative inclina-tions. The decisive royal word which could have cut through this impasse was not forthcoming. The well-liked Ferdinand whose naive sincerity inspired popular loyalty and the alternate appellations, "Ferdinand the Good Hearted" ("*Fer-dinand der Gütige*") and "Ferdy the Simp" ("*Nanderl-Trot-terl*") was incapable of effective rule due to his epileptic con-

---

35 Taken from his *Emlékiratai* (Memoirs), p. 59, as cited by Hugessen, *Political Evolution*, II, 15 and ns.

36 This paragraph is drawn from Károlyi's account which is based on *Staatskonferenz* documents. *Az 1848-diki Pozsonyi törvénycikkek az udvar előtt*, p. 23 and ns.

dition and limited mental capabilities.[37] The pathetic scene of that morning had revealed that, if not terrorized, he was at least under the power of his advisors. Among the Arch-dukes,[38] Karl, the Emperor's uncle and hero of the Napoleonic Wars, was a man of real ability, but he was excluded from public life. Karl's son, Albrecht, who had unjustly received popular blame for the bloodshed on the 13th, was inexperienced and was just beginning a military career. Johann was an elderly man who had been excluded from Court from 1813 to Franz I's death in 1835, after which he received only minor offices. He possessed Liberal and constitutional convictions and, as noted earlier, had urged Ferdinand to make concessions in early March. But his advice was ignored and he was sent down to pacify Styria on the 13th. Franz Karl, the Emperor's brother and heir-presumptive, who had spoken amicably with Kossuth earlier in the day, was not inclined to concessions. Ludwig held similar reactionary views and demonstrated no outstanding ability. Franz Josef, soon to be the camarilla's (an unofficial group dedicated to the main-tenance of absolutism) protege, was still only seventeen years of age. The absolutist feelings of his mother, the forceful Arch-duchess Sophie, were unshakable. She was apparently advised by Kolowrat, whose star was definitely on the rise, and who was at once a Czechophile and a Hungarophobe.[39]

The collective influence of these personalities created an atmosphere which was decidedly against the constitutional declarations that came from Hungary. As the night of March 16th wore on, the *Staatskonferenz* revealed itself to be a rather blind and stubborn group.[40] Faced with an acute crisis, this

---

37 Macartney, *Habsburg Empire*, pp. 239 and n. 2, 332. Despite his handicaps, Ferdinand often mustered his abilities and tried to "do good" and one cannot help but have a measure of sympathy for him as an individual who, through no fault of his own, was so unequal to the difficult role thrust on him. He was in reality badly served and then deposed for "reasons of State." Vienna was, after all, probably as cynical a town as any in this age. The fact that the people responded to him indicates he was a good person with good intentions.

38 *Ibid.*, pp. 190 and ns. 1, 2, and 3, 240, 328 and n. 3, 331 and n. 1; Tapié, *Rise and Fall of the Habsburg Monarchy*, pp. 271-72.

39 Hóman and Szekfű, *Magyar történet*, V, 318.

40 This was, after all, Thursday night, and only three days before Vienna had been in open revolt, the last signs of which had been calmed only by the promise of

collection of experienced policy makers displayed a remarkable reluctance to make a realistic appraisal of the situation.

Finally, the previously unrelenting Archduke Ludwig began to be softened by the arguments of Prince Pál Esterházy who was called in to persuade him.[41] Franz Karl also began to waver. No doubt they and the other members of the *Konferenz* were influenced by the Secret Police reports collected by Sedlnitzky from all over Hungary. They learned that anti-"Vienna" demonstrations were taking place as far away as Debrecen and Kassa.[42] Also, rumors of popular Viennese support for the Hungarian demands were rampant. One secret report stated that the famous confectionary house of Demel was boiling tar to be used in a popular rush on the Hofburg.[43] In the end, it was these fears, combined with Szőgyény's arguments and the Palatine's threat of resignation on the spot,

---

an Austrian constitution issued just the previous evening (Wednesday, March 15th). However, blindness concerning the causes and remedies for these upheavals was by no means exclusively confined to the members of the *Staatskonferenz*. For example, John Schwarz, U.S. acting Counsul at Vienna in 1848, followed exactly the line of reasoning of the subsequent "official" Habsburg explanation of the Vienna disturbances, *viz.*:

> Before we were aware of it, French emissaries were among us . . . . After peated attempts . . . to stir up insurrection . . . neither money nor exertions were wanting to seize the favorable opportunity to foment a disturbance in the capital of the monarchy . . . . The students became ready instruments . . . and thus, through the negligence of the ministers the insignificant demonstration of students of the 13th of March occasioned the overthrow of the government. I must remark that the few who fell on the 13th of March must not be looked upon as victims to the cause of liberty. As generally happens in all such convulsions, all confidence is destroyed and not only the five per cent state bonds have fallen from 115 to 50 but everyone hastens to change his bank notes to silver . . . . To make matters worse, the export of silver and gold is prohibited . . . silver coin is bought up secretly at an advance of fifteen per cent and gold at twenty per cent . . . . To compel payment of any arrears or bills of exchange, there is no possibility. The newly formed national guard affords no protection . . . payments are left . . . to the pleasure of the debtors. The outlays of the state increase every day in spite of a deduction of from five to ten per cent from the salaries of officials, no taxes are forthcoming . . . . As regards the staple articles of the United States, sales under present circumstances are scarcely to be thought of . . . . Mr. J. G. Schwarz to the Honorable James Buchanan, Vienna. June 20, 1848. *House Executive Document No. 71* 31st Congress, 1st Session, pp. 67, 68, 69, 70. See also Mr. Schwarz to the Hon. John M. Clayton, Vienna, April 21, 1849. *Ibid.*, p. 73.

41 Károlyi, *Az 1848-diki Pozsonyi törvénycikkek az udvar előtt*, p. 26.

42 *Ibid.*, p. 27.

43 *Ibid.*

which forced the issue. The predominant desire was to avoid what appeared to be Hungary's imminent separation from the Monarchy.[44] Very late in the night and with the greatest reluctance, the *Staatskonferenz* agreed to issue a favorable royal reply to the Hungarian Address. At its close, the session was characterized by Archduke Ludwig's reproachful remark to Archduke Stephan that it would be his fault as Palatine "if we lose Hungary."[45] Stephan, well aware of the great store of animosity which his actions had built for him among the Archdukes and the Court, made no reply.[46]

Unaware of this decision, the members of the Hungarian Deputation had retired well after midnight with absolutely no idea of what news the morning might bring. Within a quarter of an hour Széchenyi was roused by a messenger from the Palatine bidding him to hasten to the Hofburg. Arriving there, he found Batthyány, Kossuth, and Esterházy. Under the uneasy light of the chandeliers, the Palatine solemnly announced to the little group that the *Staatskonferenz* had just arrived at a favorable decision. Congratulations were sincerely and profusely showered on Batthyány, who was soon soundly cheered in a nearby casino.[47]

Rather typically, Széchenyi was one of the first to take his leave and walk back to his quarters. There, his relief and joy prompted him to pound thunderously on the door of the sleeping Baron József Eötvös and Count Sándor Erdődy demanding admittance: "In the name of the law!"[48] The fact that the sleeping occupants were nearly startled to death reveals more than Széchenyi's occasional sense of black humor. It was also a telling indication of the very real stakes with which they had all been playing.

Quite early on the morning of Friday, March 17th, Ferdinand did indeed sign the rescript placed before him,

---

44 *Ibid.*; Macartney, *Habsburg Empire*, p. 333.

45 Károlyi, *Az 1848-diki Pozsonyi törvénycikkek az udvar előtt*, p. 26; Horváth, *Huszonöt év*, III, 385.

46 Károlyi, *ibid.*

47 Spira, *Hungarian Count*, p. 29.

48 *Ibid.*

which contained the essential points in the Hungarian Deputation's draft of the 15th. The King indicated a favorable disposition toward "suitable legislative proposals" and directed that the "suggested laws referred to in the Address" should be submitted "for my decision without delay." However, the two points which had been added by the Hungarians after their arrival in Vienna,[49] the designation of Batthyány as Prime Minister, and the commitment that preliminary sanction for the bills currently being drafted by the Diet should be issued in advance, were both deleted. These omissions confirmed Széchenyi's earlier opinion, but they did not necessarily fault the Deputation's judgment. It was obvious that the most forceful presentation possible had been barely enough to gain royal approval. In fact, the extraordinary verbiage[50] of the royal rescript was typical of the House of Habsburg under stress. The Palatine was "invested" with "full powers to govern in my absence the Kingdom of Hungary and the Parts annexed thereto in accordance with the law and the Constitution." The crucial phrase ran as follows:

> I am disposed, subject to the maintenance of the unity of the Crown and the integrity of the link with the Monarchy, to consent to the desire of my loyal Estates for the formation of a responsible Ministry and give you at once the authority to propose for appointment suitable persons.[51]

When the Hungarian Deputation received this rescript, it was instantly regarded as a vindication of a three-hundred year national struggle against the pretensions of Habsburg absolutism and as the workable and constructive basis for a better future. The unrestrained rejoicing blocked out any thought of bad faith on the part of the dynasty, at least for the moment.[52]

---

49 *Ibid.*

50 The full text is quoted in Horváth, *Huszonöt év,* III, 386-87. A complete English translation is in Hugessen, *Political Evolution,* II, 16-17. Partial English translations are in Zarek, *Kossuth,* p. 149 and Macartney, *Habsburg Empire,* p. 333.

51 Horváth, *Huszonöt év,* III, 386-87. The "you" to whom the intermediary power of nomination of Ministers is given, is the Palatine.

52 Hugessen, *Political Evolution,* II, 17.

A party grouped about Kossuth[53] immediately appealed to the Palatine for the appointment of Batthyány as Prime Minister. The Palatine, true to his earlier commitments, went directly to the King early on this morning of the 17th. He obtained verbal consent from Ferdinand to Batthyány's appointment as Prime Minister, and then immediately wrote a letter to Batthyány entrusting him with the formation of a responsible ministry.[54] Árpád Károlyi states that Batthyány's possession of this letter caused joy among the Hungarians equal to that of the King's signature on the rescript. For the Hungarian Deputation it represented the complete victory of the mission with which it had been entrusted by the Diet. Once again the Palatine had completely upset the plans of the *Staatskonferenz*. That body had entertained hopes that, when Vienna was once again quiet, pressure might be put on the Palatine to designate a more pliable Minister than Batthyány. The King's verbal promise could have been reversed. But when these commitments became public knowledge, through the Palatine's letter to Batthyány, the prestige of the dynasty was involved and the promises could not be easily set aside.[55] The appointment was still provisional since technically Batthyány had not as yet provided the Crown with proof that he enjoyed the necessary support in the Hungarian Diet to form a government. But practically speaking, there was little question of this support. There was certainly no doubt about his support within the Deputation.

It was decided to depart for Hungary as quickly as possible. Before leaving however, the Deputation issued a manifesto to the people of Vienna, which unequivocally demonstrated that there was no desire on the part of the Deputation to sever the bonds of unity between Austria and Hungary. They also emphasized Hungary's desire to honor her fundamental obligation under the Pragmatic Sanction to provide for mutual defense:

---

53 Spira, *Hungarian Count*, p. 30.
54 Károlyi, *Az 1848-diki Pozsonyi törvénycikkek az udvar előtt*, p. 29.
55 *Ibid.*, pp. 29-31.

The bankruptcy of the godless principle of *divide et impera* which sowed the dragon's teeth of discord between us is now recognized. That tie which henceforth binds us all to the beloved reigning House . . . is no chain of servitude but the golden bonds of freedom, the maintenance of which can be assured only so long as each and all stand together. Hungarian desires have been satisfied; in the future a Hungarian Government supported by free institutions will control our destiny, and royal promise assures you that you also will henceforth enjoy similar blessings. Brothers, we shall be united in liberty, strong in our mutual understanding, powerful in our alliance, which brotherly feeling, genuine confidence and fidelity to the reigning House have cemented . . . . We exclaim as a farewell and as a final expression of our thanks, long live the reigning house, long live the Austrian people, freedom, fraternity, and the community of interests which units us all.[56]

In the midst of all this, a curious incident occurred, remembered later by Pulszky and some others.[57] A virtually unknown Hungarian engineer named Ecsegi, who was in the service of Count Keglevitch,[58] led a crowd through the streets holding a picture of Ferdinand shouting *Éljen!* (Long live). When finally persuaded to give a speech (which he delivered from the top of a cab), he stated:

Viennese! You rejoice for you are receiving a constitution and because Metternich has been dismissed. This is not enough. I tell you if you leave in office one coal carrier among those who have been your rulers, then reaction will slip in again through the door of the stove, and it will rob you of your constitution and take its revenge on you.[59]

This minor incident, one of many, went unnoticed as the Hungarian Deputation left Vienna by steampacket on the afternoon of Friday, March 17th. Once under way, it was

---

56 Hugessen, *Political Evolution*, II, 17.
57 Recorded in Zarek, *Kossuth*, pp. 149-50.
58 Gábor Keglevitch was Pest City Treasurer. Horváth, *Huszonöt év*, III, 387.
59 Zarek, *Kossuth*, p. 149.

announced to the Deputation at large that Batthyány should become Hungary's first responsible Prime Minister. The arrival of the successful Dietal Deputation in Pozsony at 6:30 p.m.[60] was one of the most memorable events in the nation''s history.[61] The Pozsony National Guard, already 1,200 strong,[62] paraded, and everyone who could move came to the dockside. Batthyány came ashore first. Kossuth followed, fell to his knees, and asked God's blessing for the work to be accomplished. He stated that the victory was not to be ascribed to any given person or party, but it had been won by all, since all had striven for it.[63]

60 Spira, *Hungarian Count*, p. 31.

61 *Ibid.*; Zarek, *Kossuth*, p. 155.

62 Urbán, "Die Organisierung des Heeres der ungarischen Revolution vom Jahre 1848," p. 109. Actually it reached a total of 1,293 enrolled between March 17th and 23rd.

63 Zarek, *Kossuth*, p. 155.

*Chapter VIII*

## THE WORK OF THE DIET AND THE FALSE RUMOR: MARCH 18TH — MARCH 25TH

By Saturday, March 18, 1848, not even the most conservative among the Magnates and those still hesitant in the Lower House could continue to doubt that a fundamental constitutional opportunity of profound importance existed.[1] This was an opportunity to reverse definitively three centuries of Habsburg illegalities and would-be absolutism, an opportunity to initiate a modernization of Hungary in a legal and "comprehensive manner." In the view of the great Liberal historian, Horváth:

> The royal rescript was completely in accord with the wishes of the nation. The country's independent government, under which provision the nation invited the Habsburg dynasty 300 years before to the throne, and which contract the Kings with their unilateral ruling had so often broken, and because of which so many times so much blood had flowed, finally by the lawful forms strictly circumscribed, had been peacefully secured.[2]

With the obscurantism of the Crown at least temporarily removed, the legislative transformation of Hungary occurring

---

1 The sensitive and just recently converted Széchenyi, whose program of non-political and gradual economic reform had made him a bitter and constant critic of Kossuth, had the generosity to admit in his self-accusatory manner "bolder and more courageous spirits, with whom higher invisible forces seem to have been allied, have placed the future of our country on a new basis which our ant-like labours would perhaps never, or only after generations, have been able to bring about." Quoted in Zarek, *Kossuth*, p. 156. Also quoted by Hugessen as having appeared in *Pesti Hírlap* on April 8, 1848. *Political Evolution*, II, 19 and n. 1. See other remarks by Széchenyi in Spira, *Hungarian Count*, pp. 30-32.

2 *Huszonöt év*, III, 387. The "blood" Horváth refers to can be most easily associated with Rákóczi's war against Habsburg absolutism (1703-1711) which resulted in some 85,000 battle casualties and some 400,000 deaths from starvation, plague, and other related causes totalling around one-half million deaths or approximately one-fifth of the entire population at that time. Király, *Hungary*, p. 46, n. 14.

in the next three weeks was effected with a swiftness in startling contrast to the decades of tedious negotations which had preceded it. It also stood, it may be justly remarked, in contrast to the proceedings of the facade constitutionalism which characterized the responsible Ministry appointed under Kolowrat's provisional presidency in Vienna.[3]

Very broadly speaking, the swiftness of this comprehensive legislative transformation was characterized by a maximum of cooperation and a minimum of obstructionism among Hungarians who held differing views ranging from conservative to radical concerning the wisdom and extent of particular bills. The general awareness of the unusual and important opportunity made all wish to make the best possible use of it.

Nevertheless, it should be noted that many intelligent and selfless Hungarians, by no means all of them conservatives, had sincere misgivings about the swiftness of events and a great concern for the solidity of this comprehensive transformation. For example, the young Eötvös, who had hurried up from Pest to take his place in the Upper House for the voting on the Address on the 14th, entertained the concern that things were moving too quickly.[4] However, despite his uneasiness, he accompanied the Dietal Deputation to Vienna, and worked indefatigably after the return to Pozsony to reconcile the interests of the differing groups. He felt that a great opportunity had come to realize the views which he had presented in his critical 1846 work, *Reform*.[5] He subsequently became a member of the Pest county executive committee and proved a valuable liaison between that *ad hoc* body and the national Diet.[6] Again, the great opposition leader whose dual commitment to constitutional legality and measured social advance is proverbial, namely, Deák, expressed the same sort

3 Hugessen, *Political Evolution*, II, 20. On the Kolowrat Ministry's beginnings, see Macartney, *Habsburg Empire*, pp. 334-35; Rath, *Viennese Revolution*, pp. 125-26.

4 Hugessen, *Political Evolution*, II, 19.

5 Mr. Blackwell to Viscount Ponsonby. Presburg, March 19, 1848, 6 a.m., *CRAH*, p. 51. *Reform* was first published in Leipzig because of Habsburg censorship. See Jones, *Five Hungarian Writers*, pp. 173 and n. 1, 174. The work has never been translated into English.

6 Spira, "A vezérmegye forradalmi választmánya 1848 tavaszán," p. 716.

of reservations.[7] He had unfortunately refused on principle to stand as a candidate for election to this historic Diet in 1847.[8] From the beginning Batthyány had wanted him in the ministry. As early as the 14th, he sent Baron Béla Wenckheim and Károly Tolnay to win Deák over, and, on March 16th, the Zala county assembly called on him to accept.[9] Deák arrived in Pozsony on the 20th, and that evening, after much persuasion during a meeting held in Batthyány's home, Deák finally agreed to accept a ministerial portfolio. However, the official announcement was withheld, and the following day the *Pesti Hírlap,* which had come out strongly for his inclusion, was still speculating about his acceptance and possible position in the Ministry.[10] In a subsequent letter to his brother-in-law, Deák expressed his misgivings. He spoke of the "feverish excitement" in Pozsony on the day of his arrival. He said he did "not approve of this instant law-making," especially concerning the bills on the abolition of the urbarium and the introduction of general taxation. He noted the pressing necessity of creating an entirely new "citizens' codex" and stated:

> The condition of the country is troublesome. Up there [Vienna] they are unable to get used to the new order of things and every matter causes more problems than we find advisable at this time; in Pest every hour might produce some thoughtless, angry outbreak which would threaten the country. At this moment nobody can have even an inkling what the most immediate future might bring. Our country is perhaps in the greatest danger it

7 Mr. Blackwell to Viscount Ponsonby. Presburg, March 22, 1848, *CRAH,* p. 51.

8 In his home county of Zala in 1843 he objected to election illegalities and violence. The numerous poor nobles had accepted Vienna's bribes and the argument that reform meant their economic demise. Unless they reversed their position on noble payment of domestic county taxes, Deák refused to stand as a candidate. Hugessen, *Political Evolution,* I, 345 and n. 3. Irányi stated that in 1847, Deák may have feared being eclipsed by Kossuth; there is no doubt, however, that he was a nationally acclaimed figure. In 1840, virtually every county elected him as an honorary official. Irányi and Chassin, *Histoire politique,* I, 174. See especially Béla K. Király's discussion in, *Ferenc Deák* ("Twayne's World Leaders Series"; Boston: Twayne Publishers, A Division of G. K. Hall and Co., 1975), pp. 93-98; 113-14. Unfortunately, this fine study was noted too late to be fully employed.

9 *Deák Ferencz beszédei,* II, 19.

10 *Ibid.,* pp. 27-38.

ever experienced. The Russians may crush us, or, again, the Austrian power, or perhaps the most horrible anarchy, only God knows. Every moment is insecure.[11]

Despite such legitimate misgivings, however, the dominant feeling from March 17th was one of forward movement. It can be truthfully stated that even with the great strain and excitement, and notwithstanding the personal interests and differences involved, the activity of the next three weeks was conducted in an absolutely constitutional and parliamentary manner.

Immediately upon the return of the Deputation from Vienna on Friday, March 17th, the Palatine publicly announced that he had appointed Batthyány provisionally as Prime Minister and charged him with the responsibility of forming a responsible ministry. He received a grudging and "provisional" approval of his actions from the *Staatskonferenz* in the form of a royal rescript on the 19th after which he formally presented the Count to a mixed session of both Houses as Hungary's first Minister.[12] In the meantime, the Lower House of the Diet without further ado had declared itself in permanent session. It worked with only short breaks the whole day of Saturday, the 18th, until midnight, and again all day Sunday. During this time it passed a series of resolutions forming a comprehensive outline for new bills as well as up-dating older proposed legislation left from the opening of the Diet in November, 1847. Most importantly, the major reform bills were brought out of the committees established by the Lower House after Kossuth's speech of March 3rd.[13]

Before proceeding to list these resolutions as supplied by Blackwell, it is necessary to affirm what was generally and popularly taught thereafter in Hungary about this period. The

11 Letter to József Oszterhueber-Tarányi, Pozsony, March 28, 1848. *Ibid.*, pp. 28-29.

12 Macartney, *Habsburg Empire*, pp. 336-37; Károlyi notes the emphasis which the *Staatskonferenz* put on "provisional" when they drew up the rescript in Vienna on the 18th. *Az 1848-diki Pozsonyi törvénycikkek az udvar előtt*, p. 32.

13 Macartney, *ibid.*, p. 337 and n. 2; Mr. Blackwell to Viscount Ponsonby. Presburg, March 19, 1848. 6 a.m., *CRAH*, p. 50; Spira, *Hungarian Count*, p. 46. See above Chapter IV, n. 2.

transformation of March 1848 has been rightfully called "an event unparalleled in . . . history . . . [when] the nobility of Hungary, of their own free will, renounced their privileges for the benefit of the whole people."[14] In the light of the preceding Reform Era and the chronology of events in early 1848, this assessment may be accepted as true in essence. Even the more radical contemporaries of the period assessed the role of the Hungarian nobility favorably. The reforming opposition "eternally merited frank admiration." Those who approved the changes at the last hour "also merit praise" for their decision to sacrifice their immediate material interests, their desire to do justice, and their understanding of their age. Both groups present a "great and very rare example: the emancipation of the plebs by the nobles themselves."[15]

This viewpoint does, however, stand in need of minor qualification due to the brief appearance in Pozsony, late on the 16th, of a mysterious, ugly, and completely false rumor concerning the events in Pest on March 15th. The rumor, presented in simplest terms, stated that Petőfi at the head of a host of peasants armed with scythes and whatnot was marching on Pozsony and raising the countryside as he went for a jacquerie similar to the slaughter which had occurred in Galicia in 1846.[16] The rumor was bolstered by the fact that it

14 Paul Ignotus, *Hungary* (New York: Praeger Publishers, 1972), p. 55.

15 Irányi and Chassin, *Histoire politique*, I, 159-60. This interpretation of the traditional Hungarian historiography appears to stand in far less need of qualification than the views of some recent Western or Hungarian Marxist historians. It is certainly true that historians in general since World War II, especially since 1948, in treating this subject have, in the words of Victor L. Tapié, "tended to move towards a Marxist interpretation and a unilateral viewpoint which placed economic and social causes in the foreground," *Rise and Fall of the Habsburg Monarchy*, p. 279, n. 36. However, as useful and as valuable as such studies are, they must lose a great deal of reality and conviction by omitting the legal, political, and constitutional aspects which were predominant in the situation.

16 This complex and still somewhat mysterious Galician event occurred in February, 1846, in the Austrian portion of partitioned Poland, and was the result of one of the perennial efforts of émigré Poles to promote a national uprising against the partitioning powers. The peasants of Galicia, who, especially in the western Vistula river valley, were in extreme straights, suffering from floods and successive years of bad harvests, subsequently claimed that their support had been solicited both by revolutionary Polish agents and then by the Austrian officialdom with promises of personal freedom and land ownership. All this is unclear, but what is clear is that the peasants in the west, especially around Tarnow, turned on the Polish nobles, slaughtering some 1,400 and bringing their bodies in carts to the

was known that the period around March 15th was a traditional market time and several thousand peasants were
camped on the *Rákosmező*, (a field) just outside Pest, where
they gathered for their customary commercial purposes. Plans
seem to have been made for Petőfi to address them, but the
rumor itself was groundless.[17]

As described above, the bloodless events of March 15th in
Pest were exclusively an urban affair spearheaded by students,
writers and nobles. Soon the city fathers and county nobles at
large adhered to it. In point of fact, the peasants around Pest,
as well as around most other Hungarian cities, particularly in
the *Alföld*, tended to be suspicious of and aloof from this
whole business.

The peasants especially suspected the budding National
Guard units as being merely a new form of the old military and
possibly a new source of taxation. Both the Hungarian
speaking and the linguistically non-Hungarian peasants
distrusted these units and only accepted them with hesita-
tion.[18]

The peasants continued in this attitude throughout the
first phase of the Hungarian "revolution." This is ironic for it
seems to belie the views of some historians who hold that one of
the major motivations for the Diet's passage of social reform
measures was its fear of peasant insurrection. Instead, the
peasants continued to regard the Guard as an "urban"
institution, primarily because very few were admitted. The
radicals, it is true, were concerned about peasant participation. The Pest county executive committee and the Pest city

---

*Kreis* (district) capital to receive their reward from the Austrians. It is of interest to
compare the differing emphasis in Macartney, *Habsburg Empire*, pp. 307 and n. 2,
308 and n. 1, 310-11, and Lewis Namier, *1848: The Revolution of the Intellectuals*
(Anchor Books ed.; Garden City, New York: Doubleday, 1964), pp. 14-15, 16 and
n. 13, 17 and n. 14, 18. The importance of this event was to bring the peasant situation into sharp focus and to increase the conviction in the Hereditary Lands and in
Hungary that something must be done about it. Macartney, *ibid.*, pp. 311-15,
Namier, *ibid.*, p. 17-19.

17 Macartney, *Habsburg Empire*, p. 337; Deme, "The Radical Left in the
Hungarian Revolution of 1848," pp. 61-67. Deme states "there is no evidence that
the radicals did try to incite the peasants against the nobility," p. 66.

18 Urbán, "Die Organisierung des Heeres der ungarischen Revolution vom
Jahre 1848," p. 111.

security committee, pushed by the more radical Youth, objected to the Diet-sponsored property qualifications for membership in the Guard. They felt it should be open to any-one who had the integrity to be entrusted with arms, including the peasants. For this reason they went beyond the Diet's authorization and invited everyone in Pest county who wished to join. The recruiting was successful enough since by mid-April the county had a guard of over 17,000. But very few indeed were peasants. Peasant support varied widely from locale to locale within the county, but on the whole active peasant participation was unusual in the five districts or *járá-sok*.[19] In Solt, Vác, and Pest *járások* and notably in the village of Izsák, the committee recruiters distributed leaflets to ex-plain the difference between the Imperial Army and the National Guard. But again and again they found the peasants indignant at the idea that they might be "conscripted" into a military unit which they stubbornly continued to regard as a burden. They wanted to know "by what authority is this being done?" and "by what right were they being imposed with new burdens?"[20] The landless or nearly landless *zsellérek*, those most eligible for the traditional form of military service, were especially uneasy. In a few areas the belief circulated that "the gentleman want to arm us against the good King"[21] to whom they attributed the recent rumors of the impending abolition of their subject status (echoes of the folk myth of Enlightened Despotism!). Obviously these peasants did not know that it was their own lords as a class, or at least a sizable portion of them, who were responsible for their impending liberation. Of course, the county executive committee did not have the legal authority, nor did it wish to force anyone to join the Guard. At this stage it was well content with the largely non-peasant volunteers.[22]

---

19 Purely administrative districts having no legal autonomy into which the counties were divided for convenience.

20 Spira, "A vezérmegye forradalmi választmánya 1848 tavaszán," p. 719. Spira bases this information, especially concerning the peasant village of Izsák, on previously unpublished archival materials, see p. 720, n. 28.

21 *Ibid.*, p. 719.

22 *Ibid.*, pp. 719-20.

On the other hand, despite the initially hesitant reaction displayed in some areas by the "peasantry" (an extremely complex "group" for a single label [23]) toward these "military" innovations, it would be false to view their general reaction to the reform measures as uniformly obstructionist. Exactly the opposite was true in many parts of Hungary during March of 1848. News of the impending abolition of the lord-subject nexus had been in the air for some time. On March 15th, many Dietal Delegates notified their counties of the Diet's decision [24] for abolition, whereupon the counties immediately announced it. [25]

As Deák correctly anticipated, [26] the necessarily hasty nature of the urbarial aboliton eventually would result in a nearly endless series of misunderstandings and disputes. It produced innumerable litigations concerning the quality and quantity of land tenure transitions. [27] In the end, although the Hungarian Law IX of 1848 abolished "completely" and "forever" the subject status or "serfdom" in Hungary, [28] the unclear material aspects of the reform were less uniform. These latter, however, were by no means negligible. [29] Out of

---

23 See István Barta's study of the highly differentiated social and economic conditions of the pre-1848 Hungarian peasantry. He notes that the term zsellér was a judicial not a social category which involuntarily brings to mind the poverty stricken and landless seasonal worker in the lowest layers of society. But, he states, in reality only a very small percentage of peasants in this category were completely without an income. He specifically warns against applying the doctrine of class warfare to the 1848 situation. "A magyar polgári reformmozgalom kezdeti szakaszának problémái," pp. 305-42, especially 308, 311.

24 Irányi and Chassin, Histoire politique, I, 138.

25 Ibid., pp. 139, 167, 195; Deák Ferencz beszédei, II, 28.

26 Deák Ferencz beszédei, II, 28-29.

27 The effect on land tenure of the process begun in 1848 continued well into the twentieth century. See Edit Fél and Tamás Hofer, Proper Peasants: Traditional Life in a Hungarian Village (Chicago: Aldine, 1969), pp. 51 and n. 57, 313ff. and passim.

28 Law IX was quite specific on this point. Blackwell, Inclosure in No. 23, Acts passed by the Hungarian Diet, CRAH, p. 68; Macartney, Habsburg Empire, pp. 338, 377, 463; Horváth, Huszonöt év, III, 507; Hóman and Szekfű, Magyar történet, V, 391; d'Eszlary, Institutions, III, 340.

29 The material aspects of the reform were not clearly spelled out by law IX, but are inferred in its provisions when read in conjunction with Laws VI and VII of 1840 and Law IV of 1844. See discussion in Ignác Acsády, A magyar jobbágyság története (History of Hungarian Villeinage) (2nd ed.; Budapest: Imre Faust, 1944), pp. 510-511, 554-56.

a total of 1,366,749 formerly subject peasant families, 568,673 or 43.7 per cent became freehold landowners of their plots and of the remaining 798,076, an estimated 600,000 *zsellér* families became freehold owners of their house, an internal section of land in a village and often of one-eighth of a former subject holding for grazing purposes. Moreover, when measured by individuals instead of families, over one-half of the formerly subject peasants in Hungary were to be beneficially affected by the material aspects of the reform due to the fact *zsellér* families were usually small and those of the "full peasants" much larger.[30]

The first general reaction throughout Hungary was spontaneous celebration and anticipation of a better future.[31] In several places during these first days, the peasants paraded through the street to music. They carried the national colors, saluted the clergy, and gathered before their lords' residences with cries of "long live" the King, the lords, and the lords' officers. On March 26th, there was an especially emotional scene close to Pest in Palota when Count Károlyi's administrator made the announcement to the subjects who had gathered for the division of the spring *robot*. In Duka, the liberated peasants were so grateful that they volunteered to work the landlord's fields for another year during difficult transition period.[32] Nor was this an isolated instance. Similar offers were made throughout Hungary during the initial euphoria[33] — at least in those areas where lord-subject relations had been good.

This feeling of kinship and amiability was broken for a while by the already mentioned false rumor of a peasant insurrection which briefly circulated in Pozsony in mid-March. While this rumor was given only brief credence, the

30 János Varga, *A jobbágyfelszabadítás kivívása 1848-ban* (The Triumph of Serf Liberation in 1848) (Budapest: Akadémiai Kiadó, 1971), pp. 338-40. The author also states that many of the former *zsellérek* officially listed as landless were in possession of vineyards and cleared lands outside the normal urbarial relationship. Cf. Statistics in Király, *Ferenc Deák*, pp. 206-207.

31 Irányi and Chassin, *Histoire politique*, I, 159, 166-67; Spira, "A vezérmegye forradalmi választmánya 1848 tavaszán, pp. 721-22.

32 Spira, *ibid.*, 721.

33 Irányi and Chassin, *Histoire politique*, I, 161.

acceptance of such a possibility constituted an inadvertent general acknowledgment that the condition of the subject peasantry demanded alleviation; a point which the Hungarian nobles of the reform-minded opposition had been pressing ever since the Diet of 1832. The rumor (augmented by Petőfi's poem, "Great Glorious Lords") was at its height just after the Pest manifestation, that is on Thursday and Friday the 16th and 17th. It served the purpose of completing the intimidation of the Magnates, as well as the conservatives in the Lower House.[34] Nonetheless, it should be remembered that Magnate resistance had actually dissolved before the opposition earlier on March 14th on receipt of the Vienna news which had brought the final passage of the Address to the Crown. The rumor simply accelerated the realization of a decision already taken. A measure of its impact is that on Saturday, March 18th, Blackwell recorded that the most haughty among the Magnates were, in effect, shaken. As the Lower House was furiously enacting the below described resolutions, they were without exception approved by the Upper House without comment.[35] During the process several Magnates could be observed conversing familiarly with the common noble Delegates of the Lower House, to whom some had previously never condescended to speak.[36] Another measure of the force of the false rumor is that shortly after the return of the succesful Dietal Deputation to Pozsony and the acknowledgement of Batthyány as Prime Minister, the Diet immediately informed Pest of the favorable decision. Accordingly, Count Keglevitch was appointed to head a deputation to Pest to explain this most recent and significant concession by the Crown.[37]

It was on Saturday, March 18th, that Pozsony began to learn that the rumor was false. Széchenyi had either learned of

34 Macartney, *Habsburg Empire*, p. 337; Irányi and Chassin, *Histoire politique*, I, 164; Deme, "The Radical Left in the Hungarian Revolution of 1848," pp. 61-66.

35 Mr. Blackwell to Viscount Ponsonby. Presburg, March 19, 1848. 6 a.m., *CRAH*, p. 50.

36 Mr. Blackwell to Viscount Ponsonby. Presburg, March 22, 1848, *CRAH*, p. 52.

37 Horváth, *Huszonöt év*, III, 387.

the Pest March 15th manifestation while still in Vienna or shortly after his return to Pozsony on the 17th.[38] Now, early on the morning of Saturday, the 18th, he discovered to his great relief that the events in Pest had been bloodless. An eye witness account of the Pest developments was excitedly related to him by his trusted colleague, Lajos Kovács, who had just arrived from the capital. Széchenyi's recurring fear of a popular appeal to violence, which would halt the advance of legal reforms, destroy the precarious consensus, and degenerate into a primitive and doomed struggle, quickly receded. He learned that:

> Although the demands embodied in the Twelve Points of Pest had been rather radical, the gulf between them and the resolutions already carried by Parliament was not unbridgeable; and that although the youthful leaders of the March movement in Pest wanted a part in the overall direction of affairs, they had no intention of forcing the Diet into the background . . . and indeed they looked forward with sympathetic anticipation to the formation of the Batthyány government.[39]

Above all, Széchenyi knew at this time that the rumor of a "peasant army" on the march was completely without foundation.

Széchenyi and Kovács hurried first to Batthyány and then to Kossuth to discuss the nature of the Pest events. They also wanted to exchange views about the major demand of the radicals, namely, that the Diet transfer itself to Pest immediately. Széchenyi, Batthyány and Kovács were initially in favor of this not unreasonable request. They reasoned that the Diet could thus demonstrate its sympathy for Pest's adamant reform stance and also reduce the danger of a split with the radicals. Only Kossuth was opposed to the idea.[40] He pointed to the exigencies of time involved and to the fact that the members of the Dietal committees were in mid-stride in their

---

38 His biographer, György Spira, has not established the moment exactly. *Hungarian Count*, p. 50.

39 *Ibid.*, p. 51.

40 *Ibid.*, p. 52.

efforts to bring out the most equitable and comprehensive bills possible under the circumstances. Kossuth also wished to preserve at this crucial juncture the influence which he was able to exercise and which a move of the Diet into the popular pressure milieu of Pest might impair.[41] Széchenyi's biographer, Spira, even goes beyond this consideration. He argues that Kossuth was concerned that the Diet would respond so extensively to the Pest radicals that moderate opinion, especially among the more conservative county nobles (to whose instructions the Delegates were still technically bound in law), would be needlessly alienated.[42] In any event, Kossuth's reasoning prevailed. The decision to reject, or more accurately, to delay this move to Pest was already taken before the delegation from the Pest security committee arrived in Pozsony the following day (the 19th).[43]

The Pest delegation had been sent off with a 4,000 man parade of the Guard[44] and was headed by the future police chief of Budapest, Pál Hajnik. Hajnik took over Vasvári's leadership since the latter had lost his voice due to extensive oratory.[45] It included, among others, Nyáry, Bulyovszky, some university students, and the impatient Petőfi with several of his zealous followers.[46] As a delegation, they were immediately received at the Sunday Circular Sitting of the Lower House, which was even then open to the public[47] and at that moment working in committees on the reform legislation. Széchenyi and his co-chairman, Imre Bíró of Arad county, were both favorably impressed with the delegation as it presented the "Twelve Points" and (on Vasvári's motion) asked that the nation's legislative body remove itself to Pest.

---

41 L. Deme, "The Radical Left in the Hungarian Revolution of 1848," pp. 78-79.

42 Spira, *Hungarian Count*, p. 52.

43 Irányi and Chassin, *Histoire politique*, I, 165.

44 Urbán, "Die Organisierung des Heeres der ungarischen Revolution vom Jahre 1848," p. 107.

45 L. Deme, "The Radical Left in the Hungarian Revolution of 1848," p. 76 and n. 23.

46 *Ibid.*; Révész, "Das Junge Ungarn 1825-1848," p. 98; Horváth, *Huszonöt év*, III, 387-88.

47 Irányi and Chassin, *Histoire politique*, I, 165.

Széchenyi recorded excerpts in his Diary entry for the day from Vasvári's (probably somewhat strained) remarks. The "grave" and "commanding" manner of the group impressed him favorably. It was not composed of destructive fanatics; Vasvári reminded him of Saint Just! [48]

At the request of the House, Kossuth was selected to reply to the Pest group. He was skillful in the given situation and succeeded in expressing the overwhelming Hungarian consensus concerning the legal structure of the State and the most promising course of action to be followed. [49] He thanked the Pest deputation for the capital's sympathy toward the reforms which the Diet had already set up as its goal. He praised the capital's efforts at keeping order while at the same time strengthening the fight for freedom. However, he also addressed some very serious, even harsh, words toward the deputation. He wished, he said, to retract the impression that the Diet's success got its motivation or even its momentum from the manifestation in Pest. He hoped that in the future the capital would discontinue the role which made it appear as a competitor to the work of the Diet. He hoped "that Pest will understand my announcement, that although I regard Pest as the heart of the nation, I cannot follow it as a law-maker." [50] The Hungarian nation, he stated, desired freedom and rights for the whole country, not just a city. He expressed the hope that they all shared in the feeling that the Diet represented the whole nation and determined the country's destiny. Kossuth concluded by stating that even now the Diet was working on those problems which were included in the "Twelve Points."

As a whole, the Pest delegation, which contained only a minority of radicals, received Kossuth's views well. They saw that the demands in the "Twelve Points" were contained in the Diet's Address to the Crown which had been proposed to and accepted by the King. Being informed of the Diet's work, they stated that Pest had no intentions of creating and abolishing

---

48 Spira, *Hungarian Count*, p. 53.
49 Information in this paragraph from Horváth, *Huszonöt év*, III, 388.
50 *Ibid.*

laws, nor of governing all of Hungary.[51] However, Kossuth's words did insult Pál Nyáry, the president of the Pest county executive committee. Apparently, in light of the executive committee's accomplishments in Pest, he entertained hopes of being offered a ministerial portfolio in the Hungarian government. Actually, he was soon offered the directorship of the Office of Statistics. But he refused, and when the Diet moved to Pest he led an opposition against Kossuth, for whom he nurtured a consistent hatred until the end.[52] Kossuth's words in general, however, had a sobering effect on the Pest deputation, including the radicals.

Very late that night, banquets were held in Pozsony in honor of the Pest deputation and the Pest manifestation. During these affairs some of those present shifted further to the Left because of their dissatisfaction over such things as the unaltered class composition of the present Diet, and its "slowness" with reform legislation. This displeasure was expressed particularly at the banquet given in honor of the Pest Youth committee, where Petőfi played an increasingly prominent part.[53]

Indeed, it was not long before the radical antagonism toward the Diet was expressed in an article appearing in the March 21st issue of *Marczius Tizenötödike* (March Fifteenth) which challenged Kossuth's analysis of the current situation. With admirable candor the radical paper (in its first issue of March 19th it had expressed its satisfaction and support for the success of the Deputation in Vienna on the 17th [54]) admitted that Kossuth (who was not specifically named) was correct when he stated that Pest did not represent all Hungary.[55] It

---

51 Irányi and Chassin, *Histoire politique*, I, 165-66.

52 Horváth, *Huszonöt év*, III, 388-89.

53 Révész, "Das Junge Ungarn 1825-1848," p. 98.

54 Concerning the Palatine's authority to appoint a responsible ministry, the paper stated: "The time has come for the affairs of Hungary to be decided at home." Spira, *Hungarian Count*, p. 22, n. 19.

55 On the orher hand, it would be difficult for the radicals to maintain that Pest represented the nation. As of April 1st, less than one-half of Hungary's cities or counties — thirty-seven and twenty-one respectively — had established fraternal contact with Pest, and only one of these had indicated a willingness to take orders from the Pest committees. See Spira, *Hungarian Count*, p. 56, n. 105; L. Deme, "The Radical Left in the Hungarian Revolution of 1848," p. 84 and n. 37.

even admitted that at present only the Diet had the legal right to do so.[56] However, the article also stated that if Pest could not claim to be the representative of the entire nation, neither could the Diet. Its Delegates had been elected by only one "caste" — the nobility — and as long as the legislature was so constituted, its moral authority was open to question.[57]

What the writers of this March 21st article in *Marczius Tizenötödike* did not make sufficiently clear is that the reforming members of the national Diet had already admitted the justice of their analysis on the 19th. On that date the Diet had passed a resolution promising its own replacement by a new popularly elected assembly as soon as the relevant bills could be devised. On the same day, before the Pest security committee in the municipal council room of the City Hall, the spokesman of the Dietal delegation from Pozsony[58] freely admitted that the current Diet represented only the nobles. He stated that he was authorized to promise a popularly-elected Parliament which would be representative of the whole nation according to the new principles of legal equality of all classes. Until then, he exhorted all to trust and obey the government of Count Batthyány.[59]

From this point on, that is from these few days of March 19th to the 25th, despite some recurrent tensions, on the whole, the relationship between the radicals of Pest and the Diet took on the aspect of a more normal political "lobbying" by the former and the exchange of differing views. As events proved, on social matters there were to be only extremely minor differences between the legislation which the Diet actually passed and what even the more extreme radicals desired. As will be shown, there was almost complete agreement in both principle and application between the reforming nobles in the Lower House and the radical demands. Indeed, after March 19th, the only residual anxiety

56 Deme, *ibid.*, p. 80.

57 *Ibid.*

58 Horváth, *Huszonöt év*, III, 387.

59 L. Deme, "The Radical Left in the Hungarian Revolution of 1848," p. 81 and n. 30.

left concerning Pest, one borne by such reformers as Deák, Eötvös, Széchenyi, and Kossuth himself, was that Pest would take some irretrievable political act unsuited to Hungary's capacity.[60] The strong nationalism of the political activists in Pest might undo all the reform work of the Diet and give the Imperial centralists in Vienna a future opportunity to intervene with the charge that all was invalidated, illegal, and treasonable.[61]

With the role of the Pest radicals and the brief effect of the false rumor placed in perspective, attention may now be turned to the Dietal resolutions which were passed rapidly by the Lower House of the Diet on Saturday, March 18, 1848, and adopted by the Upper House without opposition or comment on that day and the next. These resolutions became bills after passage by both Houses in final form and once they received royal sanction were to become the famous April Laws. First, as Blackwell recorded, in the morning, the Delegates of the Lower House in Circular Sitting spontaneously decided to abandon the practice of voting by counties. They organized themselves so that each Delegate, including also those of Free Districts, Royal Boroughs, and Cathedral Chapters, had a free vote without distinction.[62] In Blackwell's words, "they have

---

60 *Deák Ferencz beszédei*, II, 28-29.

61 This, of course, is exactly what the Imperialists in Vienna later did, but the strict observance by the Hungarians of the Pragmatic Sanction and of constitutional and legal process made the Vienna camarilla's case very transparent.

62 The haste with which this was done and the fact that constitutionally Delegates were bound by their constituents' instructions and obliged to consult with them and to receive new instructions on the new issues (a cumbersome and time-consuming procedure which many reformers, for example, Eötvös, wished to change), was certainly one reason for Deák's disapproval of the Diet's proceedings. The extraordinary circumstances both in terms of internal Hungarian pressure upon the Diet for effective action and in quickly taking advantage with a united front of the unusual opportunity vis-à-vis Vienna of receiving a fundamental affirmation of the traditional Constitution and of simultaneously modernizing the nation, rendered these constitutional objections essentially procedural rather than fundamental. This view is substantiated by the fact that no Hungarian constituency subsequently censored or recalled its Delegate for this action. Rather, there was a general understanding of the extraordinary circumstances and approval of the action. Evidently Deák, himself, shortly adopted the view that the nation had the right to alter a constitutional procedure, which was not fundamental and which affected exclusively the "*natio*" part of the corporate body politic, in furtherance of the fundamental Constitution itself. In any event, there was time between the passage of the March bills and their sanction as the April Laws, for the Delegates to

consequently formed themselves into a National Convention or Constituent Assembly." Then they proceeded to pass the following resolutions:

> A regular system of taxation for all classes without distinction to be forthwith established; the *Roboth,* the tithe of one-tenth to the Church, of one-ninth to the manor, and all other Urbarial services are abolished; the aviticity laws (*ősiség*) and the law of primogeniture to be abolished; a national guard to be immediately organized; to send all foreign (Austrian) troops out of the Kingdom; to recall Hungarian troops from the Austrian States; to incorporate the Military Frontiers with the adjacent counties; to effect a union with Transylvania and to insist on Dalmatia being incorporated with Hungary.[63]

Blackwell concluded his dispatch by saying that the Ministry was not yet formed, but it seemed likely that it would be constituted as follows: Batthyány to become the Premier; Deák the Minister of Interior; Kossuth the Minister of Finances; Eötvös the Minister of Public Instruction and Religious Worship; and Esterházy the Minister of International Affairs "i.e. of the diplomatic relations of the independent Kingdom of Hungary with the other States of the Austrian Empire."[64]

The following Tuesday (March 21st), Blackwell reported that the revolution had, in effect, been completed the previous Saturday, and that the "Liberals were very sanguine." However, on this day affairs had a more "gloomy" appearance. No ministry was yet formed. Several combinations were suggested and it was hoped things would go satisfactorily:

> Buda and Pesth are under the rule of Klauzal, one of the most celebrated Delegates at the last Diet, and also — then at least — one of the most moderate of the Liberal party: and most of the towns from which news has arrived, are

---

consult with their constituencies. Since no major objections were raised by these constituents or by the Crown concerning the procedural manner in which the Delegates originally voted the resolutions, they can be considered legal and entirely constitutional.

63 A direct citing of Blackwell's dispatch with the difference that his order of presentation has not been followed. Mr. Blackwell to Viscount Ponsonby. Presburg, March 19, 1848, 6 a.m., *CRAH,* pp. 50-51.

64 *Ibid.,* p. 51.

governed much in the same manner by Committees of Public Safety.[65]

On Wednesday, the 22nd, he reported:

Forty or fifty persons were arrested last night; most of them, it seems, are Austrians, who, after plundering the environs of Vienna, had come here for the same purpose. I never saw Presburg so quiet as it is this evening. As I came home (11 o'clock) there was scarcely a person to be seen in the streets . . . a bill has been brought in respecting the Ministry; and until it has passed through the Upper House and received the Royal sanction, Count Batthyány cannot well submit the names of his colleagues for His Majesty's approbation. According to this bill there are to be nine Ministers, viz. Prime Minister, Interior, Foreign Affairs, Finance, Public Works, Trade and Agriculture, Public Instruction, Justice, and War . . . . By a Minister of Foreign Affairs they now understand an Hungarian Minister who is to reside in Vienna, and be consulted in all transactions with foreign States in which the interests of Hungary are in any way involved.[66]

The following day, Thursday the 23rd, just five days since the Saturday resolutions, Blackwell's dispatch recorded:

This morning the bill respecting the Ministry passed the Chamber of Magnates when Count Batthyany announced that he had formed a Ministry (the arrangements having been completed during the night) and would make known the names of his colleagues previous to their being submitted to His Majesty. He then announced them in the following order: —

| | |
|---|---|
| Premier without Portefeuille | Count L. Batthyany |
| Interior (Home Department) | Szemere |
| Foreign Affairs | Prince Esterhazy |
| Finance | Kossuth |
| War | Mészáros |
| Public Works | Count Stephen Szechenyi |

65 Mr. Blackwell to Viscount Ponsonby. Presburg, March 21, 1848, *ibid.,* p. 51.

66 Mr. Blackwell to Viscount Ponsonby. Presburg, March 22, 1848, *ibid.,* pp. 51-52.

| | |
|---|---|
| Public Instruction and Religious Worship | Baron Eötvös |
| Trade, Agriculture, Manufacturing and Industry | Klauzal |
| Justice | Deak [67] |

After recording this parliamentary accomplishment, Blackwell went on to recount continuing sources of trouble. Szemere, a few days earlier, had drawn up a provisional bill on the press (Blackwell had reported on March 19th that the press was now quite free).[68] This had passed both Houses with only trifling amendments, but it caused a tremendous uproar in Pest among the Youth.[69]

> They even threaten to convoke a Diet, or more properly speaking, a National Convention at Pesth, on the plea that the present Diet is not a popular assembly; that its proceedings (since the nomination of Count Batthyany) are too dilatory; that the measures proposed are not sufficiently energetic! In one word, by all I am able to learn, they want to establish a republic, or at least "a monarchy with republican institutions" . . . . In Presburg people have been satisfied by quietly removing the Imperial arms from the Post, Salt and other public offices, leaving the doors and railings of these offices with their black and yellow stripes untouched; but at Pest the Imperial arms were torn down and thrown in the street, and in a few hours the doors and railings repainted with the national colours — red, white, and green. Of one thing I am fully convinced, which is, that if the Austrian Cabinet should attempt to render the Hungarian Ministry dependent on them . . . . your Excellency may except to see 50,000 armed Hungarians before the gates of Vienna.[70]

On Saturday, March 25th, the seventh day since the passage of the initial resolutions, Blackwell wrote that:

---

67 Mr. Blackwell to Viscount Ponsonby. Presburg, March 23, 1848, *ibid.*, p. 52.

68 Mr. Blackwell to Viscount Ponsonby. Presburg, March 19, 1848, 6 a.m., *ibid.*, p. 50.

69 They compared Szemere's proposed bill to the reactionary press law of Louis Philippe and solemnly burned copies of it in front of Pest City Hall. Zarek, *Kossuth*, p. 158; Irányi and Chassin, *Histoire politique,* I, 163-64.

70 Mr. Blackwell to Viscount Ponsonby. Presburg, March 23, 1848, *CRAH,* pp. 52-53.

A strange infatuation seems still to prevail at Vienna . . . .
They seem to imagine that because no blood has been
shed, a revolution has not taken place in this country —
that the Hungarian Government must still continue . . .
dependent on the Imperial Government. They must however renounce these ideas . . . without a moment's delay,
otherwise the country will be in a state of anarchy.

Now a bill for the organization of the Ministry and the
necessary abolition of the Hungarian Chancery, Vice-
Regal Council, in short, all the old Collegial system passes
both Houses. Count Batthyany hastens to Vienna to submit the bill, together with the names of the Ministers for
Royal sanction . . . . He is followed by Deak and the
Palatine and I presume has been joined by Prince Ester-
hazy. Count Batthyany has been in Vienna upwards of
forty-eight hours, and it would appear has not been able
to obtain the Royal sanction.[71]

In this dispatch Blackwell went on to say that the situation was
critical. In a conversation he had with Eötvös that morning the
latter had informed him that a disturbing message had been
received from Pest on the night of the 22/23rd. If the definite
confirmation of a responsible ministry were not announced
soon, the National Guard had plans to storm the royal arsenal
at Buda.[72]

As can be sensed in Blackwell's dispatch, Saturday, March
25, was part of a period of uneasy expectancy in Pozsony. The
batch of resolutions had been passed by both Houses of the
Diet the previous Saturday, the 18th. They had been finalized
by the Diet as a corpus of bills as early as Wednesday, March
22nd, and had been carried to Vienna by the Palatine,
Batthyány, and others on Thursday, the 23rd.[73] The Hungarian Diet now awaited the decision of its hereditary and
legitimate King — or more precisely, the decision of those who
advised him.

---

71 Mr. Blackwell to Viscount Ponsonby. Presburg, March 25, 1848, *ibid.*, p.
53.

72 *Ibid.*, p. 54. This may have been a bluff on the part of the Pest activists,
since the twenty-four hour deadline which they laid down had passed and no attack
on the arsenal had taken place.

73 Macartney, *Habsburg Empire*, pp. 338-39.

*Chapter IX*

## THE RESCRIPTS OF MARCH 29TH

On the basis of the royal rescript issued by Ferdinand on March 17th — pledging Hungary a responsible ministry — it was expected that "preliminary" royal sanction to the Hungarian bills would be quickly forthcoming.[1] However, the Hungarian Diet waited a full seven days for a reply (until March 29th) because behind the scenes the Imperial centralists at the Vienna Court, who never had any intention of giving up absolute political power, were desperately using this time to form a liaison with the Croatian conservatives. With the appointment of Colonel Josef Baron von Jelačić to the office of Croatian *Ban* (Governor), the centralists established contact with the Croatian-Serbian "Illyrian" movement in the Military Borders — with the object of mounting an invasion of Hungary as soon as possible.

This is a complex situation to unravel due to the secrecy with which the Court absolutists pursued their objectives, and the conflict which ensued affects national susceptibilities to the present day. It is of interest to note that the wife of Karl Franz and mother of Franz Josef, the Archduchess Sophie, appears to have been very active in the formulation of this policy.[2] Also, on March 17th, the same day the royal rescript promising a responsible ministry was issued to the Hungarian Deputation

---

1 In the period of negotiation between the Diet and the Crown over proposed legislation, preliminary sanction was extended to bills in piecemeal fashion before the formal royal sanction. In this instance, concerning the bill creating a responsible ministry, the fact that the preliminary sanction was issued in the form of a rescript (by definition an ordinance issued on the basis of existing Law and in explanation of the same) to the Palatine shows that it was drawn up on the precedent of the Palatinal Law of 1485. It constituted a public and binding royal commitment. Hugessen, *Political Evolution,* II, 26; Marczali, *Hungary in the Eighteenth Century,* p. 334, n. 1; d'Eszlary, *Institutions,* II, 116-25.

2 Zarek, *Kossuth,* p. 160.

in Vienna, a personal letter under Ferdinand's name was sent to Jelačić promising his appointment as Croatian *Ban*.[3] The appointment was evidently an early suggestion of Baron Franz Kulmer, the *főispán* of Zágráb (Agram) county in Croatia.[4] It was put through the *Staatskonferenz* by Kolowrat on March 20th.[5] On the 23rd, a royal rescript announced the appointment of Jelačić. Simultaneously, he acquired the status of Privy Councillor and was also promoted from the rank of a Colonel, commanding the first Bánát Regiment, to that of a Field Marshal and commander-in-chief in Croatia and the Military Border.[6] On the 25th, a national mass meeting in Zágráb proclaimed Jelačić *Ban* and resolved to send a Deputation to Ferdinand asking for complete independence from Hungary. They arrived in Vienna the 29th and were met with the typical Viennese obscurantism since the Court still did not feel strong enough to risk offending Hungary.

The Hungarian government, in the meantime, sent a conciliatory manifesto to Zágráb in the Hungarian and Croatian languages, proclaiming the Liberal principles which it wished to effect. Moreover, on March 28th, Kossuth delivered a speech in which he optimistically stated that "the steps taken by the Hungarian Diet have been received with grateful enthusiasm in Croatia."[7] But his statement hardly corresponded to the true situation in Zágráb, where Jelačić was conducting anti-Hungarian agitation. On March 30th, Kulmer wrote to Jelačić: "Austria will have to reconquer Hungary . . . for this purpose you must at all costs retain the loyalty of the Military border."[8]

Thus, at this early stage the Imperialists in Vienna had already formulated the plan to use the nationalisms of those living in the Lands of the Crown of St. Stephen who did not speak Hungarian as a primary language as a means to suppress

---

3 *Ibid.*, p. 161.

4 G. Rothenberg, "Jelačić, the Croatian Military Border, and the Intervention against Hungary in 1848," *Austrian History Yearbook*, I (1965), 51.

5 Macartney, *Habsburg Empire*, pp. 383-84.

6 Rothenberg, *ibid.*, p. 50; Macartney, *ibid.*, p. 384.

7 Zarek, *ibid.*, p. 162.

8 Rothenberg, *ibid.*, p. 51.

Hungarian Liberalism and to regain absolute political power. To forestall this possibility, in mid-April the Hungarian government announced that the Croatians could employ the Croatian language in official governmental communications with the central government (in local affairs this right had never been questioned), and invited Jelačić to a meeting with the hope of reaching an agreement. But this concession came too late, for Jelačić had already been secured by Vienna. His reply was to announce on April 19th the "rupture" of Hungarian-Croatian relations and to make it an offense (on April 27th) punishable by court martial to ascribe liberation of the peasants in Croatia to the Hungarian April Laws. Again in July, at a meeting in Vienna between Jelačić and Batthyány, which had been arranged by Archduke Johann it was "clear to everyone . . . that the *Ban* represented the interests of the military party"[9] and had no intention of compromising with Hungary. This became even more evident in August, when the Hungarian government issued a statement to the former *Grenzer* (Border Guards) of the Military Border, assuring them complete possession of their land, the right of choice in occupation, and the right to elect local officials. But, due to the influence of Jelačić, this plea was to no avail.[10]

Although these behind-the-scene machinations of Vienna began as early as March 1848, the Hungarians were unaware of them. They had faith in their Constitution and believed in the explicit royal word.[11] Therefore, when the Palatine and the councillor, Eduárd Zsedényi, returned from Vienna with two royal rescripts on the morning of March 29th, after six days of negotiations, expectations were high.[12] The first rescript was political and the second social in nature. The former in essence reversed the solemn royal pledge of a responsible ministry in the March 17th rescript.

When the Palatine read these rescripts at one o'clock in the afternoon before a packed hall in Pozsony, the reaction was

---

9 *Ibid.*, p. 56.

10 *Ibid.*, p. 57.

11 Hugessen, *Political Evolution*, II, 23.

12 Irányi and Chassin, *Histoire politique*, I, 181; Macartney, *Habsburg Empire*, p. 339.

first one of stunned astonishment, and then, genuine anger. [13] This Hungarian reaction appears entirely warranted and justified, because, despite the extraordinary events and the pressure under which the original rescript of the 17th had been obtained, the Crown's action on the 29th was virtually without precedent in the history of Hungary's chequered constitutional relations with the Habsburgs. On numerous occasions in the past the Habsburgs had sanctioned Hungarian Laws which they had no intention of observing in letter or spirit. They had successfully neglected the enforcement of such Laws, or had chipped away at their true intent with quibbling and argumentation over their proper application. Until the rescripts of the 29th, however, it was unknown for the Crown to extend the royal word, and then reverse itself. The action of Ferdinand's advisors on the 29th, therefore, undermined the credibility of the Crown, and by doing so, struck at the very basis of constitutional government. The Hungarians with their strong sense of constitutional procedure, had every justification in feeling provoked. They could now rightfully argue that the action taken by Vienna was itself unconstitutional. One can hardly deny that the decision concocted by the Imperial policy makers for the Hungarian rescript of the 29th was inimical to all governance. A certain degree of credibility is necessary for any effective form of government, excepting the most obvious despotism.

The first royal rescript agreed to the appointments of Széchenyi, Deák, Szemere, Eötvös and Klauzál, but stated that the Palatine's plenipotentiary powers to act for the monarch during his absence from Hungary were to be restricted to the present holder of the office and not transmitted to future officeholders. In addition, the present Palatine's powers con-

---

13 Irányi and Chassin, *ibid.*; Macartney, *ibid.*; Hugessen, *Political Evolution,* II, 22; Sándor Szilágyi, *A magyar forradalom története 1848- és 49-ben* (The History of the Hungarian Revolution in 1848 and '49) (Pest: Gusztáv Heckenast, 1850), p. 22. Zarek states Batthyány had not expected this, and even the most pro-Habsburg member of the proposed ministry, Esterházy, had not thought it possible. *Kossuth*, p. 163. Károlyi states that news had leaked out before the reading that the Palatine had not obtained everything desired, which was the reason for the great crowd, but even so, "dead silence" followed the reading. *Az 1848-diki Pozsonyi törvénycikkek az udvar előtt,* pp. 80-81.

cerning the organization of an army of national defense were rejected and reserved to the monarch:

> His Majesty clings to the principle of intimate connection which derives from the Pragmatic Sanction and to his rights with respect to the employment of the armed forces in accordance with the Law and to the nomination of officers. [14]

The rescript further stated that the sovereign, rather than the new responsible ministry, was to retain discretionary control over Hungarian tariffs and commercial policy. Also, the Diet's control over taxation must continue to be limited to extraordinary direct taxation. Other Hungarian taxes and the amount assessed to meet the expenses of the institutions serving the whole Monarchy "should remain in His Majesty's hands and be paid into a Common Treasury." [15] That is, these revenues were not to be assessed through the cooperation of the responsibile Hungarian Ministry of Finance. Finally, and most importantly, the old Hungarian Court Chancellery was to continue as before as a sort of overseer (presumably with a "right of veto") above the entire "responsible" Hungarian Ministry. [16]

---

14 Hugessen, *Political Evolution,* II, 21. The Hungarian Laws implementing the Pragmatic Sanction said nothing about the armed forces beyond an obligation to provide for the Monarchy's mutual defense. The many Hungarians Laws (Law VIII of 1715; Law C of 1723; Law XXIV of 1764; Law IX of 1792; Law I of 1802; Law VII of 1830; Law II of 1840; Laws XXII and XLIII of 1741; Law IXX of 1790) which regulated Hungary's military contribution to mutual defense made no mention of the question of command, but many did mention the appointment of Hungarian officers to Hungarian regiments, and, in general, the Diet's unquestioned right to regulate the terms of Hungarian participation.

The rescript of the 29th was, therefore, appealing to a constitutional practice and custom which had never been specifically defined or received the nation's consent in written Law. In fact, the whole thrust of Hungarian constitutional law argued against the question of command and appointment as being an exclusive *jus reservatum* of the King, while the existence of a separate Hungarian army was an entirely legal possibility. d'Eszlary, *Institutions,* III, 165-77, especially 166; Hugessen, *ibid.,* II, 42-45. After thorough study of the available records, Károlyi states that "we cannot say which member of the *Staatskonferenz* had the idea of restricting the Palatine's powers." *Az 1848-diki Pozsonyi törvénycikkek az udvar előtt,* p. 72.

15 *Deák Ferencz beszédei,* II, 33. This is an excellent point by point summary of the royal reply, 32-34.

16 *Ibid.;* Macartney, *Habsburg Empire,* p. 339; Hugessen, *Political Evolution,* II, 20-21; Hóman and Szekfű, *Magyar történet,* V, 390. This rescript was drafted sometime between March 24th and a late evening meeting of the

The second rescript, which on its face appeared almost an after-thought, was social in essence. It stated that sanction for the Diet's bill abolishing the urbarium (that is, the bill which dissolved the lord-subject *nexus* or "serfdom"), could not be implemented until the Diet had discussed and made provisions for the landlord's compensation. The Diet was advised to undertake this task immediately. The rescript also described the "dangers" and "losses" involved in immediate abolition of the subject status including the disruption of agricultural production and the possibility of a famine.[17]

This retraction, after the Crown had earlier promised sanction of the historic measure, was an open invitation to Hungarian conservatives to recant on the social issue. It was extended in the hope that it would give new courage to the reactionary elements among the Magnates and, therefore, cause a split in Hungarian solidarity vis-à-vis Vienna. The reform movement would thus either fall apart, or, if the rescript were accepted, the time and patience of the Diet would be entirely consumed in the complex financial discussion concerning compensation rates. Perhaps the negative results of the reforming efforts of the Diets of 1832-1836 and 1843-1844 would be repeated.[18] The Hungarian subject peasant was thus to be used again by the successors of Josef II as a pawn in a political struggle to buy time and to maintain an outdated form of government.

In Pozsony, these royal rescripts of the 29th were immediately printed for public consumption. The *jurati* attending the Diet quickly settled consideration of them to their own (and the general) satisfaction by publicly burning many copies on the fashionable Promenade in the Theatre Square to the cheers of a large crowd.[19] As this occurred, the Lower House

---

*Staatskonferenz* on March 26th and submitted to the King on March 27th. Major figures in the *Konferenz* during this period were Archduke Ludwig, Archduke Franz Karl, Kolowrat, Hartig, Windisch-Graetz, Ficquelmont and Jósika. According to Szőgyény, the proposal to continue the old Hungarian Court Chancellery over the new Hungarian Ministry was originally György Bartal's idea. Károlyi, *Az 1848-diki Pozsonyi törvénycikkek az udvar előtt*, pp. 59, 63, 75.

17 Macartney, *Habsburg Empire*, p. 339; Szilágyi, *A magyar forradalom története 1848- és 49-ben*, pp. 22-23.

18 d'Eszlary, *Institutions*, III, 338-39.

19 Mr. Blackwell to Viscount Ponsonby. Presburg, March 29, 1848, *CRAH*, p. 54; Irányi and Chassin, *Histoire politique*, I, 184.

hastily assembled for discussions on this latest and quite unexpected royal reversal which virtually rejected the political and social core of the reform program. [20] The debate that began in the evening lasted well into the night.

After the formal reading of the two rescripts which was interrupted more than once by storms of anger from the irate Delegates ("as if they already had an inkling of the future"), [21] the confirmed Prime Minister, Batthyány, who had just returned from Vienna "highly dissatisfied at the proceedings of the Emperor's advisors," [22] stated flatly:

> This royal answer according to my conviction does not meet our justifiable expectations (interruption here by shouts of "True, true") and therefore without any further ado I request Your Highness to use your influence to have His Majesty change his reply in such a manner that it should make true His Majesty's word that he wishes to give Hungary an independent Hungarian Ministry. Because if this does not happen, I herewith declare both in my name and that of my colleagues that we are not able to accept the Ministry and do not feel ourselves justified in doing so. [23]

At this the Palatine, in full accord, turned to the Diet with an appropriate rejoinder, ending with the promise:

> Here I solemnly give my word that all the objections concerning this matter which the responsible Ministers entrust to me, I will not only submit to His Majesty but will insist on being accepted (interruption here with

---

20 Mr. Blackwell to Viscount Ponsonby. Presburg, March 29, 1848, *CRAH*, p. 54.

21 Szilágyi, *A magyar forradalom története 1848- és 49-ben*, p. 22.

22 The dissatisfaction was shared by the Palatine and Deák who had accompanied him. Mr. Blackwell to Viscount Ponsonby. Presburg, March 29, 1848, *CRAH*, p. 54. Deák and Batthyány both felt that the *Staatskonferenz* had drafted these rescripts behind their backs just after they left Vienna, and that the *Konferenz* had deliberately deceived them. Károlyi, *Az 1848-diki Pozsonyi törvénycikkek az udvar előtt*, p. 80.

23 Szilágyi, *A magyar forradalom története 1848- és 49-ben*, p. 22. The essence of Batthyány's attitude is also given in Hugessen, *Political Evolution*, II, 21. "Your Highness" in the Batthyány speech quoted above means the Palatine Archduke Stephan.

cheers) and if I am forced to, our stand will depend on this (Long cheers). [24]

Thus, the Diet greeted with a general and enthusiastic approval the stand taken quite properly and with the necessary alacrity by the Batthyány Ministry. The Ministry threatened collective ministerial resignation, a practice so familiar in England, against "Vienna's" attempt to crush modern responsible government in Hungary at its inception. Nor, as Szilágyi's account shows, was it simply the most pronounced Liberals who were absolutely furious at this latest and most audacious attempt by the Imperialists to see just what the Hungarians might swallow; the Diet was generally incensed and united in its opposition. Széchenyi "who of late years had been regarded as a Conservative made a speech that reminded the auditors of the time when he was the fiery leader of the Opposition." [25] "Vienna" had obviously taken the wrong tack with Hungary, revealing its habitual misunderstanding of the country. This unprecedented policy of reversing a royal promise and relying on time as an ally was a tactic much better suited to the extra-Hungarian Lands of the Monarchy. The new rescripts, far from disuniting the elements of Hungary's political structure, had the predictable effect of uniting them even more than before. They strengthened Hungary's attachment to its Constitution and gathered the support of conservatives behind the movement for political and social reform. Also, the possibility of radical action mounted. As Blackwell observed, Batthyány had formed a Ministry of the most moderate men of the Liberal party (Széchenyi, Esterházy, and Eötvös were outstanding for their dynastic loyalty and attachment to the Monarchy), and only the day before Eötvös had received by courier from various parts of Hungary mes-

---

24 Szilágyi, *A magyar forradalom története 1848- és 49-ben*, p. 23. Hugessen gives an English translation of the above quoted portion of the Palatine's brief announcement, but with a different choice of words. The meaning, however, is identical; *viz.* the Palatine considered himself the constitutional instrument of the responsible Ministry and included his office in the threat of collective ministerial resignation. *Political Evolution*, II, 21.

25 Mr. Blackwell to Viscount Ponsonby. Presburg, March 29, 1848, *CRAH*, p. 54.

sages of support for the Batthyány efforts.[26] The Prime Minister's efforts had every prospect of proceeding in a constitutional and parliamentary manner and of keeping the realm under the sceptre of its legitimate sovereign prior to this tactic of the Vienna Imperialists to restore absolutism. Now, on this Wednesday evening, after Batthyány's opening statement and some general speeches, the Diet ceased its formal sitting and took up an informal session on specifics with the anger of the Delegates being "carried" to them unabated.[27]

László Madarász, the Delegate of Somogy county, delivered a furious verbal attack against Eduárd Zsedényi the hapless councillor who had signed the offending rescripts in Ferdinand's name. He concluded with a motion to punish him under ancient Laws designed to prohibit unconstitutional actions. This suggestion attracted some enthusiastic support, but was quickly tabled in favor of a more constructive consideration of the problem at hand.[28]

Kossuth, in comparison to some other Delegates, spoke only briefly,[29] but with great vehemence and very much to the point. He agreed with Madarász that the Crown councillors might be guilty of lese majesty against the nation but suggested that such action be delayed until it could be seen if they persisted in rejecting the just national demands.[30] As he continued, it was his unsurpassed ability to formulate and crystalize already-existing thoughts which in the end explained the fact that his views were accepted by the Diet and incorporated in its final official position. After protesting against yet a third reading of the two rescripts which somebody actually suggested, Kossuth truthfully stated that they were by now so well known everyone should have arrived at a definite opinion. Then he said that he would divide his remarks "dis-

---

26 *Ibid.*

27 Szilágyi, *A magyar forradalom története 1848- és 49-ben*, p. 23. See also, Irányi and Chassin, *Histoire politique*, I, 181-82.

28 *Deák Ferencz beszédei*, II, 35.

29 Mr. Blackwell to Viscount Ponsonby. Presburg, March 29, 1848, *CRAH*, p. 54.

30 Irányi and Chassin, *Histoire politique*, I, 182.

passionately" between the two.[31] He rightly chose to comment on the "social rescript" first since this was clearly "Vienna's" best effort to sow dissension in the Diet. With considerable skill he countered the intention of the Viennese policy makers. He argued that by implication the royal rescript of the 17th, which had approved the Address to the Crown had already contained the reference to the abolition of serfdom. This and even the present rescript of the 29th, already constituted an approval by the Crown of urbarial abolition. Therefore, it was clearly a matter for the nation to establish the details and method of its realization. He stated that the intrigues played in Vienna would not achieve any goal in Hungary and that for his part and in his opinion:

> The abolition of the urbarium is, in effect, already sanctioned in this rescript. However, in as much as they [Vienna advisors] still want to continue discussions about it with the stated reasons it will stop agricultural production or produce danger of famine or God knows what other disasterous pictures they may draw, I herewith declare that I am unwilling for this to go on now that this rescript already has His Majesty's sanction and the urbarium, impossible to restore, has been abolished.[32]

Technically, Kossuth's opinion was on uncertain constitutional ground since no one could state that he regarded subjection as abolished in a legal sense until the day when the bill to that effect was formally sanctioned. By every other measure, however, his observations had reason to recommend them. Abolition of subjection, with the affording of "equitable compensation,"[33] had been a specific point in the Address to

---

31 Information in the remainder of this paragraph from, Szilágyi, *A magyar forradalom története 1848- és 49-ben*, p. 23.

32 *Ibid.*

33 Mr. Blackwell to Viscount Ponsonby. Presburg, March 9, 1848. Inclosure 7 in No. 5, Representation respecting the Questions before the Diet adopted at a Circular Sitting of the Delegates March 3, 1848, *CRAH*, p. 43.
   Law XII of 1848 fixed indemnification to the landlords for their property loss of land to the former subject peasant at a sum twenty times above the current market value of the urbarial holding's annual yield. Since the peasant with few exceptions did not possess the cash, nor could he borrow it for such a transaction (which had been a large part of the difficulty under the permissive Laws of 1840), the Hungarian State was to issue long-term bonds for this purpose — the redemption

the Crown voted the 3rd and the rescript of the 17th had in response requested the presentation of "suggested Laws referred to in the Address."[34] On the 23rd a bill voted by the Diet for abolition had been submitted to the Crown. It consequently made little sense for the Crown on the 29th, seven days after the bill had been submitted, to start requesting detailed additions regarding compensation. The true motive of the Emperor's advisors, as Kossuth correctly perceived, was to delay and to divide the Diet. But the Diet in turn could exercise its constitutional right to dispute the Crown's interpretation. Moreover, as an elected Delegate Kossuth was within his rights to criticize the content of a royal rescript. Completely out of patience, he was driven to an extreme position. A bill embodying the nation's manifest will and concerning which there had supposedly existed a previous agreement in principle between Crown and nation was being obstructed by the Emperor's non-Hungarian advisors for an anti-constitutional political advantage. Hence, Kossuth argued that in this case the nation was justified in maintaining that the bill had received sanction. He urged the Diet to reject the Crown's request for revisions and to insist on its original

---

of which was to be known as cancellation of the "status debt." This Law, in reality, was only a proposed formula since the Diet avoided mention of specific sums or rate-tables, which were all deferred to the next Diet. The problems involved with this Law are obvious. First of all, the market value of agricultural produce varied in geographical location and had often fluctuated widely in the past. Secondly, endless disagreement was possible concerning what constituted a truly representative yield from one or several urbarial holdings. It depended on what was, or should be, produced, what system of crop rotation was, had been, or should be used, whether the holdings were best adapted to one or two crops annually, to mixed crops, and so on. Finally, Law XII of 1848 left the actual redemption of the status debt up in the air; it was not clear if the peasant was to make payments for all, a part, or even any of the obligation — the alternative source being revenues from the State's general taxation. It is worth note that some seven months later (September 7, 1848) the Austrian *Reichstag* passed a bill which provided the basis for eventually incorporating exactly the same formula of twenty times the cash value of a holding's annual yield as constituting the land's market value for compensation purposes. Also, it is noteworthy that whereas the former subject in the Western Lands was to pay one-third this "purchase price," the Hungarian peasant, in the end, paid nothing for his ownership of the former urbarial lands. d'Eszlary, *Institutions*, III, 340 and n. 230; Hóman and Szekfű, *Magyar történet*, V, 391; Hugessen, *Political Evolution*, II, 31; Horváth, *Huszonöt év*, III, 507; Macartney, *Habsburg Empire*, pp. 374, 439, 461-66; Blum, *Noble Landowners*, pp. 235-37; Robertson, *Revolutions of 1848*, p. 235, n. 13; Tapié, *The Rise and Fall of the Habsburg Monarchy*, pp. 287-89.

34 Hugessen, *Political Evolution*, II, 17.

bill. The necessity for the alteration or abolition of the urbarium had been generally admitted for several years, but had eluded settlement in the past. Now, on the very edge of success, Kossuth's observations had the merit of reenforcing the Diet's bold decision to cut the Gordian knot. In addition, his argument was in accordance with the enlarged scope of discretion the legislative element of the Hungarian government was to exercise in a modern system of ministerial responsibility.

Concerning the bogies of disruption, losses, and starvation, he stated, "we can only send a manifesto to the people in which we ask them from the standpoint of the general well-being — but not order them — that they should not leave their lands uncultivated, trusting this to the peoples' own good sense and patriotism."[35]

Kossuth's desire to secure the earliest possible specific royal confirmation of the abolition of the lord-subject *nexus* may be interpreted by some as uneasiness over the threat of lower class violence or some sort of class warfare. However, at least in retrospect, these developments do not appear to have been as serious or as immediate as some contemporaries feared. If a violent social disruption were imminent, Kossuth's above statement, indicating the peasants' willingness to work the land before the material aspects of the liberation were clarified, would have made little sense. Nor would it have been a viable suggestion before the Diet. Kossuth was aware that any retraction or unwarranted delay of the announced urbarial abolition would likely lead to peasant violence, a possibility which Deák frankly stated.[36] However, the Diet had previously taken its decision in favor of "comprehensive" reform, and was now unanimously against the deferment of any part of it. Therefore, on this night, the possibility of peasant violence was not immediate nor was it a primary concern among the Lower House Delegates. Blackwell's correspondence, for example, does not include a single reference to any class conflict. The all-important predominance of the political issue, as opposed

35 Szilágyi, *A magyar forradalom története 1848- és 49-ben,* p. 23.
36 *Deák Ferencz beszédei,* II, 28.

to any social issue, was automatically perceived by him when he formulated the question of a responsible ministry in the following terms:

> If Hungary really possesses a responsible Ministry, the Royal sanction ought either to have been given or refused; whereas they [i.e. the Imperial policy makers] have adopted the old collegial system of having recourse to Royal resolutions. They wish, it seems, to retain the Hungarian Chancery, when it is obvious that, with a responsible Ministry, the Chancery is superfluous.[37]

It was to this vital and central issue that Kossuth, after finishing his comments on the "social rescript," turned before the (by now nocturnal) informal sitting of the Diet. He addressed himself to it with vehemence.

He pointed out that the retention of the Hungarian Court Chancellery as a sort of overlord in Vienna would reduce the new responsible ministry to the position previously occupied by the *Consilium*,[38] which executed the orders transmitted to it by the Imperial bureaucrats of the total Monarchy's central institutions. He hardly needed to remind the Delegates that this former practice was completely illegal. Law X of 1790, for example, stated that Hungary was an independent Kingdom and expressly declared that by virtue of this in-

---

37 A knowledgeable Englishman, Mr. Blackwell was familiar with the structure and object of a responsible parliamentary government functioning in a limited, constitutional monarchy. Since Batthyány had been recognized by the Crown as responsible Prime Minister, he thus seems keenly aware of the irregularity of rescripts having been formulated and a major policy decided upon by the Crown without consultation with the new Ministry. Mr. Blackwell to Viscount Ponsonby. Presburg, March 29, 1848, *CRAH*, p. 54.

38 The *Consilium* by Laws CI and CII of 1723 was declared independent with no direct connection to the boards of government of the Habsburg Provinces, but authorized rather to communicate directly with the King. In Hungarian constitutional thought, the *Consilium* was regarded as not only the servant of the King, but also an organ of the Diet, since it was responsible for issuance of directives to the counties to observe Dietal resolutions. Constitutionally therefore, it was regarded as an advisory (on a lower level than the Chancellery) and administrative bureaucracy (the counties could, however, on proper grounds refuse to execute its directives) at the service of both Crown and Diet. Hence, in the past, Habsburg subordination of it to the orders of the Imperial governmental bodies was clearly illegal, while the King's unilateral usage of it was contrary to the meaning and spirit of the Constitution. Law XCVII of 1723 and Law III of 1764, both requiring that as soon as possible it should be transferred from Pozsony to Buda, had been ignored until Josef II's time. See Marczali, *Hungary in the Eighteenth Century*, pp. 333-38 and n. 1.

dependence as a political entity with its own Constitution, it could not be subordinated to, or rendered dependent on, any department of the Imperial government.[39] From this point of view then, this rescript of the 29th could be regarded as a daring attempt by the Emperor's advisors to elicit the Hungarian Diet's legalization of what had been even previously illegal. Such an act would have resulted in the *de jure* recognition of the subordination of the new Hungarian government to the Imperial government.[40] Kossuth's impromptu résumé[41] of the situation was accurate:

I say this rescript is an outrageous mockery and a light playing with the throne and the nation. And who is pursuing this wanton game with our country? The all-pervading spirit is that of the hated bureaucracy which should from now on remain in Vienna. The Hungarian independent Ministry could remain nothing but a lowly . . . office in their eyes, as was the *Consilium*; these men do not care for the future of the House of Austria, they do not think of the blood of citizens which may now flow in rivers at the moment the King announces "there will be no responsible Hungarian Ministry;" they trim away at the royal words, not even leaving that nimbus around the King's name, wishing to deprive it of its glory and dignity, carrying the matter so far that the people should lose their faith in the King's words. Seeing these things, I am struck to the depths of my soul at this instance that in the face of the given kingly word His Majesty should have any advisor in Hungarian matters other than the already ap-

---

39 Hugessen, *Political Evolution,* II, 21; see also, I, 191, 232.

40 Károlyi states that the *Staatskonferenz* wanted to use arms to crush Hungary, but did not have money or troops at this point. He gives an excellent example of the attitude of the traditional Imperial government toward Hungary. The members of the *Staatskonferenz* were in theory appointed by the Emperor, but at this time actually appointed themselves and enjoyed no one's confidence but their own. Yet, on March 26th, when Somssich broached the idea of inviting Batthyány and Deák to attend, the Austrian members were violently oppossed on the grounds they were "only Ministers designate and not sworn in." *Az 1848-diki Pozsonyi törvénycikkek az udvar előtt,* pp. 68, 71.

41 Szilágyi, *A magyar forradalom története 1848- és 49-ben,* pp. 23-24. Zarek, *Kossuth,* p. 163 provides a much more readable English translation of this speech than that given above which has been left fairly literal in the hope of conveying something of the incredibly compressed and torrential meaning in the Hungarian passage as well as something of Kossuth's overwhelming force with speech.

pointed first responsible Minister, Count Lajos Batthyány and retains Archduke Ludwig, who should have no influence in Hungarian matters, who has not even the slimmest right. He is not heir-apparent, he is not Palatine and as long as Count Hartig, Windisch-Graetz, and lord knows from who else's influence our matters depend, all of us must be most deeply embittered that matters are still at that point as an overruled councillor . . . .

After this and other speeches, the Delegates hammered out the Dietal resolution which was to be the formal reply to the royal rescripts, and returned for their second formal sitting for its passage late in the night.[42] There were some minor concessions to the Crown, devised by Batthyány, such as the King's right to the nomination of bishops and to appoint National Guard officers of fieldgrade.[43] But, as had been clear from the beginning, on the major issues there was not the slightest retreat. The properly and carefully worded resolution informed the monarch that as their crowned King they had thought his word inviolable. Thus, they could not really believe that he had retracted his promise concerning the approval of an independent and responsible Hungarian Ministry. Therefore, this decision must have come from the discredited bureaucracy, jeopardizing the future of the peoples united under the Austrian ruling House. The resolution stated that faith in the King suffered because of this action, and concluded with an expression of hope in the success of the Palatine's mission. As for the abolition of the *urbarium,* the Dietal resolution stated: "We look upon this as already approved and we do not see the need for debates . . . nor do we agree to its suspension."[44]

This resolution was passed unanimously by the Diet.[45] The

42 Szilágyi, *A magyar forradalom története 1848- és 49-ben,* p. 24.

43 Mr. Blackwell to Viscount Ponsonby. Presburg, March 29, 1848, *CRAH,* p. 54. See also, *Deák Ferencz beszédei,* II, 33. "The prudence of the [Hungarian] legislative assembly was therefore no less than that of the Crown and the reception given to the Viennese rescripts proves that their true meaning was immediately understood." Irányi and Chassin, *Histoire politique,* I, 183.

44 Szilágyi, *A magyar forradalom története 1848- és 49-ben,* p. 24.

45 Hugessen, *Political Evolution,* II, 21; Irányi and Chassin, *Histoire politique,* I, 182.

Palatine set out during the night for Vienna, promising again either to return no longer as Palatine or with royal approval for the ministry bill.[46] He was soon followed by Batthyány, Deák, Széchenyi and Eötvös.[47] Meanwhile, in Pozsony, the Delegates were becoming deadly adamant in their position based upon the Constitution. In the words of the contemporary, Sándor Szilágyi: "In this moment only one thought lived in their souls — in a cordial manner, or with force, by all means necessary, we shall retain the sanction of the Laws."[48]

*   *   *

While the Delegates deliberated in Pozsony on the evening of the 29th, a crowd of youths — including some National Guards — gathered in the market square and then proceeded to the residence of Baroness Meskó, where they forced an entry, hoping to find Zsedényi there.[49] The incident was mild enough, but it was the first really illegal act to occur in the city. On the following morning, Thursday, March 30th, prior to his departure for Vienna, Széchenyi brought it up at a Circular Sitting of the Diet. He scolded the lawbreakers severely. The Delegates were in agreement, although a few dissenting noises were heard. Then, Deák delivered some rather long and sobering observations, reminding his listeners that the greatness in the French Revolution did not consist of breaking into private homes, persecuting individuals or threatening personal safety. He stated that whoever approved such personal attacks (or kept silent) committed "sins against the country."[50] He reminded the Delegates of the possibility of intervention by outside enemies and emphasized the need for unity. He dismissed Madarász's motion against Zsedényi as based on "outmoded law," and said if the Delegates could not avoid the bitterness of party faction and lead others away from anarchy to the path of

---

46 Mr. Blackwell to Viscount Ponsonby. Presburg, March 29, 1848, *CRAH*, p. 55.

47 *Ibid.*, pp. 54-55; Macartney, *Habsburg Empire*, p. 339.

48 *A magyar forradalom története 1848- és 49-ben*, p. 25.

49 *Deák Ferencz beszédei*, II, 35.

50 *Ibid.*

law, then they "tear at the body of the new-born nation"[51] and were not to "be trusted with the good of the country."[52]

Deák's words quickly spread and proved to be enough to keep Pozsony quiet while the Ministers went to Vienna. But the situation in Pest was a different matter. When Pest received word of the rescripts by steampacket on the evening of the 29th, the city was almost immediately in an uproar. An impromptu open meeting was held in the Museum square and a mob began to demonstrate in front of the Imperial fortress of Buda, while the Pest security committee heatedly discussed revolution. Nyáry and Szemere, representing the new national government, had great difficulty in preventing an open insurrection.[53] Petőfi, his patience snapped, delivered passionate speeches, and widely publicized his previously moderated republican sentiments with the completion of his poem, *A királyokhoz* (To Kings).[54] The fact that open revolt and violence did not break out can be attributed only to the moderation and strength of those in positions of leadership who enjoyed popular respect, and exercised a commanding moral influence.[55]

The Pest county executive committee, which from March 19th had maintained a sort of lobby at the Pozsony Diet, arguing for a more liberal press law, the reduction of the suffrage property qualification to one hundred forints, and for other progressive measures, had already been dissatisfied enough with Vienna's delay. It was now aghast at these latest rescripts of the 29th overthrowing the very foundation of the entire reform program. In cooperation with the Pest city security committee, they provided leadership and direction to

51 *Ibid.* Deák's reference to outmoded law was to some of those of Ulászló II's reign which were also the Laws used as a constitutional precedent for the establishment of a responsible ministry. But there was no real conflict because Deák, in this context, was obviously referring to the fact that hopefully the extreme penalty of decapitation was no longer needed as a form of censure in a matter which involved a difference of opinion or a simple mistake in political judgment.

52 *Ibid.*, p. 36.

53 Irányi and Chassin, *Histoire politique*, I, 191.

54 Earlier poems, such as *V. Ferdinandhoz* (To Ferdinand V) and *A királyok ellen* (Against Kings), the last written in 1844, had remained unpublished. Jones, *Five Hungarian Writers*, p. 279.

55 Szilágyi, *A magyar forradalom története 1848- és 49-ben*, p. 25.

the popular fury by organizing a demonstration for the next day. The demonstration on March 30th filled Pest to over-flowing, and it was so thunderous that it "perhaps surpassed even the manifestation of March 15th." [56]

Pest was in such a state that if Kossuth had really been a demagogue and an aspiring dictator, he could have easily raised the excited masses of Pest with a call to revolt and marched on Vienna with a fair chance of shattering the House of Habsburg.[57] Such was the enormity of his popular prestige and the anger of even normally responsible opinion at this latest action by the Vienna clique. The camarilla had revealed momentarily, but with clarity, its true attitude toward the Hungarian Constitution. "Vienna" obviously did not regard it as a mutual and honorable compact between King and nation. For them, it was a facade structure to be manipulated for the unilateral consolidation of Imperial power.

Yet, Hungarian constitutional feeling was innate rather than superficial. In Pest, the security committee issued a proclamation on March 31st urging the inhabitants to be patient and wait a few hours for word from the Palatine. [58] As if by consensus the nation agreed to await the outcome of the

---

56 Spira, "A vezérmegye forradalmi választmánya 1848 tavaszán," p. 723.

57 "Austria," wrote Blackwell on the 29th, "is at this moment utterly power-less" and this observation was an accurate estimate. Vienna itself had simmered down considerably towards the end of the month, but Zarek's statement that the population could have been easily brought back into the streets seems accurate, especially in light of subsequent developments. Moreover, outside the Hereditary Provinces, Austria was still in trouble, especially in Lombardy where actual revolt had broken out and where military operations were under way concerning which Viennese governmental and financial circles were divided in opinion. Austria's chief difficulty at this point seems to have been the lack of military presence. As Lord Ponsonby wrote Lord Palmerston from Vienna on March 28th, the Government was already desirous of obtaining increased men and funds for the Imperial Army from Hungary. See: Mr. Blackwell to Viscount Ponsonby. Presburg, March 29, 1848, *CRAH*, p. 54; Zarek, *Kossuth*, p. 164; Macartney, *Habsburg Empire*, pp. 341-50; Viscount Ponsonby to Viscount Palmerston. Vienna, March 28, 1848, *CRAH*, p. 48. See also *ex post facto* observations of the situation at this time which have a pronounced pro-centralist viewpoint by the acting Consul of the U.S. at Vienna. Mr. J. G. Schwarz to the Honorable James Buchanan. Vienna, June 30, 1848. *House Executive Document No. 71.* 31st Congress, 1st Session, pp. 67-71, especially p. 69. Károlyi's study of the *Staatskonferenz* at this time definitely shows that a majority of its members favored crushing Hungary with troops, but troops were simply not available. *Az 1848-diki Pozsonyi törvénycikkek az udvar előtt*, p. 68.

58 Irányi and Chassin, *Histoire politique*, I, 191.

strongly phrased Dietal resolutions in Vienna. Kossuth himself was completely aware of his unique personal prestige which made him so hated in certain Vienna circles, as well as among Hungarian aristocrats. He plainly saw the opportunity before him. Speaking shortly after March 30th, he stated:

> I . . . was for some hours in a position to decide the fate of the Austrian throne . . . the blood of my countrymen would flow at my bidding. But there is no more execrable crime than to gamble with the life's blood of one's fellows and a nation's peace. [59]

Therefore, despite the provoking circumstances, Kossuth, together with the other Dietal Delegates, waited in Pozsony to see what would be the latest pleasure of the Habsburg Court toward Hungary's constitutional position. Pest remained agitated through Friday, March 31st. In the streets and the cafes there was constant discussion on the course to be adopted should the Court persist. One committee member put his name to a placard calling for nothing less than the revocation of the Pragmatic Sanction. There was talk of separation from Austria and the election of the Palatine as King. A few young people talked of a republic. Many spoke of a collision with Imperial troops. But Pest also waited the Court decision. [60] Despite the farcical attempt on the part of a clique of Viennese absolutists to reverse the agreement of the 17th between Crown and nation, Hungary displayed a sense of restraint by maintaining the Kingdom's link with the Monarchy and awaiting the results of renewed efforts to obtain a constitutional settlement with the Crown. One which would be open, straightforward, and based on good faith. However, by this juncture passions had risen to such a state that it was certain, especially since the passage of the National Guard bill, that a nation in arms would have stood behind the Hungarian Ministry if "Vienna" continued to insist upon the virtual elimination of the promised constitutional concessions of March 17th. [61]

59 Zarek, *Kossuth*, p. 164; Irányi and Chassin, *Histoire politique*, I, 185.

60 Irányi and Chassin, *Histoire politique*, I, 191.

61 G. Spira, "A vezérmegye forradalmi választmánya 1848 tavaszán," p. 723; Hugessen, *Political Evolution*, II, 22.

*Chapter X*

## THE RESCRIPT OF MARCH 31ST

Beset by the disturbances in Milan,[1] and faced with a united Hungarian resistance,[2] the Viennese Court camarilla relented. At last, the Palatine returned from Vienna to the Hungarian Diet on Friday, March 31st with the crucial and satisfactory royal rescript. Ferdinand V naturally reserved to himself all the traditional prerogatives of the Holy Crown such as the right of ennoblement and the appointment of clergy to the higher ecclesiastical offices. He accepted the concessions proposed by Batthyány and voted by the Diet on the 29th according to which he retained his traditional right of military appointments, including fieldgrade officers in the National Guard. He acknowledged the Palatine's powers of representing him with the proviso that their exercise not impair "the unity of the . . . Monarchical association."[3] To all else, however, consent was given. Ferdinand V agreed to the list of Ministers proposed by the Diet through the Palatine, including those for National Defense and National Finance; he promised, henceforth, to exercise his own executive powers only:

---

1 These had been mounting since the beginning of March. Venice fell on the 21st and in the night of 22/23rd Radetzky withdrew the Milan garrison reduced by one-third into the Quadrilateral. Charles Albert had crossed into Lombardy on the 23rd. The Hungarian regiments in Radetzky's command, by the way, remained faithful. Macartney, *Habsburg Empire*, pp. 343-44; Rothenberg, "The Habsburg Army and the Nationality Problem," p. 72. See also, Stiles, *Austria in 1848/49*, pp. 191-213, and Springer, *Geschichte Oesterreichs seit dem Wiener Frieden 1809*, I, 234-43. The latter is an especially good account of the Austrian side. In the last days of March and early April, many in Vienna had come to believe that "national freedom and the continued existence of Austria were no longer compatible," p. 243.

2 It should be remembered that Vienna maintained agents everywhere and was aware of the unity displayed in Hungary, especially of the resolution of the Pest county and city committees and the popular support they received. Károlyi, *Az 1848-diki Pozsonyi törvénycikkek az udvar előtt*, p. 4.

3 Macartney, *Habsburg Empire*, p. 339.

Through an independent Hungarian Ministry and that no enactment, appointment . . . was valid without the counter-signature of the appropriate Minister, each Minister being responsible for his official actions . . . [the Ministers' competence included] all questions which hitherto fell, *or ought to have fallen,* within the competence of the Court Chancellery, the Concilium and the Camera, including the Department of Mines . . . to all civilian, Church, fiscal . . . and military questions.[4]

The rescript of the 31st also approved the appointment of a responsible Hungarian "Minister *a latere,*" that is, a Minister of Foreign Affairs (*Külügyminiszter*) as he was commonly referred to, and subsequently styled in official documents.[5] His function was to represent Hungary effectively "in all questions of common interest to Hungary and the Hereditary Provinces."[6]

Admittedly, a certain degree of ambiguity necessarily surrounded this latter Minister's position in so far as it could be defined at this point in a rescript or subsequently in Law III of 1848. However, there appears little justification for believing that the Hungarian Diet in making provision for this Minister had any intention of establishing an autonomous rival to the Monarchy's *Haus-Hof-und Staatskanzlei.* Rather, it was in full accord with independent Hungary's obligation to contribute to the Monarchy's mutual defense as incurred under the Pragmatic Sanction (an obligation which naturally had always carried with it the necessity to cooperate in the formulation of agreement on diplomatic, defense, and Monarchic financial affairs). The new responsible Hungarian Minister of Foreign Affairs was expected to fulfill a dual function. As Blackwell had reported a few days earlier, on the one hand he was to facilitate relations between Hungary and the other States of

---

4 Quoted from *ibid.*, pp. 339-40. (Italics mine.) The full text of this rescript of March 31st is given in Szilágyi, *A magyar forradalom története 1848- és 49-ben,* pp. 25-26.

5 Viscount Ponsonby to Viscount Palmerston. — (Received May 17.) Vienna, May 12, 1848. Inclosure in No. 23. Acts passed by the Hungarian Diet, *CRAH,* p. 66. This Inclosure is a report written by Blackwell which Lord Ponsonby received and forwarded to Lord Palmerston. The author of these remarks is naturally, therefore, Mr. Blackwell.

6 Macartney, *Habsburg Empire,* p. 340; Hugessen, *Political Evolution,* II, 28.

the Austrian Empire concerning financial and military matters of mutual interest.[7] On the other hand, he was understood to be a "Hungarian Minister who is to reside in Vienna, and be consulted in all transactions with foreign States in which the interests of Hungary are in any way involved."[8] Certainly, such a Hungarian Minister, being as he was responsible to the Diet (even though there existed a constitutional precedent),[9] posed a large incursion of the legislative power into the Habsburg Imperial and Royal preserves of controlling diplomatic and military affairs. Yet the Hungarian intent was not to break away from the Monarchy, but rather to cooperate and co-ordinate a mutual policy with "Austria" as had always been defined by the Pragmatic Sanction. The real relationship and importance of the responsible Hungarian Minister of Foreign Affairs vis-à-vis Vienna could only have emerged with clarity in time under actual operating conditions conducted in circumstances of mutual cooperation.[10]

---

7 Mr. Blackwell to Viscount Ponsonby. Presburg, March 19, 1848. 6 a.m., *CRAH*, p. 51.

8 Mr. Blackwell to Viscount Ponsonby. Presburg, March 22, 1848, *ibid.*, p. 52.

9 Before the coming of the Habsburgs, as well as after the acceptance of the Pragmatic Sanction, the influence of the King was always admitted to be predominant in the conduct of foreign affairs—except in cases of a minority or incapacity. But the "nation" was also recognized in Hungarian practice as having the right to be consulted. In the fourteenth and fifteenth centuries the Grand Council usually reviewed foreign policy, and the Diet frequently made its views known. On occasion the Diet even decided questions of war and peace, as in the 1491 Peace of Pozsony.

The Palatine, who since Law XXXIII of 1492 was elected by the Diet, also had the constitutional power to conduct foreign affairs if the situation required it. He usually did so with the advice and consent of the other dignitaries of the Realm (Chief Justice, Lord Treasurer, etc.) with the advice of the Diet being proffered or solicited.

With the coming of the Habsburgs, the Diet in no way renounced its right to be consulted on foreign policy. Numerous Laws (Law I of 1536; Law IV of 1546; Law II of 1622; Law I of 1659; Law IV of 1681) required that Hungary be represented in peace negotiations with the Turks. The Habsburgs generally ignored Hungarian rights and tradition in this area. But it is worth note that in 1830s and in 1840s the Hungarian Diet refused votes of troops and monies until it received an accounting from the Crown concerning the European diplomatic situation as a means of emphasizing its rights to be consulted on foreign policy. See d'Eszlary, *Institutions*, II, 84-85, 121; Hugessen, *Political Evolution*, II, 46 and ns. 1 and 2.

10 Some confusion may arise over terminology since "foreign affairs" to Hungarians had a double meaning; first their own relations with the Hereditary Lands and, secondly, the Monarchy's relations with other States. In Vienna "foreign affairs" meant exclusively the latter. Macartney, *Habsburg Empire*, p. 340, n. 2.

In the rescript of the 31st, "Vienna" understood the meaning of the Hungarian provision for a Minister of Foreign Affairs. The predominant desire of the Court at this juncture was to placate an incensed Hungary and to secure Hungarian assistance in the military difficulties in northern Italy. All this can be sensed in the lines appearing over Ferdinand's signature:

> While I recognize the fact that the organization of home defense and the vote for military requirements belong to the sphere of action of the legislature, and that the disposition of the regular forces and their employment are within the competence of the Viceroy's Government acting through the responsible Ministry, on my part I confidently expect from the attachment . . . to my House and to the connection, consecrated by the Pragmatic Sanction, with my Empire that they will readily see that the question of the employment of the Hungarian Army beyond the limits of the Kingdom, as well as that of the appointment to military offices, can depend only on my royal decision, and that the counter-signature in such matters must consequently be entrusted to the Minister in attendance on my person.[11]

This part of the rescript of the 31st was, on its face, a legitimate constitutional position for the King to maintain. The King recognized the legislature's authority over the National Guard and over the supply and organization of Hungarian units in the regular Army. He also recognized that the effective organization and disposition (presumably within Hungary) of the regular Army fell within the competence of the Palatine acting in accordance with the Minister of War, [12] who was to be ultimately responsible to the projected Parliament elected on a classless suffrage. Beyond this, no Hungarian could legitimately deny the King's statement that under the terms of the Pragmatic Sanction Hungary had an obliga-

---

11 Hugessen, *Political Evolution,* II, 22.

12 The term actually used for this Ministry in 1848 was "*Honvédelmi minisztérium.*" Translated it means "Ministry of National (or of "Home") Defense." See remarks by Blackwell in Viscount Ponsonby to Viscount Palmerston. (Received May 17.) Vienna, May 11, 1848. Inclosure in No. 23. Acts passed by the Hungarian Diet, *CRAH,* p. 66.

tion to cooperate and in part provide for the mutual defense of the total Monarchy. It followed that for effective operations beyond the borders of Hungary, the Hungarian regiments of the Imperial Army (presumably soon to be reorganized as the Royal Hungarian Army) should be placed under the command of the King-Emperor, almost certainly a unified command which would include units from the other Lands of the Monarchy. Actually, nothing in this part of the rescript of the 31st was contradictory to Hungarian constitutional practice as handed down from Medieval times. Rather, it was a reenforcement of such practice since a King of Hungary by tradition and by Law was required to obtain the nation's consent (here represented by the counter-signature of the "Minister in attendance on my person") for the deployment of Hungarian armed forces beyond the borders of Hungary. Once the consent had been obtained, his rights of command were unquestioned. Thus, it can be seen that the military arrangements which were emerging in the terms of the rescript of March 31, 1848, were consciously based upon a very old Hungarian constitutional principle and practice. Nor does there seem to be any reason why such arrangements should not have proved effective in operation if there had existed or developed the necessary spirit of mutual trust and a sincere desire to make them work.[13]

In any event, while the military reference in the rescript of the 31st did not exactly create rapture among the most nationalistically-minded in the Diet, no motion was made against it, and it was accepted *in toto* to the accompaniment of some continued grumbling from the Left. The Diet thereupon

---

13 In Laws I and III of 1439, the Diet had carefully laid down the procedure and order the King must follow in mobilizing a national army, and throughout this and the next century, numerous Laws regulated the terms of military service outside the borders of the Kingdom. d'Eszlary, *Institutions*, II, 170 and n. 75, 172 and ns. 84 and 85, 173 and n. 92, 169-86, *passim*. See also the importance of this principle in the origin of the *Bulla Aurea* in W. Sólyom-Fekete, "The Golden Bull of Hungary," pp. 366-68, 371. Article 7 had specially stated that the army, at this time principally the nobles, was not obliged to follow the King in wars outside Hungary unless special arrangements were agreed upon. By 1843, this principle had come to mean ideally that parliamentary consent must be obtained for the participation of the Hungarian standing Army in foreign wars.

voted a temporary three million forints [14] toward the upkeep of the common services of the Monarchy, while at the same time deferring until the next Diet a request from the *Staatskonferenz* that Hungary assume responsibility for a quarter of the total Monarchy's debt and make an immediate initial payment of ten million forints. [15]

The reason for Vienna's unusual capitulation to Hungarian constitutionalism was to become apparent to the Diet soon enough. On the evening of Sunday, April 2nd, Prince Esterházy, the new Hungarian Minister of Foreign Affairs, was to receive an official application from the *Staatskonferenz* requesting troops to assist the Monarchy to retain possession of Lombardy. [16] This, in reality, was the modern opening of a long series of exchanges on military matters which were to become bitter after 1867. But the immediate feeling in Hungary on this Friday, March 31, 1848, was one of national triumph. The Palatine's first reading of the rescript before a mixed sitting of the two Houses, which had been specially called for the occasion, was met with enthusiastic and repeated cries of "long live the King" accompanied by the rattling of sabres, and cheers from the public galleries. [17] Among the more informed, the rejoicing was more sober and cautious. Yet a thoughtful enthusiasm was felt by all for this second, eleventh-hour royal retreat from absolutism. The Hungarian Constitution had been vindicated in a peaceful manner, and the way was now apparently open for its transformation into a

---

14 Converted into U.S. dollars according to the 1843 exchange rate of $0.485 to one forint ( = Gulden), this sum equalled $1,455,000.00. See Blum, *Noble Landowners,* p. 247. Despite the financial chaos caused by the Napoleonic Wars, twenty forints were theoretically stabilized since 1773 to equal one fine Cologne Mark which contained 23.39 gr. silver. Macartney, *Habsburg Empire,* p. 835.

15 Macartney, *Habsburg Empire,* p. 340. The *Staatskonferenz* was thus demanding an initial payment of $4,850,000.00. See above, n. 14. Irányi and Chassin note that measured by population and resources in 1848, Hungary should have been liable for one-third of the total Monarchy's expenditures. *Histoire politique,* I, 185. However, in the given situation, the *Staatskonferenz*'s sudden demand of a huge sum was precipitate. It should be noted that the Hungarian Diet left the door completely open for future negotiations to settle the matter more permanently.

16 Mr. Blackwell to Viscount Ponsonby. Presburg, April 3, 1848, *CRAH,* p. 55.

17 Irányi and Chassin, *Histoire politique,* I, 184.

modern instrument of responsible government. Individually and in groups, many members of both Houses called on the Palatine to thank him for the constitutional role which he had played, and many Delegates expressed their gratitude to him in the columns of Kossuth's paper, *Dietal Reports*.[18]

The Hungarian public was generally unaware of the extent of the continued malevolence which existed in the Imperial Ministries or of the intrigues of the Vienna camarilla. Expressions of gratitude and loyalty to the throne were sent from all parts of the nation.[19] Confidence and optimism in a constructive future began to be generally expressed from almost every quarter.

Even Pest, the center of extreme nationalism and social unrest, where noble and non-noble, radical and moderate, had so effectively united against Vienna's *volte-face,* very shortly accepted this latest rescript and the settlement involved with good will.[20] On March 30th rapid-fire discussion had taken place in the general meeting of the Pest county executive committee over the unacceptable rescript of the 29th and the next day many had arrived wearing red buttons as symbols of their complete and unalterable dissatisfaction. Within the committee and throughout Pest, heated discussion continued into the night of the 31st. Then Baron József Eötvös arrived from Pozsony with the news of the royal concessions and that the Diet had accepted them.[21] Kossuth sent down word with him that refusal to accept them would result in cutting Hungary away from the dynasty, and he urged acceptance because he did not want civil war. In the heated discussions which followed the receipt of this information, Nyáry, Irányi, and Petőfi held out for non-acceptance. They urged the committee to advise the Diet that the new Ministers should refuse to take up their portfolios until the Crown relinquished the right to appoint fieldgrade officers in the Guard. Others, led

18 *Ibid.,* pp. 185-86.

19 Hugessen, *Political Evolution,* II, 23.

20 Verification on this point and the information in the following paragraph is found in Spira, "A vezérmegye forradalmi választmánya 1848 tavaszán," pp. 723-24.

21 Irányi and Chassin, *Histoire politique,* I, 192.

by Irányi were concerned with stronger internal guarantees of democratic reform. They tried to raise objection to the provision that the present bills permitted nobles to retain their franchise during their lifetime, even if they could not meet the new property requirements. [22] This was the extremist position briefly held by a minority. But shortly, even these radicals came to realize that the concessions in the rescript of the 31st were substantially satisfactory and that continued objections over details, inviting the risk of armed conflict, were unwarranted. After his initial reaction, Irányi took the lead in this view, and other radicals followed suit, tearing off their red badges. Petőfi was among the last to retreat from the extremist position, stating as he did, that: "I do not wish to see my nation's youth so divided. I shall therefore untie my sword and lay it at rest but I shall not break it." [23] With this, even extremist Hungary, if not entirely satisfied, was willing to abide by, and work with, the constitutional promises as extended by the Crown in the rescript of the 31st.

In Pest, Wesselényi, the Liberal Transylvanian Magnate whose strong national convictions had made him a hero during the reform struggles of the 1830s,[24] and who had by now lost his sight, seemed to be satisfied with the newest solution. Moreover, when he addressed an excited crowd following this crisis, he seemed to express the consensus of the majority as he said: "If the chains of tyranny are to be broken, then the people must be worthy of their freedom. Anarchy is the bridge over which expelled Absolutism returns." [25]

In Pozsony, Kossuth stated:

> The King must not believe that his might is in any way impaired by the changes in the system or the concessions which he has made. His power is enhanced and now will be fulfilled the prophecy that the second founder of the House of Habsburg will be that ruler who gives his peoples a constitution. Let His Majesty come as soon as possible

22 *Ibid.*

23 *Ibid.*; Spira, "A vezérmegye forradalmi választmánya 1848 tavaszán," p. 724.

24 Barany, *Stephen Széchenyi*, pp. 271-73, 289-91, and *passim*.

25 Zarek, *Kossuth*, p. 164; Hugessen, *Political Evolution*, II, 23.

into the midst of his faithful Hungarians and convince himself that our fidelity is no empty word, but that the Hungarian can be . . . sincere, not only in winning liberty . . . but also in loyalty to his King. [26]

Preparations were already underway for the King's impending visit to Pozsony for the purpose of sanctioning as Laws the comprehensive series of reform bills which the Delegates were now bringing to drafted completion. Among the details still under consideration at this time were the requirements for the new classless franchise. As in the States of Western Europe, this franchise was to be based upon property qualifications. In the case of the formerly subject peasant, it was agreed that the suffrage was to be extended to the holders of one-quarter *telek* (the urbarial *session* or serf holding), equivalent on the average to about eight English acres. The conservative Magnates of the Upper House, experiencing something of a resurgence, attempted to increase the franchise restriction to include only holders of one-half a *sessio* or about sixteen acres. However, the noble Delegates of the Lower House refused this second invitation to retreat. They remained united on their Liberal principles and easily defeated this conservative proposal to reduce the number of eligible voters. Thus, for the peasant, the franchise remained set at approximately eight acres. [27]

Also, during this period a communication arrived from the *Staatskonferenz* proposing that the *Hofkriegsrat*[28] (War Council) retain control of Hungary's Military Border, and that the extension of the franchise into this jurisdictional area

26 Zarek, *ibid.*; Hugessen, *ibid.*

27 Mr. Blackwell to Viscount Ponsonby. Presburg, April 13, 1848, *CRAH*, p. 57.

28 With the introduction of a ministerial system to Austria in late March, the *Hofkriegstrat* had technically become the "Ministry of War of the *Gesammt-monarchie.*" In reality, however, there was virtually no change in its composition, operations, or outlook — "the war ministry in Vienna, which unlike many government offices never lost its power and determination to manage the military affairs of the empire, ignored the new arrangement and continued to issue orders." The new Minister of War, F. M. Zanini, was appointed April 2nd and lasted until April 20th. He was a former member of the *Hofkriegstrat*. He was followed on April 30th by General Count Baillet de Latour. See Macartney, *Habsburg Empire*, pp. 334, 379 and 385. Quote is from Rothenberg, "Jelačić, the Croatian Military Border, and the Intervention against Hungary in 1848," pp. 51-52.

should be delayed until the convocation of the next Diet, or perhaps more accurately speaking, the new Parliament.[29] In retrospect, this proposal can be seen as a means to aid "Vienna" in its secret plans to mount an invasion against Hungary. For the moment, however, the Hungarians remained generally unaware of moves in this direction.[30]

On the night of April 7th, a Friday, the Palatine travelled to Vienna to discuss the Border question, whose immediate importance stemmed from the presence of Border regiments in Italy. In fact, an important part of Radetzky's forces (on paper twenty-two regiments) consisted of the first line Border battalions, estimated *in toto* at 60,000 men. This situation, plus the consideration that a sizable proportion of troops

---

29 Although the Upper House remained unchanged, the responsible Ministry and new franchise for the Lower House would warrant the use of this more recognizable term for a modern legislative body, and it is preferred by most writers. Because of the evolutionary nature of the change, however, "Diet" may also be used.

30 In the interests of fairness, it is necessary to emphasize that at this point the policy of absolutist political reaction and the contemplation of an armed invasion of Hungary was the brainchild of an unstructured clique of Imperial centralists, often termed the "Court party" or the "camarilla." It was not the policy of the new Austrian Ministries, which, incidentally, were floundering about awaiting the concoction and promulgation of an Austrian constitution. Macartney, *Habsburg Empire*, pp. 335-36.

For instance, the new Austrian Minister of War, Zanini, instructed the 18,000 troops of the regiments of the Imperial Army in Hungary to swear allegiance to, and take their orders from, the new Hungarian Ministry of War, and no friction developed on this point. However, the same Minister opposed the Hungarian claim to reincorporate the Military Border into Hungary proper on the grounds that control of the area was a "reserved right" of the monarch even though the Hungarian demand was looked upon favorably enough by other Austrian Ministers. It seems quite possible that in taking this position regarding the Border, Zanini was still not privy to the extreme designs of the camarilla. Again, it seems more than an open question whether the naive Ferdinand himself had any knowledge of the plans of the camarilla. On April 2nd, he rejected those parts of a Croatian Address which contradicted Croatia's relationship to Hungary. Hugessen indicates that he may have been acting under the direction of the camarilla which was still playing for time, but that he did so with any personal deceit is doubtful.

In any event, even though (to use Rothenberg's phrase) "the military party . . . determined to save the empire and the central government . . . if necessary against the wishes of the emperor," did not emerge in the open until mid-June, there is no doubt that plans for intervention against Hungary by the camarilla had been formulated much earlier. Kolowrat, the Minister President of the Austrian Ministry at various times in this period and a prime mover in the plans of the camarilla, had written as early as May 20, 1840, and February 18, 1845, that Slav nationalism might be a useful tool against Hungarian "aspirations." Hugessen, relying on the account given by László Szőgyény, *Emlékiratai*, pp. 65-66, dates the genesis of the plan on March 21, 1848.

(nominally two battalions from each regiment) remained within the Border itself, made authority over the Border a major factor in military and political calculations.[31] If nothing else, a considerable amount of prestige was involved at this critical juncture in the Monarchy's fortunes. The new Hungarian government did claim ultimate civil jurisdiction over the Border. Nevertheless, at this point the new responsible Ministry had absolutely no intention of issuing independent military directives to the Border troops concerning disposition of forces. The Ministry did not wish to rival Vienna, nor to be injurious to the Monarchy's security. Moreover, the Border troops were a Habsburg creation,[32] and composed almost entirely of Croats and Serbs whose loyalty to the dynasty was renowned. The Palatine apparently recognized the reason of the Austrian argument that any extensive changes in the administration of the Military Border would only create needless confusion at a time when the Monarchy was conducting military operations in Italy. Consequently, the compromise which emerged was that the Border should be transferred from the *Hofkriegsrat's* authority to that of the Hungarian Ministry of War, but that the military organization of the area was to be

---

31 Each Border regiment in normal times consisted of four battalions levied according to age groups. The first and second battalions rotated on active duty while the third and fourth battalions of older men were called up only in unusual circumstances. In an extreme situation, every regiment had a "fifth battalion," the *Landesaufgebot,* which consisted of every man regardless of age. In 1848, Blackwell projected a one and a half percent increase from the 1839 official census, and estimated the total population of the Military Border at 1,350,000 souls. He further estimated that the normal peacetime establishment of 46,795 men under arms could be increased as high as 91,231 troops available for operations outside the Border, while still leaving the Border well manned. See, Macartney, *Habsburg Empire,* p. 380; Rothenberg, "Jelačić, the Croatian Military Border, and the Intervention against Hungary in 1848," pp. 46-47; Mr. Blackwell to Viscount Ponsonby. Presburg, April 13, 1848. Inclosure 2 in No. 16. Statistical Data respecting the Population, Military Force, and c., of Hungary, *CRAH,* p. 58.

32 Gunther Erich Rothenberg, *The Austrian Military Border in Croatia, 1522-1747* (Illinois Studies in the Social Sciences, Vol. XLVIII; Urbana: The University of Illinois Press, 1960), pp. 27-28; Macartney, *Hungary: A Short History,* pp. 74-75. The system, of course, was not entirely original with the Habsburgs, since from the very foundation of the Hungarian State *gyepü* or frontier areas had been assigned by Hungarian Kings to various groups (e.g. Székely of Transylvania) to act as permanent guards in return for privileges. Under King Matthias Corvinus (1458-1490) a system of frontier fortresses was maintained against the Turkish pressure. See Macartney, *ibid.,* pp. 10, 22; d'Eszlary, *Institutions,* II, 176-82, 185; Hugessen, *Political Evolution,* II, 76-79.

left undisturbed pending a future legal settlement. The Hungarian Diet was to refrain from passing any bill at the present session for the complete civil incorporation of the Border into the adjacent Hungarian counties. However, since "Vienna" recognized the Border to be a historical part of the Lands of the Hungarian Crown, the Hungarian Diet was empowered to send civil commissioners into the area to explain the new Laws. The population of the Border was understood to be included in the new franchise bill, and therefore allowed to elect representatives to the next Diet. On the Palatine's return with this compromise, the Diet honored it, and on April 12th the understanding concerning the maintenance of the current military organization was again confirmed by the Hungarians.[33]

In another late settlement, the Crown dropped its previous insistence on a detailed bill which would have laid down the exceedingly complex fiscal and procedural *formulae* necessary to compensate personal and corporate landlords for the loss of services and land resulting from the emancipation of the subject peasant. It accepted instead the Diet's general draft bills which left specific compensation tables to future arrangements and to "the honor of the nation."[34] The Hungarian common nobility thus cut the age-old Gordian Knot without any immediate provisions to ease the economic dislocation associated with such a fundamental transition.

With these last settlements agreed upon, Ferdinand, as the fifth King of Hungary of that name, accompanied by Queen Marie Anne, his brother, the Archduke Franz Karl, and his nephew, Franz Josef, made the brief trip from Vienna to Pozsony on April 10, 1848. The monarch's purpose was to give formal sanction to the corpus of reform bills prepared by the

---

33 Mr. Blackwell to Viscount Ponsonby. Presburg, April 13, 1848, *CRAH*, p. 56; Macartney, *Habsburg Empire*, p. 380.

34 Macartney, *Habsburg Empire*, p. 341; Viscount Ponsonby to Viscount Palmerston. — (Received May 17.) Vienna, May 12, 1848. Inclosure in No. 23. Acts passed by the Hungarian Diet, *CRAH*, p. 68. In this report by Blackwell he states the phrase ran: "The legislature places the indemnification of the landed proprietors under the protection shield of the national public honour" ("a nemzeti közbecsület véd-pajzsa alá helyezi").

noble Delegates of the Diet of 1847-48. He was then to close this last Diet in Hungarian history that had been elected on the basis of the noble suffrage.[35] Soon after his evening arrival, the King reviewed the National Guard and that night the city of Pozsony was illuminated in his honor.[36]

35 Viscount Ponsonby to Viscount Palmerston. — (Received April 17.) Vienna, April 11, 1848, *CRAH*, p. 56. Franz Josef, was of course, the seventeen year old son of Franz Karl and Sophie. Ponsonby's dispatch includes the sometimes ignored fact of rather obscure interest that Marie Anne accompanied her husband. She is undoubtedly usually ignored because she seems to have never, even indirectly, exercised any influence on anything. She was a daughter of Victor Emmanuel I, a Princess of Savoy, who had had the apparent misfortune of being married to epileptic Ferdinand in 1830. Though she never complained much, neither did she ever trouble herself to learn German. In Hungarian Law, by virtue of her marriage she was considered Queen, albeit with no political power. She accompanied Ferdinand after his "abdication" and died only in 1884. Macartney, *Habsburg Empire*, p. 240.

36 Irányi and Chassin, *Histoire politique*, I, 204.

## Chapter XI

## APRIL 11TH, 1848: THE SANCTION OF THE APRIL LAWS AND FUTURE PROSPECTS

The British Ambassador in Vienna, Lord Ponsonby, reported that the King was received in Hungary with acclamations.[1] At ten o'clock on the morning of Tuesday, April 11, 1848, Ferdinand V stepped into the Great Hall in Pozsony before a *sessio mixta* (joint session) of both Houses of the Hungarian Diet.[2] Accompanying him was the Palatine, Archduke Stephan. Hungary's first responsible Prime Minister, Count Batthyány, stood beside the Palatine just behind the King.[3] The fact that the two immediate heirs in the line of succession, the Archdukes, Franz Karl, and his son, Franz Josef, also stood with the group was generally regarded as further confirmation by the Crown of the frank commitments it was about to undertake.[4]

Ferdinand, speaking in Hungarian,[5] said in part:

I have come with joy into your midst for I find my beloved Hungarian people to be the same as I have always found it to be . . . from the bottom of my heart I wish happiness to my loyal Hungarians for it is in their happiness that I find my own. Therefore, that which they require for the at-

---

1 Viscount Ponsonby to Viscount Palmerston. — (Received April 19.) Vienna, April 13, 1848, *CRAH*, p. 56.

2 Horváth, *Huszonöt év*, III, 503. For the ceremony of the King's formal sanction, the Diet moved to the Palace of the Archbishop-Primate of Hungary. Irányi and Chassin, *Histoire politique*, I, 204.

3 *Ibid.*; Zarek, *Kossuth*, p. 165.

4 Hugessen, *Political Evolution*, II, 23; Horváth, *Huszonöt év*, III, 503. Before the monarch read the actual sanction, the two Archdukes joined the Queen in the gallery box from where they viewed the entire hall. Irányi and Chassin, *Histoire politique*, I, 204.

5 Zarek, *Kossuth*, p. 165. Szekfű remarks that the Hungarian language Laws of 1844 required him to do so before the Diet. Hóman and Szekfű, *Magyar történet*, V, 391.

tainment thereof I herewith grant and confirm by my Royal word to you and through you to the whole nation in whose fidelity I find my greatest joy and comfort. [6]

With this, the large hall was filled with resounding cheers which the Palatine finally quieted before delivering his own suitable and rather long reply. This was well-prepared, and he very truthfully expressed the sentiments of the nation for which his office entitled him to speak.

He stated that the present Diet, in whose final moments they were about to participate, was a momentous one, and that the bills about to be sanctioned were to renew the country. He stated that: "As something with a . . . vital strength . . . by these Laws the Hungarian Constitution achieved a new secure basis," [7] and that by these Laws the nation would be joined to the King and the Royal House in a desired union. In the future, Hungarians would show their loyalty by their actions. For the present: "One happy, grateful people surrounds your Majesty's Throne and the nation's heart never beat more loyally or more warmly for its sovereign than it does now for Your Majesty who these present Laws sanction." [8] Franz Karl, speaking up in his own name, and that of his son, Franz Josef, [9] announced: "In my opinion, all that this noble-minded people can desire for its glory and prosperity is to be found to the full in these laws, at the ratification of which I consider it a special privilege to have been present." [10]

The drafted legislation was given a final, formal reading. Then, the actual royal sanction was given to these bills of the Diet of 1847-48, thus making them Laws to be entered into the

---

6 Horváth, *Huszonöt év*, III, 503; Hugessen, *Political Evolution*, II, 23-24.

7 Horváth, *Huszonöt év*, III, 503-504. This phrase and the Palatine's remarks in their entirely are also reproduced in exactly the same form in Szilágyi, *A magyar forradalom története 1848- és 49-ben*, pp. 31-32.

8 Szilágyi, *ibid.*, p. 32; Horváth, *ibid.*, p. 503.

9 Born on August 18, 1830, this youth was at this time only seventeen years of age. In the spring of 1848 he had been serving with the Army in Italy and only recently called back to Court. At the end of the year at Olmütz (Olomouc) on December 2nd, it was he, then turned eighteen, who was proclaimed Emperor, and who was to rule the Monarchy until 1916, finishing his rule as a constitutional King of Hungary.

10 Hugessen, *Political Evolution*, II, 24.

*Corpus Juris Hungarici,* and consequently making them unalterable unless modified or replaced by subsequent Laws. The royal sanction ran:

> Having graciously listened to, and graciously granted the prayers of our beloved and faithful Dignitaries of the Church and of the State, Magnates, and Nobles of Hungary and its Dependencies, we ordain that the before-mentioned laws be registered in these presents, word for word; and as we consider these laws and their entire contents both collectively and separately fitting and suitable, we give them our consent and approbation. In exercise of our royal will, we have accepted, adopted, approved, and sanctioned them, assuring at the same time our faithful States, that we will respect the said laws, and will cause them to be respected by our faithful subjects. [11]

With the signature of Ferdinand, and the counter-signature of Batthyány, this document was also entered in the *Corpus Juris.*

Ferdinand thus formally closed the Diet at eleven o'clock on the morning of April 11, 1848. Accompanied by his wife and party, amid resounding roars of "long live!," he left the hall; followed with cheers, he and his party departed Pozsony at noon.[12] After the King's departure, honoring an old custom, the Magnates and Delegates, still in joint session removed themselves to their own hall in the Dietal buildings, where a final reading of the thirty-one Laws just sanctioned was given, and where farewell speeches were made. The Palatine referred again to the fundamental importance of their work, and stated that the new Laws could be regarded as the initial structure resting on the firm basis of the Constitution, which would one day become a great cathedral. The final speech was delivered, most appropriately according to custom, by the *Personalis,* the presiding officer of the Lower House,

11 Theresa Pulszky, *Memoirs of a Hungarian Lady* (Philadelphia: Lea and Blanchard, 1850), p. 229.

12 Szilágyi, *A magyar forradalom története 1848- és 49-ben,* p. 32; Irányi and Chassin, *Histoire politique,* I, 206. Mr. Blackwell is more reserved in his description — the King's departure was "received with the usual manifestations of popular satisfaction." Mr. Blackwell to Viscount Ponsonby. Presburg, April 13, 1848, *CRAH,* p. 56.

János Zarka. He expressed his grateful thanks to the Palatine, the Magnates, and the Delegates for their assistance in accomplishing this great reconstruction.[13] Then the Magnates and elected Delegates, who had been the legally constituted Hungarian political nation until the sanction of these Laws, dispersed.

When the King and his party returned the same afternoon to Vienna,[14] the British Ambassador wrote that it appeared that in the future the Emperor would reside for a considerable part of each year in Pozsony or "Pesth."[15] The transfer of the first Hungarian responsible Ministry to the capital began on the afternoon of the following day, Wednesday, April 12th.[16] Its arrival was formally celebrated in the illuminated twin-city on April 14th — a celebration highlighted by a parade of the City's 7,000-man National Guard.[17]

Blackwell intentionally remained in Pozsony until April 18th. He arranged his trip to Budapest,[18] the new seat of the Hungarian legislature, in order to travel on the same packet which carried the Palatine, who, as the event proved, was "received in an enthusiastic manner."[19] Blackwell found the situation in Pest, which just two weeks previously had been a step from secession, to be calm, orderly, positive, and optimistic.[20] The Imperial black and yellow had been replaced on gates, sentry-boxes, barracks, and public

---

13 Szilágyi, *A magyar forradalom története 1848- és 49-ben*, p. 32; Horváth, *Huszonöt év*, III, 504.

14 Horváth, *ibid.*

15 Viscount Ponsonby to Viscount Palmerston. — (Received April 19.) Vienna, April 13, 1848, *CRAH*, p. 56.

16 Zarek, *Kossuth*, p. 165; Horváth, *Huszonöt év*, III, 504.

17 Urbán, "Die Organisierung des Heeres der ungarischen Revolution vom Jahre 1848," p. 110.

18 Blackwell's usage of the term (below, n. 19) indicates that it was becoming more popular. The date officially set by the new Ministry for its use was April 10, 1848.

19 The information on the conditions in Budapest are taken directly from the eyewitness account in Mr. Blackwell to Viscount Ponsonby. Pesth, April 25, 1848, *CRAH*, pp. 63-64.

20 Mr. Blackwell's observations correspond with other accounts, for example, that of Ferenc Pulszky, who, when he visited Vienna just shortly after this in late April, was struck by the disorder and unsettled conditions there as compared to Budapest. See Macartney, *Habsburg Empire*, p. 378, n. 1.

buildings in general, with the Hungarian tri-colors. He observed that the troops of the Hungarian regiments of the Habsburg Imperial Army continued to wear the black and yellow cockade and their officers the black and yellow sashes until the new Hungarian War Ministry should authorize the expected change on markings from "F.I." (Ferdinand I, Emperor of Austria) to "F.V." (Ferdinand V, King of Hungary). He detected the existence of a lingering republican sentiment among the former youthful activists, as well as the existence of a feeling held by this group that Hungary would be better rid of her obligations under the Pragmatic Sanction as a State completely detached from the Monarchy. Blackwell emphasized that these sentiments were peculiar only to a minority group. The Ministers were "sincerely desirous of re-taining the Hungarian Crown in the House of Habsburg;" moreover, the radical sentiments were not being actively pressed. The students of the University had resumed their studies and the general feeling was one of deep satisfaction with all that had been achieved. The new Ministry had issued an order which enjoined those organizing a public meeting to submit in writing a twenty-four hour notice of its purpose, and making persons liable at law for the use of inflammatory language or treating at length questions beyond the purpose for which the meeting was gathered. Blackwell thought that this decision of the Ministry was constitutionally questionable at the moment, and claimed that it was adopted after news reached Hungary of the measures taken by the British govern-ment respecting the Chartist meetings on Kennington Com-mon. He observed that the Ministry's action had the beneficial effect of discouraging any renewal of the occasional, minor, anti-Jewish outbursts which had occurred in some cities during the previous month.[21] One significant sign of constitutional

---

[21] In the cities, some German and Serbian merchants and artisans resented the fact that the reform bills would grant legal equality to Jews. On March 20th one such anti-Jewish outburst had occurred in Pozsony, which, although it was quickly repressed, did mar the reform movement. Irányi and Chassin, *Histoire politique*, I, 168. See also Salo W. Baron, "The Impact of the Revolution of 1848 on Jewish Emancipation," *Jewish Social Studies*, X (1949), 195-248; Steven Béla Várdy, "The Origins of Jewish Emancipation in Hungary: The Role of Baron Joseph Eötvös," *Ungarn-Jahrbuch*, (1975).

change, he recorded, was that the ceremonial gold key recently held by the Chamberlain of the now-abolished Royal Hungarian Court Chancellery had been turned over to the National Museum "as the relic of a by-gone age." Another expression which characterized this feeling of beneficial change was supplied by the young contemporary, Sándor Szilágyi, when he wrote two years later of the Diet's work: "You cannot deny the creators' knowledge of the subject, their thoroughness, and the clever use they made of the advantages. It is undeniable that the reform ideas were incorporated in the already drafted Laws." [22] Blackwell's dispatch, both in its general tone and in its factual context, indicates that there was not even the slightest popular suspicion that the recent agreement between King and nation would not be honored. The *ad hoc* Pest committees had been dissolved, and the tumultuous public meetings which had been held daily in late March were now things of the past. In this regard, Blackwell praised the "salutory effect" of the energy displayed by the new responsible Ministry in assuring a "Democratic spirit." He noted that, along with the disappearance of the collegial system of government, the use of "Excellency" as the title of officeholders was discontinued in favor of the simple, *Miniszter úr*, that is, "Mr. Minister," [23] as the official address to be made to the head of a Hungarian Ministry.

The only really adverse news which Blackwell recorded was that in Croatia and Slavonia, the Slav political leaders were refusing to accept the authority of the new Hungarian Ministry on the grounds that the new Laws of 1848 had received a royal sanction extorted by intimidation. The observation had all the merit of censuring the role played by the English Commons in bringing out the Reform Act of 1832, or regretting the "transgressions" committed by the English legislature against the Crown's prerogatives in the seventeenth and eighteenth centuries. A Hungarian Ministerial Council held on April 23rd

---

22 *A magyar forradalom története 1848- és 49-ben,* p. 33.

23 Those familiar with the Hungarian language are, of course, aware that "*úr*" also means "lord," "husband," "master," "owner," "proprietor," and so on. Like the English, "Mr.," the German, "Herr," or the French, "Monsieur," *úr,* obviously owes little to democratic or egalitarian concepts.

by now attributed this state of affairs to agitation secretly sponsored somewhere in the Viennese Imperial bureaucracy. The Hungarian Ministry had summoned the *Ban* of Croatia to Budapest with the object of reaching some sort of agreement with the disaffected Croats, and a Royal Commissioner from a respected Serb family had been sent down to south Hungary to discuss Serb grievances.[24] Aside from these complaints originating on Hungary's periphery, the majority of Hungarian counties were generally quite peaceful.

For the present, Blackwell found talk centering mostly on the one million forints authorized by the recently closed Diet. The Ministry was empowered to emloy 800,000 for the development of railways, and 200,000 for the regulation of rivers. The Ministry was very occupied with raising this as quickly as possible and making arrangements for its proper expenditure. Even this was regarded as only an interim measure until a long-range, stable, and well-planned project could be authorized by the next Diet. Much discussion centered around a plan which had been published by Széchenyi in February whereby a twelve million forint sum was

---

24 Jelačić had slightly earlier refused a similar proposal by the Hungarian government. Now it was fast becoming one of his statesmanly tactics to return letters unopened. On April 27th, he refused to accept a communication from the Hungarian government and placed a battalion on war-footing. Rothenberg, "Jelačić, the Croatian Military Frontier, and the Intervention against Hungary in 1848," p. 52; Macartney, *Habsburg Empire*, pp. 384-85. However, to avoid a distortion the reader should be reminded that neither the influence of Jelačić nor the schemes of the Vienna Imperialists entirely explain the deterioration of Croatian-Hungarian relations. The Hungarian language Laws of 1844 and the limited political and territorial status allowed a Greater Croatia by other Hungarian Laws in 1848 also played a part in the unfolding situation. On August 27, 1848, the Hungarian Council of Ministers declared itself ready to see Croatia separate, but wished to retain the port of Fiume for Hungary and access to the sea. A few days later, on August 31st, Kossuth stated that Croatia might separate completely and go its way if the Croats so desired. But Jelačić was evidently so confident of victory and determined to expand Croatia's territory that his response was the invasion of Hungary on September 11th. Z. I. Tóth, "The Nationality Problem in Hungary in 1848-1849," p. 257. The Serbian situation deteriorated after mid-April, and by May sporadic incidents of unrest and violence were general in both the Border and south Hungary proper. On these, and the activity of the Hungarian Commissioner, Count Péter Csernovics (Temes county *főispán*), see pp. 65, 68-69, and *passim* in Endre Arató, "Die Bauernbewegungen und der Nationalismus in Ungarn im Frühling and Sommer 1848," *Annales Universitatis Scientiarum Budapestinensis de Rolando Eötvös Nominatae,* Sectio Historica, IX (1967), 61-103.

to be raised over a twelve-year period with little apparent risk, 800,000 of which would be devoted to navigation, 1,200,000 for turnpike roads, and 10,000,000 for railways. A rail network of 1,400 English miles was suggested which would connect the extremities of the Lands of the Holy Crown. In the new Ministry's eyes this project would bring about the commercial development and material improvement of all the peoples of historic Hungary.

The tone of this and of other dispatches by Blackwell was positive and optimistic. Elections for the new Diet, or Parliament, were set for June, 1848, and Blackwell thought that the legislature, which was to meet in Budapest in August, "will probably make almost as sweeping reforms as those that have been made by the present Diet since the Revolution." [25]

25 Mr. Blackwell to Viscount Ponsonby. Presburg, April 13, 1848, *CRAH*, p. 57.

## EPILOGUE

By the end of 1848 the camarilla prevailed upon the dynasty to renounce its sanction of the April Laws. Since this was done in a unilateral manner, it was by definition constitutionally illegal. In March, 1849, Hungary was subordinated to an octroyed Imperial constitution which was itself never fully implemented and eventually withdrawn (1851). Thus, driven by the dynasty into an impossible position, Hungarians took up arms in defense of the April Laws and the Hungarian Constitution — all technically in the name of Ferdinand V, who had been deposed on December 2, 1848, in favor of Franz Josef. Many Hungarians did so with great enthusiasm, and others with the greatest sadness and utmost reluctance, a feeling which was even intensified on the latters' part by the Hungarian declaration of independence on April 14, 1849. For several desperate months in 1849, Hungary stood completely alone against Imperial troops augmented by armed bands drawn from the dissident nationalities. Yet the nation achieved truly remarkable military successes against them in a war whose dimensions and duration were entirely unexpected. However, with the entry of Russian troops in force, the Hungarian cause was impossible to maintain, and after the surrender at Világos on August 13, 1849, the country was subjected to neo-absolutism accompanied by an unprecedented and ruinous taxation.

Thus, the Hungarian struggle which began in early 1848, failed to secure modernization and constitutional governance, though it required the invading armies of two of Europe's largest autocracies to crush it. This was a time when many in Western Europe were becoming disillusioned with "bourgeois revolutions" and the results of "Liberalism in the hands of selfish men."[1] Therefore, it is regrettable that the promising developments which occurred in Hungary between March 3rd and April 11, 1848, no longer provided an example of successful reform on the Continent. The realization and implementation of the Hungarian reforms remained unfulfilled for eighteen years because autocratic interests had suppressed one of Europe's few truly indigenous Constitutions.

---

1 Irene Collins, *Liberalism in Nineteenth Century Europe* (London: The Historical Association, 1967), p. 12.

# SELECTED BIBLIOGRAPHY
# OF HUNGARIAN HISTORY
## 1780-1849

It is believed that the entries in this bibliography provide the interested reader with a list of sources which are particularly useful for an understanding of the events which occurred in Hungary in March and April 1848. It is further hoped, despite the fact that this bibliography is by no means comprehensive, that these entries may be helpful in some manner to those who wish to pursue a study of some aspect of Hungarian development, constitutional, political, social or economic from the late eighteenth to the mid-nineteenth centuries. The reader's attention is directed toward the first classification, "Published Primary Sources," which contains works whose authors personally experienced the period of which they wrote as well as any book or article which contains substantial or significant contemporary documents, letters, etc. Nor should the researcher overlook the collection of theses and doctoral dissertations. In the area of books, English language studies, which often do not reflect a Hungarian viewpoint, predominate. The total of available Hungarian studies is barely indicated while the substantial studies done recently by German and Austrian historians which are relatively easy to find are largely omitted here. Coverage of articles which have appeared in English language journals to 1974 is to some degree adequate; articles in German language journals are at least provided as a sampling. Those articles appearing in Hungarian language journals between roughly 1950 and 1970 are believed to constitute a representative picture.

Those who wish broader collections than contained in this bibliography will not of course neglect the current guides such as *Historical Abstracts* nor the older bibliographies such as that contained in the last volume of Hóman and Szekfű's classic *Magyar történet*. In addition, the excellent bibliography in Carlisle A. Macartney's rather recent *Habsburg Empire 1790-1918* is recommended as well as the excellent current bibliographies, reviews of the literature and announcements in past and present issues of the *Austrian History Yearbook*. Hungarian historians are naturally aware of the numerous excellent bibliographies produced by pre- and post-Marxist Hungarian historiography, an example of the latter being the multi-volume *Magyar történeti bibliográfia* brought out in the 1950s under the editorship of Zoltán I. Tóth. However, not everyone may have as yet become familiar with the lists of bibliographies and guides to source material contained in Domokos Kosáry's newer *Bevezetés*, the first volume of which appeared in 1970.

With this much stated concerning the limitations of the present bibliography, it must be quickly added that it is naturally believed that the entries are significant ones for the study of Hungary in the given period. These entries have been selected primarily with the English language researcher in mind and they represent a modest attempt to begin to fill the gap which has been habitually left by many Western scholars who depend almost exclusively on the old Austrian centralist accounts and the newer Slavic and Roumanian historiographies. The correction of this imbalance is essential for without honest attempts to represent the Hungarian viewpoint and to assess the significance of the Hungarian State in the Habsburg Monarchy, the historical experience of all the Danubian peoples must necessarily suffer from degrees of distortion.

## I. Published Primary Sources

Andics, Erzsébet. *A Habsburgok és Romanovok szövetsége* (The Habsburg and Romanov Alliance). Budapest: Akadémiai Kiadó, 1961.

— — —. *A nagybirtokos arisztokrácia ellenforradalmi szerepe 1848-49-ben* (The Counterrevolutionary Role of the Great Estate Owner Aristocracy in 1848-49). 2 vols. Budapest: Akadémiai Kiadó, 1952-65.

"Anglo-Hungarian Documents 1841-1850," *South Eastern Affairs,* I (1931), 136-41, 143-45, 147-49.

*Austria and the Austrians.* 2 vols. London: 1837.

"Austria and the Austrians," *The London Quarterly Review,* LXIV, no. 129 (December, 1838), 126-47.

Barany, George. "The Opening of the Hungarian Diet in 1843: A Contemporary American Account," *Journal of Central European Affairs,* XXII, no. 2 (July, 1962), 153-60.

Barta, István. "Adatok a gácsi posztógyár reformkori történetéhez," (Data Relating to the History of the Cloth Factory at Gács During the Age of Reform), *Történelmi Szemle,* IV, no. 1 (1961), 113-22.

— — —. "A kormány parasztpolitikája 1849-ben" (The Government's Peasant Policy in 1849), *Századok,* XC, nos. 1-2 (1956), 5-68.

— — —. (ed.). *Kossuth Lajos ifjúkori iratok: törvényhatósági tudósítások* (Louis Kossuth's Early Writings: Governmental Law Reports). Vol. VI: *Kossuth Lajos összes munkái* (The Complete Works of Louis Kossuth). Budapest: Akadémiai Kiadó, 1966.

— — —. (ed.). *Kossuth Lajos kormányzóelnöki iratai.* (The Writings of Louis Kossuth as Head of Government). Budapest: Akadémiai Kiadó, 1955.

— — —. (ed.). *Kossuth Lajos az országos honvédelmi bizottmány élén* (Louis Kossuth at the Head of the National Defense Committee). 2 vols. Budapest: Akadémiai Kiadó, 1952-53.

— — —. (ed.). *Kossuth Lajos az utolsó rendi országgyűlésen* (Louis Kossuth at the Last Feudal Diet). Vol. XI: *Kossuth Lajos összes munkái* (The Complete Works of Louis Kossuth). Budapest: Akadémiai Kiadó, 1951.

Beck, Wilhelmine von. *Personal Adventures during the Late War of Independence in Hungary.* London: 1850.

Beér, János (ed.). *Az 1848/49 évi népképviseleti országgyűlés* (The 1848-49 Popular Representative Assembly). Budapest: Akadémiai Kiadó, 1954.

Birányi, Ákos. *Pesti forradalom Martius 15-19* (Revolution in Pest March 15-19). Pest: Mihály, Magyar, 1848.

Böhm, Jakob. "Die Deutsche Legion im ungarischen Freiheitskampf 1848/49," *Zeitschrift für Militärgeschichte,* VI, no. 1 (1967), 81-96.

Brace, Charles. *Hungary in 1851.* New York: 1852.

Bright, Richard. *Travels from Vienna through Lower Hungary: with Some Remarks on the State of Vienna During the Congress in the Year 1814.* Edinburgh: A. Constable and Company, 1818.

Czörnig, Carl von. *Ethnographie der österreichischen Monarchie.* 3 vols. Vienna: 1849-1857.

Deák, Imre (ed.). *1848: A szabadságharc története levelekben, ahogyan a kortársak látták* (1848: The History of the War of Independence in Letters as Seen by Contemporaries). Budapest: Sirály Könyvkiadó, 1942.

Degré, Alajos. "A magyarországi vármegyei levéltárak története" (History of the Archives of the Counties of Hungary), *Levéltári Szemle,* XIV, no. 4 (1964), 96-119.

Desprez, Hippolyte. "Les Paysans de l'Autriche," *Revue des deux mondes,* XX, Fifth Series (1847), 234-68.

Drage, Geoffrey. *Austria-Hungary.* London: John Murray, 1909.

Elliot, C. B. *Travels in the Three Great Empires of Austria, Russia, and Turkey.* 2 vols. London: R. Bentley, 1838.

*1832/6-dik évi ország-gyűlésen alkotott törvény czikkelyek* (Law Articles of the Diet of 1832-36). Po'sonyban (Pozsony): Országgyűlési nyomtatványok Kiadóinál, n.d.

Ember, Győző (ed.). *Iratok az 1848-i magyarországi parasztmozgalmak történetéhez* (Documents on the History of Peasant Movements in Hungary in 1848). Budapest: Közoktatásügyi Kiadóvállalat, 1959.

Engels, Friedrich. *The German Revolutions.* Edited and with an Introduction by Leonard Krieger. Chicago: The University of Chicago Press, 1967.

Eötvös, József. *Reform.* 2nd ed. Pest: Mór Ráth Publisher, 1868.

Fekete, Sándor and László, József (eds.). *Vasvári Pál válogatott írásai* (Selected Writings of Paul Vasváry). Budapest: Művelt Nép Könyvkiadó, 1956.

Fényes, Elek. *Magyarország statisztikája* (The Statistics of Hungary). 3 vols. Pest: Trattner-Károlyi, 1842.

— — —. *Statistik des Königreich Ungarn.* I. Theil, Pest: 1843.

Geréb, László (ed.). *Táncsics Mihály válogatott írásai* (Selected Writings of Michael Tancsics). Budapest: Táncsics Könyvkiadó, 1954.

Görgei, Arthur. *My Life and Acts in Hungary in the Years 1848-1849.* 2 vols. London: 1852.

Great Britain. Parliament. House of Commons. *Sessional Papers* 1851, Vol. LVII: *Correspondence Relative to the Affairs of Hungary, 1847-1849*

Presented to Both Houses of Parliament by Command of Her Majesty August 15, 1850.

Guter Rat für Österreich, mit Bezugnanme auf das Programm der liberalen Partie in Ungarn. Leipzig: 1847.

Hartig, Franz Graf von. Genesis der Revolution in Österreich im Jahre 1848. 2nd ed. Leipzig: Friedrich Fleischer, 1850.

Helfert, Josef A. von. Geschichte der österreichischen Revolution. 2 vols. Freiburg im Breisgau: 1907-1909.

Horváth, Eugene. "Kossuth and Palmerston: 1848-1849," The Slavonic Review, IX, no. 27 (March, 1931), 612-31.

Horváth, Mihály. Magyarország függetlenségi harczának története 1848 és 1849-ben (History of Hungary's War for Independence in 1848 and 1849). 3 vols. Geneva: Miklós Puky Press, 1865.

— — —. Huszonöt év Magyarország történelméből 1823-1848 (Twenty-five Years from the History of Hungary 1823-1848). 3 vols. 3d ed. Budapest: Mór Ráth Publisher, 1886.

Hübner, Alexander Grafen von. Ein Jahr meines Lebens: 1848-1849. Leipzig: F. A. Brockhaus, 1891.

Irányi, Daniel and Chassin, C. L. Histoire politique de la Révolution de Hongrie 1847-1848. 2 vols. Paris: Pagnerre, 1849-1860.

Jakab, Elek. Szabadságharczunk történetéhez: visszaemlékezések 1848-49-re (From the History of Our War for Independence: Recollections from 1848-1849). Budapest: Lajos Aigner, 1881.

Jelavich, Charles and Barbara Jelavich. The Habsburg Monarchy: Toward a Multinational Empire or National States. "Source Problems in World Civilization." New York: Rinehart and Company, 1956.

Jókai, Mór. Életemből (From My Life). 2 vols. Budapest: Révai Testvérek, 1898.

K. k. Direction der administrativen Statistik. Tafeln zür Statistik der österreichischen Monarchie, 1829-1859. Vienna: 1846, part I, table 2, p. 2.

Károlyi, Árpád. Az 1848-diki Pozsonyi törvénycikkek az udvar előtt (The Reform Laws of 1848 before the Court). Budapest: Magyar Történelmi Társulat, 1936.

— — —. Németújvári gróf Batthyány Lajos első magyar miniszterelnök főbenjáró pöre (The Treason Trial of the First Hungarian Prime Minister, Count Louis Batthyány of Németújvár). 2 vols. Budapest: Magyar Történelmi Társulat, 1932.

203

Kecskeméti, Károly. "Témoignages français sur la Hongrie a l'époque de Napoléon 1802-1809," *Fontes Rerum Historiae Hungaricae in Archivis Extraneis* (1960), 1-173.

Király, Béla K. *Hungary in the Late Eighteenth Century.* New York and London: Columbia University Press, 1969.

Klapka, György. *Memoirs of the War of Independence in Hungary.* 2 vols. London: Gilpin, 1850.

Kohn, Hans. *The Habsburg Empire 1804-1918.* New York: D. VanNostrand Company, Inc., 1961.

Kónyi, Manó (ed.). *Deák Ferencz beszédei* (Francis Deák's Speeches). 6 vols. Budapest: Franklin-Társulat, 1882-1898. Especially Vol. I, 1829-1847; Vol. II, 1848-1861.

Kosáry, Domokos. *Bevezetés Magyarország történetének forrásaiba és irodalmába* (Introduction to the Sources and Literature of the History of Hungary), Vol. I: *1. Általános Rész I-II* (1. General Part I-II). In A Magyar Tudományos Akadémia Történettudományi Intézete. Budapest: Tankönyvkiadó, 1970.

Kossuth, Louis. *L'Europe, l'Autriche, et la Hongrie.* 3rd ed. Brussels: 1859.

— — —. *Meine Schriften aus der Emigration.* 3 vols. Pressburg: 1880-1882.

Langsdorff, Emile. "La Hongrie: La Diète et les Réformes sociales," *Revue des deux mondes,* XXIV, Fifth Series (1848), 745-61.

Le Play, Pierre Guillaumet Frédéric. *La Réforme sociale en France deduite de l'observation comparée des Peuples européens.* 3 vols. 7th ed. Paris: Dentu, 1887.

Macartney, C. A. (ed.). *The Habsburg and Hohenzollern Dynasties in the Seventeenth and Eighteenth Centuries.* New York: Walker and Company, 1970.

Márkus, Dezső et al. (ed.). *Corpus Juris Hungarici Magyar Törvénytár.* 3 vols.; Budapest: 1896-1900.

— — —. (ed.). *1836-1868. évi törvényczikkek* (Law Articles of 1836-1868). Budapest: Franklin Társulat, 1896.

Mehring, Franz (eds.). *Aus dem literarischen Nachlass von Karl Marx. Friederich Engels und Ferdinand Lassalle.* Stuttgart: 1902.

Metternich, Clemens. "The Opposition in the Diet of Pressburg," Docs. 784 and 785 in Vol. IV: Richard Metternich (ed.). *Memoirs of Prince Metternich.* 5 vols. London: Bentley and Son, 1880-1882. pp. 248-59.

Mézáros, Lázár. *Élettörténete* (Autobiography). n.p.: n.d.

Nyerges, Anton N. *Petőfi*. Edited by Joseph M. Értavy-Baráth. In *State University of New York College at Buffalo's Program in East European and Slavic Studies*, no. 5. Buffalo, New York: Hungarian Cultural Foundation, 1973.

Paget, John. *Hungary and Transylvania with Remarks on their Condition, Social, Political and Economical*, 2 vols. From the New London ed. Philadelphia: Lea and Blanchard, 1850.

Palmer, R. R. and Kenez, Peter. "Two Documents of the Hungarian Revolutionary Movement of 1794," *Journal of Central European Affairs*, XX, no. 4 (January, 1961), 423-42.

Pap, Dénes (ed.). *A magyar nemzetgyűlés Pesten 1848-ban* (The Hungarian National Assembly in Pest in 1848). 2 vols. Budapest: Mór Ráth, 1888.

Pardoe, Julia. *The City of the Magyar or Hungary and Her Institutions in 1839-40*. 3 vols. London: George Virtue, Ivy Lane, 1840.

Patton, A. A. *Highlands and Islands of the Adriatic, including Dalmatia, Croatia, and the Southern Provinces of the Austrian Empire*. 2 vols. London: Chapman and Hall, 1849.

Petri, Anton Peter. "Die belagerten Festungen Arad und Temeschwar in den Jahren 1848/49," *Südostdeutsches Archiv*, VIII (1965), 113-39.

Pichler, Adolf. *Das Sturmjahr. Erinnerungen aus den März und Oktobertagen 1848*. Berlin: Meyer und Wunder, 1903.

Pillersdorf, Baron (Franz Xaver). *Austria in 1848 and 1849: The Political Movement in Austria During the Years 1848 and 1849*. Trans. George Gaskell. London: Richard Bentley, 1850.

Pridham, Charles. *Kossuth and Magyar Land; or Personal Adventures during the War in Hungary*. London: 1851.

Pulszky, Ferenc. *Életem és Korom* (My Life and Times). 2 vols. Budapest: Franklin Társulat, 1884. Also published as Franz Pulszky, *Meine Zeit, mein Leben*. 3 vols. Pressburg-Leipzig: C. Stampfel, 1880-1883.

Pulszky, Theresa. *Memoirs of a Hungarian Lady*. Philadelphia: Lea and Blanchard, 1850.

Riesbeck, Baron. *Travels Through Germany*. Translated by Reverend Mr. Maty. London: T. Cadell, 1787.

Silagi, Denis. "Zur Geschichte der ersten madjarischen gelehrten Gesellschaft 1779," *Südostforschungen*, XX (1961), 204-24.

Sinkovics, István (ed.). *Kossuth Lajos az első magyar felelős minisztériumban* (Louis Kossuth in the First Responsible Hungarian Ministry). Budapest: Akadémiai Kiadó, 1957.

― ― ―. (ed.). *Kossuth Lajos 1848-49-ben* (Louis Kossuth in 1848-49). Vol. XII: *Kossuth Lajos összes munkái* (The Complete Works of Louis Kossuth). Budapest: Akadémiai Kiadó, 1957.

Somssics, Pál. *Das Legitime Recht Ungarns und seines Königs.* Vienna: 1850.

Spira, György. "Egy pillantás a hitel írójának hitelviszonyaira" (A Glance at Conditions of Credit of the Author of Hitel), *Történelmi Szemle,* VI, nos. 3-4 (1963), 344-54.

Stiles, William Henry. *Austria in 1848-49.* 2 vols. New York: Harper and Brothers, 1852.

Szabo de Bartfa, Ladislas (Bártfai Szabó László). "Documents: Count Stephen Széchenyi's Correspondence with his English Friends," *South Eastern Affairs,* I (1931) 130-35.

Széchenyi, István. *Stadium.* Budapest: Gondolat Kiadó, 1958.

Szilágyi, Sándor. *A magyar forradalom története 1848- és 1849-ben* (History of the Hungarian Revolution in 1848 and 1849). Pest: Gusztáv Heckenast, 1850.

Szőgyény-Madich, Ladislaus. *Emlékiratai* (Reminiscences). 3 vols. Budapest: 1861.

Táncsics, Mihály. *Életpályám* (The Course of My Life). Budapest: Révai Könyvkiadó, 1949.

Tolnai, György. "A parasztipar kialakulása és tőkés iparra fejlődése Magyarországon 1842-1849" (The Development of Peasant Industry and its Conversion to Capitalism in Hungary 1842-1849), *Századok,* XC, nos. 4-6 (1956), 709-35.

Townson, Robert. *Travels in Hungary with a Short Account of Vienna in the Year 1793.* London: Printed for G. G. and J. Robinson, 1797.

Trocsányi, Zsolt. "Wesselényi Miklós fogsága" (The Imprisonment of Miklós Wesselényi), *Századok,* XCV, nos. 2-3 (1961), 281-99.

U.S. House of Representatives. *House Executive Document No. 71. Correspondence of John George Schwarz Consul of the United States at Vienna.* 31st Cong., 1st Sess., July 22, 1850.

Varga, János. "A bihari nemesség hitelviszonyai a polgári forradalom előtt" (The Credit of the Nobility in Bihar County before the Bourgeois Revolution), *Történelmi Szemle,* I, nos. 1-2 (1958), 21-54.

Vinczi, Károlyné. "Földeak község levéltárának leltára 1838-ból" (Contents of the Archives of the Village-Town of Földeak), *Levéltári Szemle,* XVI, no. 3 (1963), 660-64.

Vukovics, Sebő. *Emlékiratai* (Memoirs). Budapest: Az Athenaeum R. Társulat Kiadása, 1894.

Waldapfel, Eszter (ed.). *A forradalom és szabadságharc levelestára* (Collection of Letters of the Revolution and War of Independence). 4 vols. Budapest: Közoktatásügyi Kiadó-Gondolat, 1950-65.

Werbőczi, István. *Hármaskönyve- Tripartitum.* Pest: Magyar Tudós Társaság, 1844. (One of the numerous editions before and after; first published in Vienna, 1517.)

II. Secondary Sources

A. Books

Acsády, Ignác. *A magyar jobbágyság története* (The History of Hungarian Villeinage). 2nd ed. Budapest: Imre Faust, 1944.

Andics, Erzsébet. *Metternich und die Frage Ungarns.* Budapest: Akadémiai Kiadó, 1973.

Andrássy, Gyula. *A magyar állam fennmaradásának és alkotmányos szabadságának okai* (The Cause for the Continued Upholding of the Hungarian State and Its Constitutional Liberties). 3 vols. Budapest: 1901.

Artz, Frederich. *Reaction and Revolution 1814-1832.* New York: Harper and Brothers, 1934.

Auerbach, B. *Les Races et les Nationalities en Autriche-Hongrie.* 2nd ed. Paris: F. Alcan, 1917.

Baráth, Tibor. "Histoire de la Presse hongroise," *Bulletin of the International Committee of the Historical Sciences,* VII (1935), 243-66.

Barany, George. *Stephen Széchenyi and the Awakening of Hungarian Nationalism, 1791-1841.* Princeton, New Jersey: Princeton University Press, 1968.

Bibl, Viktor. *Der Zerfall Österreichs.* 2 vols. Vienna: Rikola Verlag, 1922-1924.

Bidermann, Hermann Ignac. *Geschichte der österreichischen Gesammt-Staats-Idee.* 2 vols. Innsbruck: Wagner, 1867-1889.

Blum, Jerome. *Noble Landowners and Agriculture in Austria 1815-1848: A Study in the Origins of the Peasant Emancipation of 1848.* Baltimore: The Johns Hopkins Press, 1948.

Bődy, Paul. *Joseph Eötvös and the Modernization of Hungary 1840-1870: A Study of Ideas of Individuality and Social Pluralism in Modern*

Politics. In *Transactions of the American Philosophical Society,* new series, Vol. LXII, Pt. 2. Philadelphia: The American Philosophical Society, 1972.

Braham, Randolph L. (ed.). *Hungarian-Jewish Studies.* 2 vols. New York: World Federation of Hungarian Jews, 1966-1969,

Breunig, Charles. *The Age of Revolution and Reaction 1789-1850.* "The Norton History of Modern Europe." New York: Norton, 1970.

Burghardt, Andrew F. *Borderland: A Historical and Geographical Study of Burgenland, Austria.* Madison: University of Wisconsin Press, 1962.

Coxe, William. *History of the House of Austria.* Vol. III. 3rd ed. London: George Bell and Sons, 1882.

Crankshaw, Edward. *The Fall of the House of Habsburg.* New York: Popular Library, 1963.

— — —. *Maria Theresa.* New York: The Viking Press, 1969.

Csizmadia, Andor. *A magyar választási rendszer 1848-1849-ben: Az első népképviseleti választások* (The Hungarian Electoral System in 1848-1849: The First Popular Representative Elections). Budapest: Közgazdasági és Jogi Könyvkiadó, 1963.

Denis, Ernest. *La Question d'Autriche: les Slovaques.* Paris: Delagrabe, 1917.

Eckhart, Ferenc. *A bécsi udvar gazdaságpolitikája Magyarországon 1780-1815* (The Economic Policy of the Viennese Court in Hungary, 1780-1815). Budapest: Akadémiai Kiadó, 1956.

— — —. *A bécsi udvar gazdaságpolitikája Magyarországon Mária Terézia korában* (The Economic Policy of the Viennese Court in Hungary in the Age of Maria Theresa). Budapest: Budavári Tudományos Társaság, 1922.

— — —. "La Révolution de 1848 en Hongrie et la Cour de Vienne," *Actes du Congrès Historique du Centenaire de la Révolution de 1848.* Paris: 1948.

Eisenmann, L. *Le Compromis austro-hongrois.* Paris: Société nouvelle de Librairie et d'édition G. Bellais, 1904.

Eötvös, József. "Viola in Court" from *The Village Notary.* Vol. IX: *Warner's Library of the World's Best Literature.* New York: Knickerbocker Press, 1917.

d'Eszlary, Charles. *Histoire des Institutions publiques hongroises.* 3 vols. Paris: Librairie Marcel Rivière et Cie, 1959-1965.

‒ ‒ ‒. *La pragmatique sanction hongroise et celles des pays et des provinces héréditaires des Habsburg.* Paris: Librairie général de droit et de jurisprudence, 1952.

Fél, Edit and Hofer, Tamás. *Proper Peasants: Traditional Life in a Hungarian Village.* Chicago: Aldine Publishing Company, 1969.

Gabriel, Astrik L. *The Mediaeval Universities of Pécs and Pozsony: Commemoration of the 500th and 600th Anniversary of their Foundation 1367-1467-1967.* Frankfurt am Main: Josef Knecht, 1969.

Gazi, Stephen. *A Histoty of Croatia.* New York: Philosophical Library, 1973.

Gogolák, Ludwig von. *Beitrage zur Geschichte des slowakischen Volkes,* Vol. III: *Zwischen zwei Revolutionen (1848-1919).* In *Buchreihe der Südostdeutschen Historischen Kommission,* Vol. XXVI. Munich: R. Oldenbourg Verlag, 1972.

Goodwin, Albert (ed.). *The European Nobility in the Eighteenth Century: Studies of the Nobilities of the Major European States in the pre-Reform Era.* New York: Harper and Row, 1967. (First published in 1953, London: A. and C. Black, Ltd.).

Grünwald, Béla. *A régi Magyarország 1711-1825* (The Old Hungary 1711-1825). Budapest: Franklin Társulat, 1888.

Hamerow, Theodore S. *Restoration, Revolution and Reaction: Economics and Politics in Germany 1815-1871.* Princeton, New Jersey: Princeton University Press, 1958.

Hantsch, Hugo. *Die Geschichte Österreichs.* 2. vols. Graz: "Styria" steirische Verlagsanstalt, (Vol. I, 1937) 1950.

Headley, P. C. *The Life of Louis Kossuth.* Auburn, New York: Derby and Miller, 1852.

Hitchens, Keith. *The Rumanian National Movement in Transylvania 1780-1849.* Cambridge, Mass.: Harvard University Press, 1969.

‒ ‒ ‒. *Studien zur modernen Geschichte Transsilvaniens.* Cluj: Darcia Verlag, 1971.

Hóman, Bálint and Szekfű, Gyula. *Magyar történet* (Hungarian History). 5 vols. 7th ed. Budapest: Királyi Magyar Egyetemi Nyomda, 1941-1943.

Ignotus, Paul. *Hungary.* New York: Praeger Publishers, 1972.

Jászi, Oscar. *The Dissolution of the Habsburg Monarchy.* Chicago: The University of Chicago Press, 1929.

209

Johnson, William M. *The Austrian Mind: An Intellectual and Social History 1848-1938*. Berkeley, Calif.: University of California Press, 1972.

Jones, D. Mervyn. *Five Hungarian Writers*. London: Oxford University Press, 1966.

Kann, Robert A. *A History of the Habsburg Empire, 1526-1918*. Berkeley, Calif.: University of California Press, 1974.

— — —. *The Multinational Empire: Nationalism and National Reform in the Habsburg Monarchy 1848-1918*. 2 vols. New York: Octagon Books, 1970.

— — —. *A Study in Austrian Intellectual History*. New York: Frederick A. Praeger, 1960.

Kapper, S. *Die serbische Bewegung in Südungarn*. Berlin: Verlag von Franz Dunder, 1851.

Kent, Sherman. *Electoral Procedures under Louis Philippe*. New Haven: Yale University Press, 1937.

Kerner, Robert J. *Bohemia in Eighteenth Century*. New York: Macmillan Company, 1932.

Kimball, Stanley B. *The Austro-Slav Revival: A Study of Nineteenth-Century Literary Foundations*. In *Transactions of the American Philosophical Society,* new series, Vol. LXIII, Pt. 4. Philadelphia: The American Philosophical Society, 1973.

Király, Béla K. *Ferenc Deák*. "Twayne's World Leaders Series." Boston: Twayne Publishers: A Division of G. K. Hall and Co., 1975.

Kiszling, Rudolf, *et al. Die Revolution im Kaisertum Österreich 1848-1849*. 2 vols. Vienna: Universum Verlag, 1948.

Klaniczay, Tibor, *et al. History of Hungarian Literature*. London: Collat's, 1964.

Knatchbull-Hugessen, C. M. *The Political Evolution of the Hungarian Nation*. 2 vols. London: The National Review Office, 1908.

Kohn, Hans. *The Idea of Nationalism: A Study in its Origins and Background*. 2nd ed. New York: Macmillan, 1961.

— — —. *Pan-Slavism Its History and Ideology*. 2nd ed. revised. New York: Vintage Books, 1960.

Komlós, John H. *Louis Kossuth in America 1851-1852*. In *State University of New York College at Buffalo's Program in East European and Slavic Studies,* no. 4. Buffalo, New York: East European Institute, 1973.

Köpeczi Béla and Balázs, Éva H.(eds.). *Paysannerie francaise, paysannerie hongroise XVI-XX siècles.* Budapest: Akadémiai Kiadó, 1973.

Kosáry, Dominic G. *A History of Hungary.* Cleveland and New York: The Benjamin Franklin Bibliophile Society, 1941.

— — —. "L'aspect social de la révolution de 1848 en Hongrie" in *Actes du Congrès historique du Centenaire de la Révolution.* Translated by R. R. Palmer. New York: Vintage Books, 1947.

Kosáry, Dominic G. and Várdy, Steven Béla. *History of the Hungarian Nation.* Vol. II of Hungarian Heritage Books. Astor Park, Florida: Danubian Press, Inc., 1969.

Kranzberg, Melvin (ed.). *1848 A Turning Point?* In *Problems in European Civilization.* Boston: D. C. Heath and Company, 1959.

Kune, Julian. *Reminiscences of an Octogenarian Hungarian Exile.* Chicago: author, 1911.

Langer, William L. *Political and Social Upheaval 1832-1852.* "The Rise of Modern Europe." New York: Harper and Row, Publishers, 1969.

Leger, Louis Paul Marie. *Histoire de l'Autriche-Hongrie.* Paris: Hachette, 1879.

Lengyel, Márta S. *Reformersors Metternich Ausztriájában* (The Fate of a Reformer in Metternich's Austria). In *Értekezések a Történeti Tudományok Köréből,* no. 47. Budapest: Akadémiai Kiadó, 1969.

Leslie, R. F. *The Age of Transformation 1789-1871.* Harper Colophon ed. New York: Harper and Row, 1967.

Lettrich, Jozef. *History of Modern Slovakia.* New York: F. A. Praeger, 1955.

Lingelbach, William E. *Austria-Hungary.* New York: P. F. Collier and Son, 1913.

Lorenz, Ottokar. *Joseph II, und die belgische Revolution nach den Papieren des Generalgouverneurs Grafen Murray.* Vienna: 1862.

Lowell, Abbott Lawrence. *Governments and Parties of Continental Europe.* 2 vols. Boston: Houghton-Mifflin, 1896.

Lustkandl, Wenzel. *Das ungarisch-österreichische Staatsrecht.* Vienna: W. Baumuller, 1863.

Macartney, C. A. *The Habsburg Empire 1790-1918.* New York: The Macmillan Company, 1969.

— — —. *Hungary.* London: Ernest Benn Limited, 1934.

— — —. *Hungary and Her Successors: The Treaty of Trianon and its Consequences 1919-1937*. London: Oxford University Press, 1937.

— — —. *Hungary: A Short History*. Chicago: Aldine Publishing Company, 1962.

Mamatey, Victor S. *Rise of the Habsburg Empire, 1526-1815*. In *Berkshire Studies in History*. New York: Holt, Rinehart, and Winston, 1971.

Marczali, Henrik. *Az 1790-91. évi országgyűlés* (The Diet of 1790-91). 2 vols. Budapest: Akadémiai Kiadó, 1907.

— — —. *Ungarisches Verfassungsrecht*. Tubingen: Mohr, 1910.

— — —. *Hungary in the Eighteenth Century*. New York: Arno Press and the New York Times, 1971.

May, Arthur J. *The Hapsburg Monarchy 1867-1914*. New York: W. W. Norton, 1968.

Mérei, Gyula and Spira, György. (eds.). *Magyarország története 1790-1849: a feudálizmusról a kapitalizmusra való átmenet korszaka* (History of Hungary, 1790-1849: The Era of Transition From Feudalism to Capitalism). Budapest: Tankönyv Kiadó, 1961.

Miskolczy, Gyula. *A kamarilla a reformkorszakban* (The Camarilla in the Reform Era). Budapest: Franklin, n.d.

— — —. *A magyar nép történelme: A mohácsi vésztől az első világháborúig* (History of the Hungarian People from the Mohács Disaster to the First World War). Roma: Anonymous, 1956.

— — —. *Ungarn in der Habsburger Monarchie*. Vienna: Herold Verlag, 1959.

Molnár, Erik, *et al. Magyarország története* (History of Hungary). 2 vols. Budapest: Gondolat Könyvkiadó, 1971.

Nagy, István. *A magyar kamara 1686-1848* (The Hungarian Treasury 1686-1848). Budapest: Akadémiai Kiadó, 1971.

Namier, Lewis. *1848: The Revolution of the Intellectuals*. Anchor Books ed. Garden City, New York: Doubleday and Company, Inc., 1964.

Obermann, Karl. *Die ungarische Revolution von 1848/49 und die Demokratische Bewegung in Deutschland*. In *Veröffentlichungen der Kommission der Historiker der DDR und der VR Ungarn*, No. 1. Budapest: Akadémiai Kiadó, 1971.

Pacatianu, T. V. *Certea de aur sau luptele politice-nationale ale Romanilor de sub Coronana ungara* (The Golden Book or the Political Struggles of the Roumanians under the Hungarian Crown). 4 vols. Sibiu: 1889-1906.

Padover, Saul K. *The Revolutionary Emperor: Joseph the Second, 1741-1790.* New York: Robert O. Balou, 1933.

Popea, N. *Memorialul Archiepiscopului si Metropolitilui Andreiu baron de Saguna.* Sibiu: 1889.

Pragay, János. *The Hungarian Revolution.* New York: Putman, 1850.

Radványi, Egor. *Metternich's Projects for Reform in Austria.* The Hague: Martinus Nijhoff, 1971.

Rath, R. John. *The Viennese Revolution of 1848.* Austin: University of Texas Press, 1957.

Redlich, Joseph. *Das österreichische Staats-und Reichsproblem.* Leipzig: P. Reinhold, 1920.

— — —. *Emperor Francis Joseph of Austria.* New York: The Macmillan Company, 1929.

Reményi, Joseph. *Hungarian Writers and Literature.* Edited and with introduction by August J. Molnar. New Brunswick, New Jersey: Rutgers University Press, 1964.

Révész, László. *Die Anfänge des ungarischen Parlamentarismus.* In *Südosteuropäische Arbeiten,* No. 68. Munich: R. Oldenbourg, 1968.

Robertson, Priscilla. *Revolutions of 1848: A Social History.* Harper Torchbook ed. New York: Harper and Brothers, 1960.

Rothenberg, Gunther Erich. *The Army of Francis Joseph.* West Lafayette, Indiana: Purdue University Press, 1976.

— — —. *The Austrian Military Border in Croatia, 1522-1747.* "Illinois Studies in the Social Sciences." Vol. XLVII. Urbana: The University of Illinois Press, 1960.

— — —. *The Military Border in Croatia 1740-1881: A Study of an Imperial Institution.* Chicago: The University of Chicago Press, 1966.

Sayous, Édouard. *Histoire des Hongrois et de leur Littérature politique de 1790 à 1815.* Paris: Librairie Germer-Baillière, 1872.

Schlessinger, Max. *The War in Hungary.* London: 1850.

Seton-Watson, R. W. *Racial Problems in Hungary.* London: A. Constable and Co., Ltd., 1908.

Silagi, Denis. *Der grösste Ungar: Graf Stephan Széchenyi.* Munich: Herold, 1967.

213

Sinor, Denis. *History of Hungary.* New York: Frederick A. Praeger Publishers, 1959.

Spira, György. "Le grand jour (Le 15 Mars, 1848)," *Études Historiques 1970 publiées à l'occasion du XIII Congrès International des Sciences Historiques par la Commission Nationale des Historiens Hongrois.* 2 vols. Budapest: Akadémiai Kiadó, 1970.

— — —. *A Hungarian Count in the Revolution of 1848.* Translated from the Hungarian by Thomas Land. Translation revised by Richard E. Allen. Budapest: Akadémiai Kiadó, 1974. (First published in 1964: Budapest, Akadémiai Kiadó under the title, *1848 Széchenyije és Széchenyi 1848-a,* The Széchenyi of 1848 and Széchenyi's 1848.)

— — —. *A magyar forradalom 1848-49-ben* (The Hungarian Revolution in 1848-49). Budapest: Gondolat, 1959.

Spira, György and Szűcs, Jenő (eds.). *A negyvengyolcas forradalom kérdései* (The Questions of the Revolution of 1848). In *Értekezések a Történeti Tudományok Köréből.* Új sorozat 77. Budapest: Akadémiai Kiadó, 1976.

Springer, Anton. *Geschichte Oesterreichs seit dem Wiener Frieden 1809.* 2 vols. Leipzig: S. Hirzel, 1863-65.

Springer, Rudolph (Karl Renner). *Grundlagen und Entwicklungsziele der österreichisch-ungarischen Monarchie.* Vienna: 1906.

Sproxton, Charles. *Palmerston and the Hungarian Revolution.* Cambridge: At the University Press, 1919.

Srbik, Heinrich Ritter von. *Metternich; der Staatsmann und der Mensch.* 2 vols. Munich: F. Bruckmann, 1925.

Steed, Henry Wickham. *The Habsburg Monarchy.* London: Constable and Co., 1913.

Steinacker, Harold. "Das Wesen der madjarischen Nationalismus," in Friedrich Walter and Harold Steinacker (eds.). *Die Nationalitätenfrage im alten Ungarn und die Südostpolitik Wiens.* Munich: Oldenbourg, 1959.

Sugar, Peter F. and Lederer, Ivoj (eds.). *Nationalism in Eastern Europe.* "Far Eastern Russian Institute Publications on Russia and Eastern Europe Number 1." Seattle: University of Washington Press, 1969.

Szekfű, Gyula. *Három Nemzedék és ami utána következik* (Three Generations and What Followed After). Budapest: Királyi Magyar Egyetemi Nyomda, 1935.

— — —. (ed.). *A magyarság és a szlávok* (The Hungarian People and the Slavs). Budapest: Kiadja a Budapesti Kir. Magyar Pázmány Péter

Tudományegyetem Bölcsészeti Karának Magyarságtudományi Intézete és a Franklin-Társulat Magyar Irodalmi Intézet és Könyvnyomda, 1942.

— — —. *A mai Széchenyi* (The Present Day Széchenyi). Budapest: A Magyar Kulturális Egyesületek Szövetsége, 1935.

— — —. *Der Staat Ungarn: Eine Geschichtesstudie.* Berlin: Deutsche Verlag-Anstalt, 1918.

Szilágyi, Sándor (ed.). *A magyar nemzet története* (The History of the Hungarian Nation). 10 vols. Budapest: Athenaeum, 1895-1898.

Szőcs, Sebestyén. *A kormánybiztosi intézmény kialakulása 1848-ban* (The Formation of the Institution of Government Commissioners in 1848). In *Értekezések a Történeti Tudományok Köréből,* no. 65. Budapest: Akadémiai Kiadó, 1972.

Tapié, Victor-L. *The Rise and Fall of the Habsburg Monarchy.* Translated by Stephen Hardman. New York: Praeger Publishers, 1971.

Taylor, A. J. P. *The Habsburg Monarchy 1809-1918.* First published by Hamish Hamilton, Ltd., London: 1948. New York: Harper and Row, 1965.

Tezner, Friedrich. *Der österreichische Kaisertitel.* Vienna: A Holder, 1889.

— — —. *Die Wandlungen der österreichisch-ungarischen Reichidee.* Vienna: Manz, 1905.

Tefft, Benjamin F. *Hungary and Kossuth.* 3d ed. Philadelphia: J. Ball, 1852.

Thirring, Gusztáv. *Magyarország népessége II. József korában* (The population of Hungary in the Era of Joseph II). Budapest: Magyar Tudományos Akadémia, 1938.

Turba, Gustav. *Die Grundlagen der Pragmatischen Sanktion.* Pt. 1: *Ungarn.* Leipzig: Franz Deuticke, 1911.

Várady, Géza. *Ezernyolcszáznegyvennyolc, te csillag* (One Thousand-Eight-Hundred and Forty Eight, You Star). In *Magyar Historia Series.* Budapest: Gondolat, 1976.

Várdy, Ágnes Huszár. *A Study in Austrian Romanticism: Hungarian Influences in Lenau's Poetry.* In *State University of New York College at Buffalo's Program in East European and Slavic Studies,* no. 6. Buffalo, New York: Hungarian Cultural Foundation, 1974.

Várdy, Steven Béla. *Hungarian Historiography and the Geistesgeschichte School.* In Studies by Members of the Árpád Academy. Cleveland, Ohio: Árpád Academy, 1974.

— — —. *Modern Hungarian Historiography.* In East European Monographs. Boulder, Colorado and New York: East European Quarterly and Columbia University Press, 1976.

Varga, János. *A jobbágyfelszabadítás kivívása 1848-ban* (The Triumph of Serf Liberation in 1848). Budapest: Akadémiai Kiadó, 1971.

Waldapfel, Eszter. *A független magyar külpolitika 1848-1849* (The Independent Hungarian Foreign Policy 1848-1849). Budapest: Akadémiai Kiadó, 1962.

Wangermann, Ernst. *The Austrian Achievement, 1700-1800.* In *History of European Civilization Library* series. London: Thames and Hudson Ltd., 1973.

— — —. *From Joseph II to the Jacobin Trials: Government Policy and Public Opinion in the Habsburg Dominions in the Period of the French Revolution.* Oxford: Oxford University Press, 1959.

Weber, Johann. *Eötvös und die Nationalitätenfrage.* In *Südosteuropäische Arbeiten,* No. 64. Munich: Oldenbourg, 1966.

Whitridge, Arnold. *Men in Crisis: The Revolution of 1848.* New York: Scribner's, 1949.

Wieser, Friedrich von. *Über Vergangenheit und Zukunft der österreichischen Verfassung.* Vienna: 1905.

Woodward, Llewellyn. *The Age of Reform 1815-1870.* Vol. XIII of *The Oxford History of England.* Edited by Sir George Clark. Oxford: Clarendon Press, 1962.

Wright, William E. *Serf, Seigneur, and Sovereign.* Minneapolis: University of Minnesota Press, 1966.

Zarek, Otto. *Kossuth.* Translated from the German by Lynton Hudson. London: Selwyn and Blount, Paternoster House, 1937.

Zeman, Z. A. B. *The Break-up of the Habsburg Empire 1914-1918: A Study in National and Social Evolution.* London: Oxford University Press, 1961.

B. Doctoral Dissertations and Masters' Theses

Andai, Ferenc. "L'histoire de la révolution hongroise de 1848 à 1849 et les rapports avec les Slavs." M.A. thesis, University of Montreal, 1963.

Barany, George. "The Emergence of Széchenyi and Hungarian Reform until 1841." Unpublished Ph.D. dissertation, Department of History, University of Colorado, 1960.

216

Bődy, Paul. "Baron Joseph Eötvös and the Reconstruction of the Habsburg Monarchy 1848-1867." Unpublished Ph.D. dissertation, Department of History, University of Notre Dame, 1962.

Castle, Edith. "Zu Zedlitz Berichterstattung in der 'Augsburger Allgemeine Zeitung': Der ungarische Landtag von 1839/40." University of Vienna, 1933.

Cushing, G. F. "Széchenyi, Kossuth and National Classicism in Hungarian Literature." University of London, 1953.

Deme, László. "The Radical Left in Hungarian Revolution of 1848." Unpublished Ph.D. dissertation, Department of Political Science, Columbia University, 1969.

Handlery, George de Poor. "General Arthur Görgey and the Hungarian Revolution of 1848-49." Unpublished Ph.D. dissertation, Department of History, University of Oregon, 1968.

Hermann, Eva. "Die Buchstadt Leipzig und ihre Rolle bei der Vorbereitung der bürgerlichen Revolution von 1848 in Ungarn." University of Leipzig, 1964.

Hildas, Peter Ivan. "The Russian Intervention in Hungary in 1849." M.A. thesis, McGill University, 1967.

Hochbaum, Julius. "Metternich und der ungarische Landtag: 1811 bis 1812." University of Vienna, 1935.

Király, Béla Kálmán. "1790 Society in Royal Hungary." Unpublished Ph.D. dissertation, Department of History, Columbia University, 1966.

Komlos, John. "Louis Kossuth in America." M.A. thesis, University of Northeastern Illinois, 1972.

Kramar, Zoltán. "The Road to Compromise, 1849-1867: A Study of the Habsburg-Hungarian Constitutional Struggle in its Terminal Phase." Unpublished Ph.D. dissertation, Department of History, University of Nebraska, 1967.

Krol, Anna Maria. "Die Stellungnahme der Wiener Journalistik des Jahres 1848 zu den Vorgänger in Ungarn." University of Vienna, 1950.

Kurat, Y. Tek. "The European Powers and the Question of Hungarian Refugees of 1849." University of London, 1958.

Kurucz, Jenő. "Die Opposition der Jugend als philosophische Strömung in der deutschen Philosophie des 19. Jahrhunderts und als politische Aktion in der Ungarnrevolution." University of Saarbrücken, 1958.

Lenz, Henry. "The German Cultural Influence in Hungary Before the Eighteenth Century." Unpublished Ph.D. dissertation, Department of Education, Ohio State University, 1967.

Pastor, Leslie Peter. "Young Széchenyi: The Shaping of a Conservative Reformer, 1791-1832." Unpublished Ph.D. dissertation, Department of History, Columbia University, 1967.

Péter, László F. "The Antecedents of the Nineteenth-Century Hungarian State Concept: An Historical Analysis." Oxford University, 1967.

Pfeffermann, Emanuel. "Baron Nikolaus Wesselényi und der Wiener Hof 1830-1835." University of Vienna, 1923.

Rock, Kenneth W. "Reaction Triumphant: The Diplomacy of Felix Schwarzenberg and Nicholas I in Mastering the Hungarian Insurrection, 1848-1850." Unpublished Ph.D. dissertation, Department of History, Stanford University, 1968.

Sik, Zoltán. "Kirchenpolitik in Ungarn unter dem Fürstprimas Josef von Kopácsy (1838-1847)." University of Vienna, 1939.

Strobach, Wolfgang. "Ungarn im Spiegel der öffentlichen Meinung Wiens 1848." University of Vienna, 1947.

Stroup, Edsel Walter. "Hungary in March and Early April, 1848." M.A. thesis, The University of Akron, 1975.

Szabo, Gertrude. "Die Revolution des Jahres 1848 in der Österreichisch-Ungarischen Monarchie in Spiegel der Memoiren und Tagebücher der Zeitgenossen." University of Vienna, 1948.

Várdy, Steven Béla. "Baron Joseph Eötvös: The Political Profile of a Liberal Hungarian Thinker and Statesman." Unpublished Ph.D. dissertation, Department of History, Indiana University, 1967.

Weiss, Eva. "The Revolution of 1848 in Austria-Hungary." M.A. thesis, McGill University, 1966.

Zeidler, Maria-Jolanda. "Vorgeschichte und Verlauf des ungarischen Landtages 1825/27." University of Vienna, 1940.

## C. Pamphlets

Collins, Irene. *Liberalism in Nineteeth-Century Europe.* London: The Historical Association, no. 34, 1967. First published 1957.

Erickson, John. *Panslavism.* London: The Historical Association, 1964.

### D. Articles

Adams, Meredith Lentz. "The Habsburg Monarchy, Austria and Hungary as Treated in the Journal of Central European Affairs," *Austrian History News Letter*, no. 3 (1962), pp. 32-55.

Andics, Erzsébet. "Kossuth en lutte contre les ennemis des réformes et de la révolution," *Studia Historica*, XII (1954), 1-169.

— — —. "Der Widerstand der feudalen Kräfte in Ungarn am Vorabend der bürgerlichen Revolution des Jahres 1848," *Acta Historica*, IV, no. 1 (1955), 151-210.

Andritsch, Johann. "Gráf István Széchenyi: Ein Lebensbild aus dem Vormärz," *Österreich in Geschichte und Literatur*, XV (1971), 88-105.

Apponyi, Comte Albert. "Origine, Caractère et Évolution de l'Idée monarchique en Hongrie," *South Eastern Affairs*, I (1931), 81-91.

Arató, Endre. "Die Bauernbewegungen und der Nationalismus in Ungarn im Frühling und Sommer 1848," *Annales Universitatis Scientiarum Budapestinensis de Rolando Eötvös Nominatae.* Sectio Historica. IX (1967), 61-103.

Balázs, E. H. "Die Lage der Bauernschaft und die Bauernbewegungen 1780-1787," *Acta Historica.* III, no. 3 (1956), 293-325.

Balogh, Joseph. "John Paget," *The Hungarian Quarterly*, VI no. 1 (Spring, 1940), 65-81.

Barany, George. "The Awakening of Magyar Nationalism Before 1848," *Austrian History Yearbook*, III (1966), 19-54.

— — —. "Hoping against Hope: The Enlightened Age in Hungary," *The American Historical Review*, LXX, no. 2 (April, 1971), 319-57.

— — —. "The Hungarian Diet of 1839-40 and the Fate of Széchenyi's Middle Course," *Slavic Review*, XXII, no. 2 (June, 1963), 285-303.

— — —. "Hungary from Aristocratic to Proletarian Nationalism," in Sugar, Peter F. and Lederer, Ivo J. (eds.). *Nationalism in Eastern Europe.* "Far Eastern and Russian Institute Publications on Russia and Eastern Europe Number 1." Seattle: University of Washington Press, 1969.

— — —. "Hungary: the Uncompromising Compromise," *Austrian History Yearbook*, III, part I (1967), 235-303.

— — —. " 'Magyar Jew or Jewish Magyar'? (To the Question of Jewish Assimilation in Hungary)," *Canadian-American Slavic Studies/Revue Canadienne-Américaine d'Études Slaves*, VIII, no. 1 (Spring, 1974), 1-44.

— — —. "The Opening of the Hungarian Diet in 1843," *Journal of Central European Affairs*, XXII, no. 2 (July, 1962), 153-60.

— — —. "The Széchenyi Problem," *Journal of Central European Affairs*, XX, no. 3 (October, 1960), 252-69.

Bariska, Michel. "Les Lecteurs françaises de Louis Kossuth," *Nouvelle Revue de Hongrie*, XXVIII (1935), 167-73.

Baron, Salo W. "The Impact of the Revolution of 1848 on Jewish Emancipation," *Jewish Social Studies*, XI (1949), 195-248.

Barta, István. "Balásházy János pályafordulása" (The Turn in the Career of János Balásházy), *Történelmi Szemle*, I, nos. 1-2 (1958), 3-20.

— — —. "István Széchenyi," *Acta Historica*, VII (1960), 63-101.

— — —. "Kossuth alföldi toborzó körútja 1848 őszén" (Kossuth's Recruiting Trip across the Great Plain in the Autumn of 1848), *Századok*, LXXXV, nos. 1-3 (1951), 149-66.

— — —. "Kölcsey politikai pályakezdete" (The Beginning of Kölcsey's Political Career), *Századok*, XCIII, nos. 2-4 (1959), 253-302.

— — —. "A magyar polgári reformmozgalom kezdeti szakaszának problémái" (Problems of the Opening Phase of the Hungarian Bourgeois Reforms), *Történelmi Szemle*, VI, nos. 3-4 (1963), 305-42.

— — —. "Széchenyi István. Halálának századik évfordulójára" (Stephen Széchenyi. On the Centenary of his Death), *Századok*, XCIV (1960).

Benda, Coloman (Kálmán). "Les Jacobins hongrois," *Annales Historiques de la Révolution française*, XXXI (January-March, 1959), 38-60.

— — —. "A Kőszegi Jakobinusok" (The 'Jacobins' of Kőszeg), *Századok*, XCIII, nos. 2-4 (1959), 524-41.

— — —. "Nationalgefühl und Nationalitätenkampfe in Ungarn am Anfang des 19. Jahrhunderts," *Anzeiger der philosophisch-historischen Klass 1971*, pp. 43-56.

— — —. "La Question paysanne et la Révolution hongroise en 1848," *Études d'histoire moderne et contemporaire*, II (1948), 231-42.

Benes, Vaclav. "The Slovaks in the Habsburg Empire: A Struggle for Existence," *Austrian History Yearbook*, III, pt. 2 (1967), 335-64.

Beregi, Theodore. "Montesquieu et la Hongrie," *Revue Politique et Parlementaire*, CCXXI (January-March, 1957), 293-96.

Bernhard, Paul P. "Joseph II and the Jews: The Origins of the Toleration Patent of 1782," *Austrian History Yearbook*, IV-V (1968-1969), 101-19.

Bernath, Mathias. "Ständewesen und Absolutismus im Ungarn des 18. Jahrhunderts," *Südostforschungen*, XXII (1963), 347-55.

Blum, Jerome. "The Rise of Serfdom in Eastern Europe," *The American Historical Review*, LXII, no. 4 (July, 1957), 807-36.

— — —. "Transportation and Industry in Austria, 1815-1848," *Journal of Modern History*, XV, no. 1 (March, 1943), 24-38.

Borsody, S. "Modern Hungarian Historiography," *Journal of Modern History*, XXIV, no. 4 (December, 1952), 398-405.

Campbell, John C. "Comments," *Austrian History Yearbook*, III, p. 2 (1967), 477-83.

Coulter, H. L. "The Hungarian Peasantry 1948-1956," *The American Slavic and East European Review*, XVIII, no. 4 (December, 1959), 539-54.

Cushing, G. F. "The Birth of National Literature in Hungary," *Slavonic and East European Review*, XXXVIII, no. 91 (June, 1960), 459-75.

— — —. "Books and Readers in 18th Century Hungary," *Slavonic and East European Review*, XLVII, no. 108 (January, 1969), 57-77.

— — —. "Problems of Hungarian Literary Criticism," *The Slavonic and East European Review*, XL, no. 95 (June, 1962), 341-55.

Deák, István. "Comments," *Austrian History Yearbook*, III, pt. 1 (1967), 303-308.

— — —. "The Month of Defiance: Revolutionary Hungary in September, 1848," *East Central Europe/L'Europe du Centre-Est*, I, no. 1 (1974), 35-53.

Deme, László. "The Society for Equality in the Hungarian Revolution of 1848," *Slavic Review*, XXXI, no. 1 (March, 1972), 71-88.

Djordjevic, Dimitrije. "The Serbs as an Integrating and Disintegrating Factor," *Austrian History Yearbook*, III, pt. 2 (1967), 48-82.

Edwards, Tudor. "Vienna: The Biedermeier Age and the Revolutionary Aftermath," *History Today*, X (October, 1960), 668-77.

Ember, Győző. "Die absolute Monarchie der Habsburger als Hindernis der ungarischen nationalen Entwicklung," *Acta Historica*, IV, nos. 1-3 (1955), 73-109.

221

— — —. "Der österreichische Staatsrat und die ungarische Verfassung 1761-1768," *Acta Historica,* VI, nos. 1-2 (1960), 114.

— — —. "Les Archives et L'Historiographie en Hongrie," *Acta Historica,* IV, no. 1-3 (1955), 319-43.

"The Enlightened Absolutism, 1715-1815," *South Eastern Affairs,* I (1931), 104-13.

d'Eszlary, Charles. "L'Administration et la Vie urbaine dans la Hongrie occupée par les Turcs au cours du XVI et XVII Siècles," *I.B.L.A.:* *Revue d'Institute des belles lettres arabes* (1956), 351-68.

— — —. "The Magna Carta and the Assises of Jerusalem," *The American Journal of Legal History,* II (1958), 189-214.

— — —. "La Situation des Serfs en Hongrie de 1514 à 1848," *Revue D'Histoire économique et sociale,* XXXVIII, no. 4 (1960), 385-417.

Falk, Minna. "Alexander Bach and the *Leseverein* in the Viennese Revolution of 1848," *Journal of Central European Affairs* VIII (1948), 139-59.

Fasel, G. W. "The French Election of April 23, 1848: Suggestions for a Revision," *French Historical Studies,* V (1968), 285-98.

Fellner, Fritz and Gottas, Friedrich. "Habsburg Studies in Europe," *Austrian History Yearbook,* III, pt. 3 (1967), 296-307.

Ficker, A. "Gebietsveranderungen der österreichisch-ungarischen Monarchie 1790-1877," Bureau der k. k. statistischen Central-Commission, *Statistische Monatschrift,* IV (1878).

Fischer-Galati, Stephen. "The Rumanians and the Habsburg Monarchy," *Austrian History Yearbook,* III, pt. 2 (1967), 430-49.

"Foundations of Magyar Society," *The Slavonic and East European Review,* XI, 369-95.

Ghermani, Dionisie. "Sozialer und nationaler Faktor der siebenbürgischen Revolution von 1848 bis 1849 in der Sicht der rumänischen Geschichtswissenschaft nach 1945," *Ungarn-Jahrbuch,* II (1970), 108-129.

Gogolak, Ludwig. "Das Problem der Assimilation in Ungarn in der Zeit von 1790-1918," *Südostdeutsches Archiv,* IX (1966), 1-44.

Grössing, Helmuth. "Ein Generalstabschefbericht der Belagerung Wiens im Oktober 1848," *Wiener Geschichtsblätter,* XXVII (1972), 309-14.

— — —. "Josip Jellačić, Banus von Kroatien, und sein Wiener Berichterstatter im Jahre 1848," *Jahrbuch des Vereins für Geschichte der Stadt Wien* XXVII (1971), 135-48.

― ― ―. "Die ungarische Verfassung und der Konstitutionalismus des Jahres 1848. Aus den Berichten eines Hofrats der obersten Polizeihofstelle vom ungarischen Reichstag 1847-1848," *Mitteilungen des Instituts für österreichische Geschichtsforschung*, LXXXI (1973), 304-36.

Grunwald, Constantin. "La grande Plaine," *Les Annales politiques et littéraires*, CXIV (10 Juillet, 1939), 36-39.

Hanák, Peter. "Hungary in the Austro-Hungarian Monarchy: Preponderancy or Dependency?," *Austrian History Yearbook*, III, p. 1 (1967), 260-302.

― ― ―. "Recent Hungarian Literature on the History of the Austro-Hungarian Monarchy, 1849-1918: A Historiographical Survey," *Austrian History Yearbook*, I (1965), 151-63.

Handlery, George. "Revolutionary Organization in the Context of Backwardness: Hungary's 1848," *East European Quarterly*, VI, no. 1 (March, 1972), 44-61.

Hantsch, Hugo. "Metternich und das Nationalitätenproblem," *Der Donauraum*, XI (1966), 51-61.

Haraszti, Éva H. "Contemporary Hungarian Reactions to the Anti-Corn Law Movement," *Acta Historica*, VIII, nos. 3-4 (1961), 382-403.

― ― ―. "Széchenyi and England," *The New Hungarian Quarterly*, VIII, no. 25 (Spring, 1967), 156-64.

Hauptmann, Ferdinand. "Banus Jellačić und Feldmarschall Fürst Windisch-Gratz," *Südostforschungen*, XV (1956), 372-402.

Havranek, Jan. "The Development of Czech Nationalism," *Austrian History Yearbook*, III, pt. 2 (1967), 223-60.

Heckenast, Desider. "Hungarian Universities — Past and Present," *Études Slaves et Est-Européennes*, II, Part I (Spring, 1957), 31-39.

Heckenast, Gusztáv. "Magyarország ipara 1726-ban" (Hungarian Industry in 1726), *Történelmi Szemle*, XIV, nos. 3-4 (1971), 320-29.

― ― ―. "Les Roturiers intellectuels en Hongrie 1780-1848," *Revue d'histoire comparée*, VII, n.s. (1948), 53-76.

Hildas, Peter I. "The First Russian Intervention in Transylvania in 1849," in *Eastern Europe Historical Essays*, edited by H. C. Schlieper. Toronto: New Review Books, 1969.

Hitchins, Keith. "Andreiu Saguna and the Restoration of the Rumanian Orthodox Metropolis in Transylvania 1846-1868," *Balkan Studies*, VI, no. 1 (1965), 1-20.

— — —. "The Early Career of Andreiu Saguna 1808-1849," *Revue des Études Roumaines*, IX-X (1965), 47-76.

Holborn, Hajo. "The Final Disintegration of the Habsburg Monarchy," *Austrian History Yearbook*, III, pt. 3 (1967), 189-205.

Holotik, Ludovit. "The Slovaks: An Integrating or a Disintegrating Force?," *Austrian History Yearbook*, III, pt. 2 (1967), 365-93.

Hoover, Arlie. "The Habsburg Monarchy, as Treated in Other U.S. Journals Than 'The Journal of Central European Affairs'," *Austrian History News Letter*, no. 4 (1963), 51-73.

Horváth, Eugene. "Russia and the Hungarian Revolution (1848-9)," *The Slavonic and East European Review*, XII, no. 36 (April, 1934), 628-43.

Horváth, Robert. "The Scientific Study of Mortality in Hungary before the Modern Statistical Era," *Population Studies: A Journal of Demography*, XVII (November, 1963), 187-97.

Iványi, Béla. "From Feudalism to Capitalism: The Economic Background to Széchenyi's Reform in Hungary," *Journal of Central European Affairs*, XX, no. 3 (October, 1960), 270-87.

Janossy, Dénes A. "Great Britain and Kossuth," *Archivum Europae centro-orientalis*, III (1937), 53-190.

Jelavich, Charles. "The Croatian Problem in the Habsburg Empire in the Nineteeth Century," *Austrian History Yearbook*, III, pt. 2 (1967), 83-115.

Jurčić, Hrvoje. "Das ungarisch-kroatische verhältnis im Spiegel des Sprachenstreites 1790-1848," *Ungarn-Jahrbuch*, III (1971), 69-87.

Király, Béla K. "The Young Ferenc Deák and the Problem of the Serfs 1824-1836," *Südostforschungen*, XXIX (1970), 91-106.

Klima, A. "Industrial Development in Bohemia 1648-1781," *Past and Present: A Journal of Scientific History*, XI (April, 1957), 87-97.

Kohn, Hans. "Was the Collapse Inevitable?," *Austrian History Yearbook*, III, pt. 3 (1967), 250-63.

Koltay-Kastner, Eugenio. "L'Ungheria nel Risorgimento italiano," *Ungheria d' oggi*, no. 2 (1969), 37-45.

Komlos, John. "Dissertations on Hungarian History completed since 1920," *Austrian History Yearbook*, IX-X (1973-1974), 260-93.

Korbuly, Dezső. "Der ungarische Adel im 19. Jahrhundert," *Österreichische Osthefte*, XIV (1973), 37-48.

Kosa, John. "The Early Period of Anglo-Hungarian Contact," *The American Slavic and East European Review*, XIII, no. 3 (October, 1954), 414-31.

————. "Hungarian Society in the Time of the Regency (1920-1944)," *Journal of Central European Affairs*, XVI, no. 3 (October, 1956), 253-65.

Kosáry, Domokos. "Széchenyi in Recent Western Literature," *Acta Historica*, IX, no. 3 (1963), 255-78.

————. "Széchenyi az újabb külföldi irodalomban" (The Image of Széchenyi in Recent Foreign Literature), *Századok*, XCVI, nos. 1-2 (1962), 275-92.

Krizman, Bogdan. "The Croatians in the Habsburg Monarchy in the Nineteenth Century," *Austrian History Yearbook*, III, pt. 2 (1967), 116-58.

Krnjevic, Juraj. "The Croats in 1848," *Slavonic and East European Review* (1948), 106-14.

Langsam, Walter Consuelo. "Emperor Francis II and the Austrian 'Jacobins,' 1792-1796," *American Historical Review*, L, no. 3 (April, 1945), 471-90.

Lanyi, Ladislas. "Napoléon et les Hongrois," *Annales historiques de la Révolution francaise*, XXVII, new series (October-December, 1955), 360-69.

Lekai, Louis J. "Historiography in Hungary," *Journal of Central European Affairs*, XIV, no. 1 (April, 1954), 3-18.

Lewis, Stanley. "Some Aspects of Tanya Settlement in Hungary," *Scottish Geographical Magazine*, LIV, no. 6 (November, 1938), 358-67.

Lukinich, Imre. "American Democracy as Seen by the Hungarians of the Age of Reform (1830-1848)," *Journal of Central European Affairs*, VIII, no. 3 (October, 1948), 270-81.

Maass, Ferdinand. "Maria Theresia und der Josephinismus," *Zeitschrift für Katholische Theologie*, LXXIX, no. 2 (1957), 201-13.

————. "Die österreichischen Jesuiten zwichen Josephinismus und Liberalismus," *Zeitschrift für Katholische Theologie*, LXXX, no. 1 (1958), 66-100.

Mamatey, Victor S. "Legalizing the Collapse of Austria-Hungary at the Paris Peace Conference," *Austrian History Yearbook*, III, pt. 3 (1967), 206-37.

Marki, Sándor. "La Hongrie et la Révolution française," *Revue historique de la Révolution francaise et de l'Empire*, IV (1913), 216-22.

McCagg, William O. Jr. "Hungary's 'Feudalized' Bourgeoisie," *The Journal of Modern History*, XLIV, no. 1 (March, 1972), 65-78.

Menczer, Béla. "Joseph Eötvös and Hungarian Liberalism," *The Slavonic and East European Review*, XVIII, no. 51 (April, 1939), 527-38.

— — —. "The Legacy of Metternich," *Contemporary Review*, (July, 1959), 36-39.

— — —. "Ungarischer Konservatismus," in Gerd-Klaus Kaltenbrunner (ed.), *Rekonstruktion des Konservatismus* (Freiburg: Romback, 1972), 219-40.

Merei, Gyula. "L'Essor de L'Agriculture Capitaliste en Hongrie dans la première Moitié du XIX Siècle," *Revue d'Histoire Modern et Contemporaine*, XII (January-March, 1965), 51-64.

— — —. "Mezőgazdasági árútermelés és a parasztság helyzete Magyarországon a feudalizmus válságának elmélyülése idején" (The Production of Agricultural Goods and the Situation of the Peasantry in Hungary During the Deepening Feudal Crisis), *Századok*, XC, nos. 4-6 (1956), 591-616.

Novotny, Alexander. "Austrian History from 1848-1938 as Seen by Austrian Historians Since 1945," *Austrian History News Letter*, no. 4 (1963), 18-50.

Otetea, Andrei. "The Rumanians and the Disintegration of the Habsburg Monarchy," *Austrian History Yearbook*, III, pt. 2 (1967), 450-76.

Petrovich, Michael B. "Comments," *Austrian History Yearbook*, III, pt. 3 (1967), 129-35.

Probszt, Gunther von. "Die Finanzierung der ungarischen Revolution von 1848-49 durch Papiergeld," *Südostforschungen*, XXVII (1968), 346-61.

Rath, R. John. "Public Opinion During the Viennese Revolution of 1848," *Journal of Central European Affairs*, VIII, no. 2 (July, 1948), 160-80.

— — —. "Students, Revolutions and the Conflict of Generations: Vienna, 1848," *The Humanities Association Review*, XXIV, no. 4 (Fall, 1973), 246-54.

— — —. "Training for Citizenship in Austrian Elementary Schools During the Reign of Francis I," *Journal of Central European Affairs*, IV, no. 2 (July, 1944), 147-64.

— — —. "The Viennese Liberals of 1848 and the Nationality Problem," *Journal of Central European Affairs*, XV, no. 3 (October, 1955), 227-29.

226

Reich, Emil. "The Magyar County. A Study in the Comparative History of Municipal Institutions," *Transactions of the Royal Historical Society,* New Series, VII (1893), 372-53.

Reinerman, Alan. "The Return of the Jesuits to the Austrian Empire and the Decline of Josephinism, 1820-1822," *Catholic Historical Review,* LII, no. 3 (October, 1966), 372-90.

Révész, László. "Das Junge Ungarn 1825-1848," *Südostforschungen,* XXV (1965), 72-119.

— — —. "Nationalitätenfrage und Wahlrecht in Ungarn 1848-1918," *Ungarn-Jahrbuch,* III (1971), 88-122.

— — —. "Polen und Ungarn 1830-1848," *Ungarn-Jahrbuch,* I (1969), 74-98.

Rock, Kenneth W. "Schwartzenberg Versus Nicholas I, Round One: The Negotiation of the Habsburg-Romanov Alliance Against Hungary in 1849," *Austrian History Yearbook,* VI-VII (1970), 109-41.

Rothenberg, Gunther E. "The Austrian Army in the Age of Metternich," *Journal of Modern History,* XL, no. 2 (June, 1968), 155-65.

— — —. "The Habsburg Army and the Nationality Problem in the Nineteenth Century, 1815-1914," *The Austrian History Yearbook,* III, Part I (1967), 70-87.

— — —. "Jelačić, the Croatian Military Border, and the Intervention against Hungary in 1848," *Austrian History Yearbook,* I (1965), 45-73.

Rudnytsky, Ivan L. "The Ukrainians in Galicia under Austrian Rule," *Austrian History Yearbook,* III, pt. 2 (1967), 394-429.

Schroeder, Paul. "The Status of Habsburg Studies in the United States," *Austrian History, Yearbook,* III, pt. 3 (1967), 267-95.

Simons, Thomas W., Jr. "The Peasant Revolt of 1846 in Galicia: Recent Polish Historiography," *Slavic Review,* XXX, no. 4 (December, 1971), 795-817.

Sólyom-Fekete, William. "The Golden Bull of Hungary 1222-1972," *The Quarterly Journal of the Library of Congress,* XXIX, no. 4 (October, 1972), 363-75.

— — —. "The Hungarian Constitutional Compact of 1867," *The Quarterly Journal of the Library of Congress,* XXIV, no. 4 (October, 1967), 287-308.

Spiesz, Anton. "Die Wirtschaftspolitik des Wiener Hofes gegenüber Ungarn im 18 Jahrhundert und im Vormärz," *Ungarn-Jahrbuch,* I (1969), 60-73.

Spira, György. "L'Alliance de Lajos Kossuth avec la Gauche radicale et les Masses populaires de la Révolution hongroise de 1848-1849," *Acta Historica*, II (1953), 49-150.

————. "La dernière generation des serfs de Hongrie," *Annales*, XXII (1968), 353-67.

————. "1848 nagyhete Pesten" (The Holy Week of 1848 in Pest), *Száza-dok*, CVIII, no. 2 (1974), 323-67.

————. "A pesti forradalom baloldalának harca a kormánnyal meg a pol-gársággal 1848 májusában" (The Struggle of the Pest Revolutionary Left with the Government and the Bourgoisie in May of 1848), *Törté-nelmi Szemle*, XIV, nos. 3-4 (1971), 330-55.

————. "Széchenyi tragikus útja" (Széchenyi's Tragic Path), *Történelmi Szemle*, VII, nos. 3-4 (1964), 583-95.

————. "Über die Besonderheiten der ungarischen Revolution von 1848/49," *Österreichische Osthefte*, XII (1970), 168-77.

————. "A vezérmegye forradalmi választmánya 1848 tavaszán" (The Re-volutionary Executive Committee of the Leading County in the Spring of 1848), *Századok*, XCVIII, no. 4 (1964), 713-54.

Spira, Thomas. "Aspects of the Magyar Linguistic and Literary Renais-sance during the Vormärz," *East European Quarterly*, VII, no. 2 (Summer, 1973), 101-24.

————. "The Growth of Magyar National Awareness. The Impact of Education and Religion before the Age of Reform," *Österreichische Osthefte*, XIV, no. 1 (1972), 49-60.

————. "Problems of Magyar National Development under Francis I (1792-1835)," *Südostforschungen*, XXX (1971), 51-73.

Steinacker, Harold. "Österreich-Ungarn und Östeuropa," *Historische Zeit-schrift*, CXXVIII (1923), 400-20.

Stranjakovic, Dragoslav. "La collaboration des Croates et des Serbes en 1848-1849," *Le monde slave*, XII, no. 9 (January-June, 1935), 394-404.

Sugar, Peter F. "The Influence of the Enlightenment and the French Re-volution in Eighteenth Century Hungary," *Journal of Central European Affairs*, XVII, no. 4 (January, 1958), 333-55.

————. "The Rise of Nationalism in the Habsburg Empire," *Austrian History Yearbook*, III, pt. 1 (1967), 91-120.

————. "The Southern Slav Image of Russia in the Nineteenth Century," *Journal of Central European Affairs*, XXI, no. 1 (April, 1961), 45-52.

228

Szabo, Ervin. "Aus den Parteien und Klassenkämpfen in der ungarischen Revolution von 1848," *Archiv für die Geschichte des Sozialismus,* VII (1919), 258-307.

Szenczi, N. J. "Great Britain and the War of Hungarian Independence," *The Slavonic and East European Review,* XVII, no. 51 (April, 1939), 556-70.

Thomson, S. Harrison. "A Century of a Phantom Pan-Slavism and the Western Slavs," *Journal of Central European Affairs,* XI, no. 1 (January, 1951), 57-77.

― ― ―. "The Czechs as Integrating and Disintegrating Factors in the Habsburg Empire," *Austrian History Yearbook,* III, pt. 2 (1967), 203-22.

Tihany, Leslie C. "The Austro-Hungarian Compromise 1867-1918: A Half Century of Diagnosis: Fifty Years of Post-Mortem," *Central European History,* III, no. 2 (June, 1969), 114-38.

― ― ―. "Bibliography of Post-Armistice Hungarian Historiography," *The American Slavic and East European Review,* VI, nos. 16-17 (May, 1947), 158-78.

Tilkovszky, Loránt. "Balásházy János élete és munkássága" (The Life and Work of János Balásházy), *Századok,* XCVI, nos. 3-4 (1962), 409-39.

Tóth, Zoltán I. "The Nationality Problem in Hungary in 1848-1849," *Acta Historica,* IV, no. 4 (1955), 235-77.

― ― ―. "Quelques Problèmes de L'État multinational dans La Hongrie d'avant 1848," *Acta Historica,* IV, nos. 1-3 (1955), 123-49.

Turczynski, Emanuel. "The National Movement in the Greek Orthodox Church in the Habsburg Monarchy," *Austrian History Yearbook,* III, pt. 3 (1967), 83-128.

Urbán, Aladár. "Die Organisierung des Heeres der ungarischen Revolution vom Jahre 1848," *Annales Universitatis Scientiarum Budapestinensis de Rolando Eötvös Nominatae Sectio Historica,* IX (1967), 106-30.

― ― ―. "Zehn kritische Tage aus der Geschichte der Batthyány-Regierung" *Annales Universitatis Scientiarum Budapestinensis de Rolando Eötvös Nominatae Sectio Historica,* II (1960), 91-124.

Urbanitsch, Peter. "In Remembrance," *Austrian History Yearbook,* IV-V (1968-1969), 575.

Valjavec, Fritz. "Die Josephinischen Wurzeln des Österreichischen Konservativismus," *Südostforschungen,* XIV (1955), 166-75.

— — —. "Die neue Széchenyi-Literatur und ihre Problem," *Jahrbücher für die Geschichte Osteuropas*, IV (1939), 90-110.

Várdy, Steven Béla. "The Age of Romanticism: The Historical Setting to Lenau's Life and Works," in A. H. Várdy, *A Study in Austrian Romanticism Hungarian Influences in Lenau's Poetry* (State University College at Buffalo, Program in East European and Slavic Studies. Publication No. 6). Buffalo: Hungarian Cultural Foundation, 1974, pp. 11-26.

— — —. "Baron Joseph Eötvös on Liberalism and Nationalism," *Studies for a New Central Europe*, Ser. 2, no. 1 (1967-1968), pp. 65-73.

— — —. "Baron Joseph Eötvös: Statesman, Thinker, Reformer," *Duquesne Review*, XIII, no. 2 (Fall, 1968), pp. 107-119.

— — —. "The Hungarian Economic History School: Its Birth and Development," *The Journal of European Economic History*, IV, no. 1 (Spring, 1975), pp. 121-136.

— — —. "The Origins of Jewish Emancipation in Hungary: The Role of Baron Joseph Eötvös," *Ungarn-Jahrbuch*, VII (1975).

— — —. "The Social and Ideological Make-up of Hungarian Historiography in the Age of Dualism, 1867-1918," *Jahrbücher für Geschichte Osteuropas*, Neue Folge, XXIV, no. 2 (1976), 208-217.

Vucinich, Wayne S. "Jelačić and the Frontier in Modern History," *Austrian History Yearbook*, I (1965), 68-72.

— — —. "The Serbs in Austria-Hungary," *Austrian History Yearbook*, III, pt. 2 (1967), 3-47.

Wagner, Francis S. "Széchenyi and the Nationality Problem in the Habsburg Empire," *Journal of Central European Affairs*, XX, no. 3 (October, 1960), 290-311.

Walter, Friedrich. "Aufklärung und Politik am Beispiele österriechs," *Österreich in Geschichte und Literatur*, IX, no. 7 (September, 1965), 347-60.

— — —. "Die Beteiligung der magyarischen Protestanten an der Revolution 1848-49," in *Gedenkschrift für Harold Steinacker*. In *Buchreihe* der Südostdeutschen Historischen Kommission, Vol. XVI. Munich: Oldenbourg, 1966, pp. 267-76.

— — —. "Die Ursachen des Scheiterns der madjarischen Waffenhilfe für die Wiener Oktober-Revolutionare 1848," *Südostforschungen*, XXII (1963), 377-400.

Wandruszka, Adam. "Die historische Schwäche des Bürgertums," *Wort und Wahrheit,* XI, no. 10 (1956), 763-69.

Wendycz, Piotr S. "The Poles in the Habsburg Monarchy," *Austrian History Yearbook,* III, pt. 2 (1967), 261-86.

Wright, William E. "The Initiation of *Robota* Abolition in Bohemia," *Journal of Central European Affairs,* XVIII, no. 3 (October, 1958), 239-53.

Young, Ian. "Russians in Hungary 1849," *History Today,* VII (April, 1957), 238-42.

Zollner, Erich. "The Germans as an Integrating and Disintegrating Force," *Austrian History Yearbook,* III, pt. 1 (1967), 201-33.

Zwitter, Fran. "The Slovenes and the Habsburg Monarchy," *Austrian History Yearbook,* III, pt. 2 (1967), 159-88.

# INDEX

Absolutism, 10, 14, 31f., 35, 44, 46, 50, 51, 53, 62, 63, 77, 85, 113, 115, 120, 122, 128, 129, 132, 136, 156, 158, 164, 174, 180, 184, 190.
"Academic Legion," 77
Academy of Sciences, see Hungarian Academy of Sciences
Address to the Crown: quoted in part, 65-69; passed, 81-82; question of revision, 81, 90-91; mentioned, 62, 65, 70, 72, 73, 80, 81, 82, 83, 84, 85, 86, 87, 89, 97, 99, 101, 102, 110, 116, 121, 122, 123, 125, 128, 131, 132, 137, 145, 148, 165
"Advice to Hungarian Agriculturalists," 45
Ágoston, József, 114
Albert of Habsburg, King of H., 21
Albrecht, Archduke, 76, 77, 78, 129
alispán, 33, 106, 109, 110
Alföld, 141
Almásy, Count Móric, 110
Andics, Erzsébet, 71, 120
Andrássy, Count Gyula, 89
Andrew (Endre), III King of H., 20, 27
Andrew (Endre) II, King of H., 19
Anjou Kings, 20
Apponyi, Count György, 57, 62, 72, 73, 80, 120, 123
April Laws, 13, 14, 69, 80, 86, 151, 158, 193; sanction of, 189-190; dynasty' renunciation of, 196
Arad County, 95, 147
Archbishop-Primate of Hungary, palace of, 188
Archdukes, Austrian, 29, 57, 129, 131
Army, see Imperial Army, Royal Hungarian Army
Árpád, 18
Árpád dynasty, 19, 20
Artisans, 93, 114
Ausburger Zeitung, 58
Austria, Lower, 74
Austria, Upper, 31
Austrian centralist historians, 11, 29, 124, 126
Austrian Civic Guards, 77

Austrian Councillors, 129, 159, 162, 164
Austrian History Yearbook, 200
Austrian Ministers, 60, 71, 123, 184
Austrian Ministry, 120, 128, 137, 154, 181, 184
Austrian National Bank, 60, 68
Austrian National Guard, 77, 130
Austrian Netherlands, 36
Austrian professors, 76
Austrian Reichsrat, 78, 166
Austrian Secret Police, 41, 45, 72, 80, 84, 96, 99, 108, 130
Austrian students, 75, 76, 77, 83, 130
Avenue of the Lords, 111
aviticitas (ősiség), Law of, 7, 21, 45, 152
Bakócz, Tamás, 22
Balásházy, János, 45
Balogh, Kornél, 61
Balogh, Péter, 1790 Program of, 36, 37, 40
Bán of Croatia, 156, 157, 158, 194
Bánát Regiment, 1st, 157
banknotes, 43, 60, 61, 62, 63, 130
banks, 53, 100, 101
banquets in Pozsony, 149
Bárány, George, 50
Baranya County, 25
Barta, István, 10, 42, 143
Basel, 18
Batal, György, 161
Batthyány, Count Lajos, 61, 62, 88, 89, 90, 96, 115, 117, 118, 119, 123, 127, 131, 132, 133, 135, 138, 139, 145, 146, 150, 152, 153, 154, 155, 158, 159, 162, 163, 164, 168, 169, 170, 171, 175, 188, 190
Belgrade, 21, 24
Bihar County, 115
bills, see Dietal bills
Bíró, Imre, 147
Black Sea, 94
Blackwell, Joseph Andrew, 54, 58, 60, 61, 65-68, 81, 82, 88, 139, 145, 151, 152, 154, 155, 163, 167-168, 173, 176, 185, 186, 190, 191-195

233

H., 37ff., 41; Franz I and H., 42-43; tactics in H. in 1840s, 57; in 1848, 87, 96, 98, 113, 115, 118, 121, 122, 125, 126, 130, 132, 159, 173, 174, 177
Hajnik, Pál, 114, 147
Hajnóczy, József, 58
Hartig, Count Franz, 60, 123, 128, 161, 170
Hatvani Street, 104
Haugwitz, Baron Friedrich Wilhelm von, 31
*Haus-Hof-und Staatskanzlei,* 176
Hereditary Provinces, see Habsburg Monarchy
*Hetilap,* 46
*Hírnök,* 46
historiography, see Austrian centralist historians, Hungarian Marxist historiography, Western historiography
*Hitel* (Credit), 45
Hofburg, 76, 78, 79, 121, 130, 131
*Hofkriegsrat,* 183, 185
Holovich, Boldizsár, 108
Holy Roman Empire, 19, 24
Horváth, Mihály, 14, 82, 97, 99, 100, 103, 111, 136
Hugessen, see Knatchbull-Hugessen, C.M.
Hungarian Academy of Sciences, 45, 95, 106
Hungarian Bodyguard, see Royal Hungarian Guard
Hungarian Civic Guards, 87, 88
Hungarian "manifesto" to Vienna of March 17th, 134
Hungarian Marxist historiography, 7, 8, 10, 11, 71, 140
Hungarian Ministers, 88, 91, 115, 117, 123, 132, 133, 135, 138, 149, 152, 153, 155, 162, 164, 168, 170, 172, 175, 176, 178, 181, 188, 192, 193
Hungarian Ministry, 118, 133, 138, 139, 146, 149, 150, 152, 153, 154, 156, 157, 158, 160, 161, 163, 168, 169, 170, 174, 176, 185, 191, 192, 193-195
Hungarian National Guard, 80, 100, 101, 106, 109, 111, 112, 115, 141, 142, 147, 174, 178, 181, 187; appointment of officers, 170, 175
"Hungarian Revolution of 1848"; nature of, 7-8, 14, 83, 103, 130
Hungarian students, 87, 88, 96, 104, 141, 147, 192
Hungary: conquest of, 19; Christianity in, 19; recognition as a European State, 19; liberation of from Turks, 26; area of, 48; declaration of independence, 99, 196
Hunyadi, János, Regent of Hungary, 21
Hunyadi, Mátyás, sees Matthias Corvinus

"Illyrian" movement, 156
"Illyrian Provinces," 43
impeachment, 23, 91
Imperial Army, 26, 34, 36, 44, 76, 77, 78, 101, 110, 111, 112, 120, 142, 152, 173, 174, 175, 179, 184, 189, 192, 196
industrialization, 46, 75, 95
interest rate, 45
Irányi, Dániel, 100, 105, 127, 140, 180, 181-182
Irinyi, József, 97, 100, 101, 105, 107, 113, 114
"Iron Gates," 94
Istanbul, 94
Italian troops (of Imperial Army), 77, 111
Italy, 178, 184, 185, 189
*ítélőmester,* 90
Izsák, 142

Jacobins, Austrian, Hungarian, 42, 98
*járások,* 142
Jelačić, Baron Josef von, 156, 157, 158, 194
*Jelenkor,* 46
Jenifer, Daniel, 95
Jews, 75, 112, 192
*jobbágy,* see peasants
Johann, Archduke, 74, 120, 129, 158
Jókai, Mór, 100, 101, 104, 113
Josef Barracks, 112
Josef, Archduke Palatine, 45, 85, 94
Josef (Joseph) II, 35-36, 38, 54, 94, 161, 168
Josef (Joseph) I, Emperor, King of H., 28
Jósika, Baron Samuel, 123, 124, 161
judges, 114
Judiciary, judicial powers, 23, 34, 38, 74, 95, 114
July Monarchy, 49
*jurati,* see "Dietal Youth"
*Juridisch-Politischer Leseverein,* 74, 77
Jurisics, Miklós, 25
jury trials, 75, 82, 100, 102
*jus resistendi,* 27

242

Szemere, Bertalan, 55, 89, 153, 154, 159, 172
Szentkirályi, Mór, 90
Szepessy, Ferenc, 109
Szigetvár, 25
Szilágyi, Sándor, 162, 163, 171, 193
Szőgyény, László (later, Szőgyény-Marich, László), 120, 121, 123, 124, 125, 128, 130, 161, 184

Táncsics, Mihály, 105, 106, 109, 111, 112
Tapié, Victor—L., 140
tariffs, 32, 45, 53, 67, 126, 160
Tarnow, 140
Tartars, 24
*Tavernicus* (Lord High Treeasurer), 70, 72
taxation, 23, 25, 32-33, 34, 36, 39, 43-44, 53, 141, 160, 196; introduction of a system of general, 54, 59, 56, 62, 66, 89, 100, 106, 118, 138, 152
Taylor, A.J.P., 13, 95
Telek, see urbarial holding
Teleki, Count László, 62, 89
Temes County, 194
Temesvár, Bánát of, 26
Tezner, Friedrich, 124
Thököly, Imre, rebellion of, 26
Tisza river, 45, 94
Tolnay, Károly, 138
Tormássy, János, 98
Török, Count Bálint, 95
Tóth, Zoltán I., 14, 200
Transylvania, 48, 82, 100, 105, 119, 123, 152, 182, 185
Transylvanian Counties, 56
Transylvanian Saxons, 124
travelogue genre, 47
Treasury, see Royal Hungarian Treasury
Trefort, Ágoston, 114
Trevelyan, G.M., 9
tribal migrations, European, 18
tribes, Hungarian, 18
*Tripartitum*, 23, 24, 126
Turks, 20, 21, 22, 24, 25, 26, 36, 54, 105, 124, 125, 126, 177
"Twelve Points," 100, 101, 102, 104, 105, 106, 107, 108, 109, 114, 146, 147, 148

Ulászló I, see Wladislaw I
Ulászló II, see Wladislaw II
United States, 94, 130
University of Gratz, 75
University of Pest, 95, 104, 192

University of Vienna, 75
Upper Hungary, 47, 51
urbarial abolition, 7, 52, 59, 62, 66, 80, 88-89, 100, 105, 117, 138, 142, 143, 152, 161, 165, 170
urbarial holding, 144, 165-166, 183
urbarial reform, 56, 58
*urbarium* of 1767, 32

Vác *járás*, 142
Váci Street, 110
Vahót, Imre, 114
Vajda, János, 110
Vasvár, Treaty of, 26
Vasvári, Pál, 97, 100, 105, 113, 147, 148
Vay, Baron Miklós, 85, 119
*Védegylet*, 96
Venice, 175
Verbőczi, see Werbőczy, István
Victor Emmanuel I, 187
Vice-Regal Council, see *Consilium*
Vienna, 54, 60, 70, 73, 74, 75, 80, 82, 83, 86, 87, 89, 92, 94, 112, 116, 117, 118, 120, 121, 127, 128, 129, 130, 132, 133, 137, 138, 139, 145, 146, 153, 155, 157, 162, 171, 172, 173, 175, 184, 191
Vienna aesenal, 112
Vienna, 1606 Peace of, 125
Viennese Civic Guard, 77
Viennese students, 75, 76, 83
Viennese workers, 75, 76, 83
*Világ*, 46
Világos, surrender at, 196
*Village Notary*, 65, 89
Vistula river valley, 140
*Vormärz*, 74
Vörösmarty, Miklós, 114

wages (Viennese), 75
Weiss, Johann, 105
Wenckheim, Baron Béla, 138
Werbőczy (Verbőczi), István, 23, 24, 51, 126
Western historiography, 11, 12, 15, 140
Wesselényi, Baron Miklós, 69, 95, 182
Wesselényi, Ferenc, Conspiracy of, 26
Windisch-Graetz, Prince Alfred, 78, 119, 122, 123, 161, 170
Wirkner, Baron Ludwig von, 84, 87, 126
Wladislaw (Ulászló) I of Jagiello, King of H., 21
Wladislaw (Ulászló) II of Jagiello, King of H., 27, 172; decree of 1507, 124, 125

243

*Ferdinand V., King of Hungary*
*1835—1848 (abdicated)*
*b. 1793 — d. 1875*

NÁDORI ESKÜ

*Archduke Stephan takes the Oath as Hungarian Palatine before King Ferdinand V, and both Houses of the Hungarian Diet, November 12, 1847, the Primate's Palace, Pozsony, Hungary.*

*Count István Széchenyi*
*1791—1860*

*Lajos Kossuth*
*1802—1894*

*Ferenc Deák*
*1803—1876*

*Baron József Eötvös*
*1813—1871*

*László Szőgyény*
*(later László Szőgyény-Marich)*
*1806—1893*

*Gábor Klauzál*
*1804—1866*

*Pál Nyáry*
*1806—1871*

*Leopold von Rottenbiller*
*1806—1870*

*Sándor Petőfi*
*1823—1849*

*Buda and Pest in 1848*

*The Hungarian National Museum completed in 1847 as the major work of Mihály Pollack.*

*Váci Street in Pest, the center of the capital's expanding commercial life in 1848.*

*Pozsony in 1848*

*Pozsony in 1848*

*The Hofburg, Vienna*

A Királyi Helytartótanáts épülete az Úrutszában.
königliches Stadthattereygebände in der Herrngasse.

*The Royal Consilium Building, Buda*

# Mit kíván a
# magyar nemzet.

## Legyen béke, szabadság és egyetértés.

1. Kívánjuk a' sajtó szabadságát, censura eltörlését.
2. Felelős ministeriumot Buda-Pesten.
3.' Évenkinti országgyűlést Pesten.
4. Törvény előtti egyenlőséget polgári és vallási tekintetben.
5. Nemzeti őrsereg.
6. Közös teherviselés.
7. Urbéri viszonyok megszüntetése.
8. Esküdtszék. képviselet egyenlőség alapján.
9. Nemzeti Bank.
10. A' katonaság esküdjék meg az alkotmányra, magyar kato-
náinkat ne vigyék külföldre, a' külföldieket vigyék el
tólünk.
11. A' politikai statusfoglyok szabadon bocsáttassanak.
12. Unio.

# Egyenlőség, szabadság, testvériség!

*Megjelent 1848. Mart. 15. tették 'Landerer 's Heckenast
nyomdájában, mint elő szabad nyomtatvány.*

*The Twelve Points*

# Nemzeti dal.

Talpra, magyar, hí a' haza!
Itt az idő, most vagy soha!
Rabok legyünk vagy szabadok?
Ez a kérdés, válaszszatok! —
A' magyarok istenére
Esküszünk,
Esküszünk, hogy rabok tovább
Nem leszünk.

Rabok voltunk mostanáig,
Kárhozottak ősapáink,
Kik szabadon éltek haltak,
Szolgaföldben nem nyughatnak.
A' magyarok istenére
Esküszünk,
Esküszünk, hogy rabok tovább
Nem leszünk.

Sehonnai bitang ember,
Ki most, ha kell, halni nem mer,
Kinek drágább rongy élete,
Mint a haza becsülete.
A magyarok istenére
Esküszünk.
Esküszünk, hogy rabok tovább
Nem leszünk.

Fényesebb a' láncznál a' kard.
Jobban ékesíti a' kart.
És mi még is lánczot hordtunk!
Ide veled, régi kardunk!
A magyarok istenére
Esküszünk.
Esküszünk, hogy rabok tovább
Nem leszünk.

A' magyar név megint szép lesz,
Méltó régi nagy híréhez,
Mit rá kentek a' századok,
Lemossuk a' gyalázatot.
A magyarok istenére
Esküszünk.
Esküszünk, hogy rabok tovább
Nem leszünk.

Hol sírjaink domborúlnak,
Unokáink leborúlnak,
És áldó imádság mellett
Mondják el szent neveinket.
A magyarok istenére
Esküszünk,
Esküszünk, hogy rabok tovább
Nem leszünk.

*The*
*National*
*Song*

## Petőfi Sándor.

*Az 1848ᵈⁱᵏ marczius 15ᵉⁿ kivívott sajtó-
szabadság után legeslegelőször nyomatott
példány s így a magyar szabadság első beteljes
Petőfiainé.*

259

*Map of Hungary in 1848*

# ERRATA

page 34, line 11 for *Concilium*
    read *Consilium*

page 52, line 6 for *cautions*
    read *cautious*

page 72, line 23 for *Travernicus*
    read *Tavernicus*

page 72, line 28 for
         *Count Antal Széchenyi*
    read *Count Antal Szécsen*

page 83, note 8 last line for *that*
    read *than*

page 156, line 18 for *Karl Franz*
    read *Franz Karl*

page 160, note 14 line 5 for
         *Law IXX of 1790*
  read *Law XIX of 1790*